Design America

SMALL HOME Plans

The plans in our Design America Series have been created by many of the nation's top architects and designers. No matter what your tastes, you're sure to find several homes you would be thrilled to call your own.

Design America Small Home Plans including Vacation Homes is a collection of best-selling vacation style and small home plans. These plans cover a wide range of architectural styles in a popular range of sizes. A broad assortment is presented to match a wide variety of lifestyles and budgets. Each design page features floor plans, a front view of the house, interior square footage of the home, number of bedrooms, baths, garage size and foundation types. All floor plans show room and exterior dimensions.

Plan #563-0271 on page 71

Technical Specifications - At the time the construction drawings were prepared, every effort was made to ensure that these plans and specifications meet nationally recognized building codes (BOCA, Southern Building Code Congress and others). Because national building codes change or vary from area to area some drawing modifications and/or the assistance of a professional designer or architect may be necessary to comply with your local codes or to accommodate specific building site conditions. We advise you consult with your local building official for information regarding codes governing your area.

Plan #563-0717 on page 144

Blueprint Ordering - Fast and Easy - Your ordering is made simple by following the instructions on page 9. See page 8 for more information on which types of blueprint packages are available and how many plan sets to order.

Your Home, Your Way - The blueprints you receive are a master plan for building your new home. They start you on your way to what may well be the most rewarding experience of your life.

CONTENTS

Design America Small Home Plans including Vacation Homes is published by Home Design Alternatives, Inc. (HDA, Inc.) 4390 Green Ash Drive, St. Louis, MO 63045. All rights reserved. Reproduction in whole or in part without written permission of the publisher is prohibited. Printed in U.S.A © 2002. Artist drawings shown in this publication may vary slightly from the actual working drawings. Some photos are shown in mirror reverse. Please refer to the floor plan for accurate layout.

House shown on front cover is Plan #563-0717 and is featured on page 144.

Our Blueprint Packages Offer...

Quality plans for building your future, with extras that provide unsurpassed value, ensure good construction and long-term enjoyment.

A quality home - one that looks good, functions well, and provides years of enjoyment - is a product of many things - design, materials, craftsmanship. But it's also the result of outstanding blueprints - the actual plans and specifications that tell the builder exactly how to build your home.

And with our BLUEPRINT PACKAGES you get the absolute best. A complete set of blueprints is available for every design in this book. These "working drawings," are highly detailed, resulting in two key benefits:

- *Better understanding by the contractor of how to build your home, and...*

- *More accurate construction estimates.*

When you purchase one of our designs, you'll receive all of the BLUEPRINT components shown here - elevations, foundation plan, floor plans, sections and details. Other helpful building aids are also available to help make your dream home a reality.

COVER SHEET

This sheet is the artist's rendering of the exterior of the home. It will give you an idea of how your home will look when completed and landscaped.

FLOOR PLANS

These plans show the placement of walls, doors, closets, plumbing fixtures, electrical outlets, columns, and beams for each level of the home.

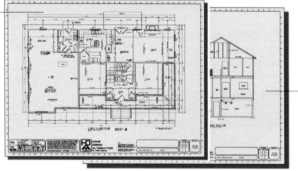

INTERIOR ELEVATIONS

Interior elevations provide views of special interior elements such as fireplaces, kitchen cabinets, built-in units and other special features of the home.

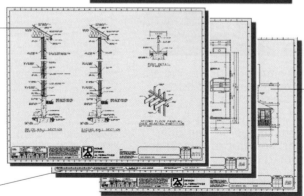

FOUNDATION PLAN

The foundation plan shows the layout of the basement, walk-out basement, crawl space, slab or pier foundation. All necessary notations and dimensions are included. See plan page for the foundation types included. If the home plan you choose does not have your desired foundation type, our Customer Service Representatives can advise you on how to customize your foundation to suit your specific needs or site conditions.

SECTIONS

Sections show detail views of the home or portions of the home as if it were sliced from the roof to the foundation. This sheet shows important areas such as load-bearing walls, stairs, joists, trusses and other structural elements, which are critical for proper construction.

EXTERIOR ELEVATIONS

These drawings illustrate the front, rear and both sides of the house, with all details of exterior materials and the required dimensions.

DETAILS

Details show how to construct certain components of your home, such as the roof system, stairs, deck, etc.

QUICK AND EASY CUSTOMIZING
MAKE CHANGES TO YOUR HOME PLAN IN **4** STEPS

HERE'S AN **AFFORDABLE** AND **EFFICIENT** WAY TO MAKE CHANGES TO YOUR PLAN.

BEFORE
Plan 2829

Customized Version of Plan 2829

AFTER

1 **Select the house plan that most closely meets your needs.** Purchase of a reproducible master is necessary in order to make changes to a plan.

2 **Call 1-800-373-2646 to place your order.** Tell the sales representative you're interested in customizing a plan. A $50 refundable consultation fee will be charged. You will then be instructed to complete a customization checklist indicating all the changes you wish to make to your plan. You may attach sketches if necessary. <u>If you proceed with the custom changes the $50 will be credited to the total amount charged.</u>

3 **FAX the completed customization checklist** to our design consultant at 1-866-477-5173 or e-mail **custom@drummonddesigns.com.** Within *24-48 business hours you will be provided with a written cost estimate to modify your plan. Our design consultant will contact you by phone if you wish to discuss any of your changes in greater detail.

4 **Once you approve the estimate,** a 75% retainer fee is collected and customization work gets underway. Preliminary drawings can usually be completed within *5-10 business days. Following approval of the preliminary drawings your design changes are completed within *5-10 business days. Your remaining 25% balance due is collected prior to shipment of your completed drawings. You will be shipped five sets of revised blueprints or a reproducible master, plus a customized materials list if required.

*Terms are subject to change without notice.

MODIFICATION PRICING GUIDE

CATEGORIES	Average Cost from... to
Adding or removing living space (square footage)	Quote required
Adding or removing a garage	$400 $680
Garage: Front entry to side load or vice versa	Starting at $300
Adding a screened porch	$280 $600
Adding a bonus room in the attic	$450 $780
Changing full basement to crawl space or vice versa	Starting at $220
Changing full basement to slab or vice versa	Starting at $260
Changing exterior building material	Starting at $200
Changing roof lines	$360 $630
Adjusting ceiling height	$280 $500
Adding, moving or removing an exterior opening	$55 per opening
Adding or removing a fireplace	$90 $200
Modifying a non-bearing wall or room	$55 per rooom
Changing exterior walls from 2"x4" to 2"x6"	Starting at $200
Redesigning a bathroom or a kitchen	$120 $280
Reverse plan right reading	Quote required
Adapting plans for local building code requirements	Quote required
Engineering stamping only	Quote required
Any other engineering services	Quote required
Adjust plan for handicapped accessibility	Quote required
Interactive illustrations (choices of exterior materials)	Quote required
Metric conversion of home plan	$400

Note: Any home plan can be customized to accommodate your desired changes. The average prices specifed above are provided only as examples for the most commonly requested changes, and are subject to change without notice. Prices for changes will vary according to the number of modifications requested, plan size, style, and metod of design used by the original desinner. To obtain a detailed cost estimate, please contact us.

Home Plans Index

Plan Number	Square Feet	Price Code	Page	Material List Available
563-0101	1,039	AA	56	✓
563-0102	1,246	A	330	✓
563-0103	1,351	A	143	✓
563-0104	1,359	A	65	✓
563-0105	1,360	A	33	✓
563-0106	1,443	A	109	✓
563-0108	1,516	B	79	✓
563-0109	1,565	B	278	✓
563-0110	1,605	B	310	✓
563-0111	1,582	B	291	✓
563-0112	1,668	C	17	✓
563-0113	1,992	C	317	✓
563-0118	1,816	C	181	✓
563-0162	1,882	D	286	✓
563-0163	1,772	C	126	✓
563-0167	2,282	D	134	✓
563-0171	2,058	C	282	✓
563-0172	1,643	B	254	✓
563-0173	1,220	A	107	✓
563-0174	1,657	B	10	✓
563-0176	1,404	A	304	✓
563-0181	1,408	A	270	✓
563-0186	1,442	A	206	✓
563-0189	2,177	C	240	✓
563-0190	1,600	C	30	✓
563-0191	1,868	D	224	✓
563-0192	1,266	A	96	✓
563-0194	1,444	A	285	✓
563-0195	988	AA	87	✓
563-0196	1,314	A	38	✓
563-0198	1,416	A	244	✓
563-0200	1,343	A	60	✓
563-0201	1,814	D	168	✓
563-0202	1,958	D	300	✓
563-0203	1,475	B	286	✓
563-0206	1,889	C	42	✓
563-0207	1,550	B	115	✓
563-0209	1,556	B	296	✓
563-0211	1,835	C	145	✓
563-0212	1,707	C	321	✓
563-0213	2,059	C	185	✓
563-0214	1,770	B	242	✓
563-0215	1,846	C	87	✓
563-0216	1,661	B	94	✓
563-0217	1,360	A	108	✓
563-0218	1,998	D	238	✓
563-0221	1,619	B	153	✓
563-0222	2,358	D	302	✓
563-0224	2,461	D	187	✓
563-0227	1,674	B	206	✓
563-0228	1,996	C	51	✓
563-0229	1,676	B	325	✓
563-0237	1,631	B	203	✓
563-0239	1,496	A	52	✓
563-0241	829	AAA	303	✓
563-0242	717	AAA	58	✓
563-0243	581	AAA	44	✓
563-0244	1,994	D	335	✓
563-0246	1,539	B	151	✓
563-0249	1,501	B	29	✓
563-0251	1,407	A	260	✓
563-0253	1,458	A	250	✓
563-0254	1,732	B	337	✓
563-0255	1,340	A	312	✓
563-0258	1,438	A	140	✓
563-0260	1,261	A	72	✓
563-0265	1,314	A	91	✓
563-0267	1,453	A	64	✓
563-0268	1,135	AA	36	✓
563-0269	1,428	A	108	✓
563-0270	1,448	A	277	✓
563-0271	1,368	A	71	✓
563-0272	1,283	A	154	✓
563-0273	988	AA	73	✓
563-0274	1,020	AA	310	✓
563-0275	1,270	A	148	✓
563-0276	950	AA	323	✓
563-0277	1,127	AA	103	✓
563-0278	2,847	E	223	✓
563-0281	1,624	B	50	✓
563-0282	1,642	B	98	✓
563-0283	1,800	D	53	✓
563-0291	1,600	B	86	✓
563-0293	1,595	B	166	✓
563-0294	1,655	B	142	✓
563-0295	1,609	B	25	✓
563-0296	1,396	A	142	✓
563-0297	1,320	A	67	✓
563-0312	1,921	D	46	✓
563-0316	1,824	C	305	✓
563-0320	2,228	D	289	✓
563-0340	2,153	C	179	✓
563-0342	2,089	C	260	✓
563-0357	1,550	B	225	✓
563-0362	1,874	C	208	✓
563-0370	1,721	C	15	✓
563-0372	1,859	C	81	✓
563-0375	1,954	C	150	✓
563-0378	2,180	C	157	✓
563-0379	1,711	B	196	✓
563-0381	2,045	C	125	✓
563-0382	1,546	B	274	✓
563-0383	1,813	C	283	✓
563-0384	2,013	C	267	✓
563-0393	1,684	B	313	✓
563-0394	1,558	B	123	✓
563-0395	1,803	C	166	✓
563-0396	1,880	C	218	✓
563-0410	1,742	B	78	✓
563-0413	2,182	C	292	✓
563-0415	1,492	A	61	✓
563-0416	1,985	C	84	✓
563-0419	1,882	C	180	✓
563-0420	1,941	C	228	✓
563-0425	2,076	C	207	✓
563-0441	1,747	B	275	✓
563-0442	1,950	C	216	✓
563-0447	1,393	B	60	✓
563-0448	1,597	C	318	✓
563-0450	1,708	B	11	✓
563-0461	828	AAA	28	✓
563-0462	1,028	AA	113	✓
563-0475	1,711	B	191	✓
563-0477	1,140	AA	16	✓
563-0478	1,092	AA	45	✓
563-0479	1,294	A	136	✓
563-0480	1,618	B	324	✓
563-0483	1,330	A	269	✓
563-0484	1,403	A	13	✓
563-0485	1,195	AA	303	✓
563-0486	1,239	A	243	✓
563-0487	1,189	AA	106	✓
563-0488	2,059	C	132	✓
563-0489	1,543	B	147	✓
563-0490	1,687	B	251	✓
563-0491	1,808	C	175	✓
563-0492	1,829	C	199	✓
563-0493	976	AA	40	✓
563-0494	1,085	AA	129	✓
563-0495	987	AA	328	✓
563-0496	977	AA	111	✓
563-0497	1,107	AA	23	✓
563-0498	954	AA	120	✓
563-0499	858	AAA	27	✓
563-0500	1,134	AA	135	✓
563-0502	864	AAA	336	✓
563-0503	1,000	AA	55	✓
563-0505	1,104	AA	43	✓
563-0507	1,197	AA	229	✓
563-0510	1,400	A	73	✓
563-0512	1,827	C	209	✓
563-0515	1,344	A	262	✓
563-0516	2,015	C	127	✓
563-0518	1,705	B	20	✓
563-0520	1,720	B	92	✓
563-0523	1,875	C	163	✓
563-0536	1,664	B	265	✓
563-0539	1,769	B	14	✓
563-0542	1,832	C	146	✓
563-0543	1,160	AA	139	✓
563-0548	1,154	AA	116	✓
563-0549	1,230	A	298	✓
563-0582	800	AAA	285	✓
563-0583	1,000	AA	96	✓
563-0584	1,300	A	74	✓
563-0585	1,344	A	32	✓
563-0586	1,664	B	241	✓
563-0587	1,120	AA	99	✓
563-0650	1,020	AA	281	✓
563-0651	962	AA	306	✓
563-0652	1,524	B	246	✓
563-0653	1,563	B	12	✓
563-0656	1,700	B	118	✓
563-0657	914	AA	233	✓
563-0659	1,516	B	224	✓
563-0660	1,321	A	328	✓
563-0661	1,712	B	67	✓
563-0668	1,617	B	332	✓
563-0669	1,358	A	151	✓
563-0670	1,170	AA	26	✓
563-0673	1,805	C	182	✓
563-0676	1,367	A	25	✓
563-0678	1,567	B	85	✓
563-0679	1,466	A	320	✓
563-0680	1,432	A	248	✓
563-0681	1,660	B	193	✓
563-0683	1,426	A	141	✓
563-0686	1,609	B	82	✓
563-0687	1,596	B	26	✓
563-0688	1,556	B	225	✓
563-0690	1,400	A	219	✓
563-0692	1,339	A	230	✓
563-0693	1,013	AA	154	✓
563-0694	1,285	A	105	✓
563-0697	924	AA	201	✓
563-0698	1,143	AA	48	✓
563-0699	1,073	AA	88	✓
563-0702	1,558	B	69	✓
563-0710	2,334	D	188	✓
563-0711	1,575	B	221	✓
563-0717	1,268	A	144	✓
563-0718	1,340	A	201	✓
563-0723	1,784	B	245	✓
563-0724	1,969	C	294	✓
563-0726	1,428	A	128	✓
563-0727	1,477	A	242	✓
563-0731	1,761	B	211	✓
563-0732	1,384	A	18	✓
563-0757	1,332	A	261	✓
563-0764	896	A	126	✓
563-0765	1,000	AA	212	✓
563-0766	990	AA	68	✓
563-0767	990	AA	235	✓
563-0769	1,440	A	159	✓
563-0790	2,397	D	307	✓
563-0795	1,399	A	21	✓
563-0806	1,452	A	274	✓
563-0807	1,231	A	59	✓
563-0808	969	AA	315	✓
563-0809	1,084	AA	33	✓
563-0810	1,200	A	314	✓
563-0811	1,161	AA	244	✓
563-0813	888	AAA	69	✓
563-0814	1,169	AA	315	✓
563-1101	1,643	B	329	✓
563-1117	1,440	A	110	✓
563-1120	1,232	A	107	✓
563-1163	2,087	C	95	✓
563-1216	1,668	B	50	✓
563-1220	1,540	B	312	✓
563-1229	1,610	B	327	✓
563-1233	1,948	C	247	✓
563-1248	1,574	B	71	✓
563-1253	1,996	C	276	✓
563-1267	1,800	C	239	✓
563-1276	1,533	B	254	✓
563-1293	1,200	A	222	
563-AMD-1135	1,467	A	270	✓
563-AMD-2163	1,978	E	22	✓
563-AMD-2175	1,464	C	93	✓
563-AMD-2189	1,994	D	249	
563-AMD-2229	2,287	E	49	
563-AP-1002	1,050	AA	148	
563-AP-1205	1,296	B	123	
563-AP-1410	1,496	A	275	
563-AP-1612	1,643	B	256	
563-AP-1912	1,985	C	89	
563-AX-1160	1,416	A	214	✓
563-AX-1340	1,352	A	210	✓

Home Plans Index

Plan Number	Square Feet	Price Code	Page	Material List Available
563-AX-1500	1,677	B	308	✓
563-AX-7836	1,303	A	97	✓
563-AX-7944	1,648	B	112	✓
563-AX-8162	1,496	A	226	✓
563-AX-8470	1,637	B	174	✓
563-AX-98366	1,029	AA	173	✓
563-BF-1314	1,375	A	104	
563-BF-DR1108	1,150	AA	103	
563-BF-DR1109	1,191	AA	48	
563-BF-DR1311	1,984	C	144	
563-CHD-11-27	1,123	AA	250	
563-CHD-13-61	1,379	A	100	
563-CHD-14-18	1,429	A	64	
563-CHD-15-54	1,612	B	287	
563-CHD-20-51	2,084	C	198	
563-CHP-1332A	1,363	A	99	
563-CHP-1532A1	1,520	B	333	
563-CHP-1632A	1,649	B	284	
563-CHP-173332	1,743	B	192	
563-CHP-173333	1,779	B	178	
563-CHP-2132B	2,172	C	164	
563-DB1963	1,347	A	110	✓
563-DB2638	2,103	C	290	✓
563-DB2761	1,341	A	36	✓
563-DB3010	1,422	A	216	✓
563-DBI-4948	1,758	B	83	✓
563-DBI-8013	1,392	A	140	✓
563-DBI-8061	2,119	C	204	✓
563-DBI-8077	1,858	C	119	✓
563-DDI-92201	1,888	C	169	
563-DDI-95219	1,251	A	268	
563-DDI-95220	1,584	B	220	
563-DDI-96217	1,770	B	316	
563-DDI-100213	2,202	D	80	
563-DDI-100214	2,104	C	197	
563-DH-864G	864	AAA	264	
563-DH-1377	1,377	A	94	
563-DH-1716	1,716	B	160	
563-DH-1786	1,785	B	124	
563-DH-2005	1,700	B	90	
563-DL-16053L1	1,605	B	104	
563-DL-17104L1	1,710	B	306	
563-DL-17353L1	1,735	B	146	
563-DL-19603L2	1,960	C	76	
563-DR-2160	1,199	AA	320	✓
563-DR-2250	1,103	AA	59	✓
563-DR-2801	1,760	B	162	✓
563-DR-2939	1,480	A	236	✓
563-DR-3906	1,442	A	202	✓
563-ES-125	1,605	B	301	✓
563-FB-327	1,281	A	311	
563-FB-1076	1,080	AA	29	✓
563-FB-1132	1,342	A	102	✓
563-FB-1148	1,491	A	34	✓
563-FB-1175	1,467	A	70	
563-FB-1217	1,583	B	117	
563-FB-3484	1,290	A	55	
563-FDG-4044	1,577	B	194	
563-FDG-7913	1,702	B	183	
563-FDG-8673	1,604	B	52	
563-FDG-9035	1,760	B	217	
563-GH-10515	2,015	C	165	✓
563-GH-20501	1,908	C	189	
563-GH-24319	1,710	B	75	✓
563-GH-24705	1,562	B	39	
563-GH-26112	1,487	AA	186	
563-GH-34003	1,146	AA	43	✓
563-GH-35008	1,291	A	213	
563-GM-1253	1,253	A	256	✓
563-GM-1333	1,333	A	31	✓
563-GM-1780	1,780	B	338	✓
563-GM-1815	1,815	C	47	✓
563-HDS-1576	1,576	B	276	
563-HDS-1627	1,627	B	19	
563-HDS-1679	1,679	B	331	
563-HDS-1697	1,703	B	319	
563-HDS-1750-B	1,750	B	253	
563-HDS-1758-3	1,787	B	293	
563-HDS-1768	1,768	B	63	
563-HDS-1817	1,817	C	76	
563-HDS-15712	1,565	B	98	
563-HP-B698	1,700	B	234	✓
563-HP-C316	1,997	C	259	✓
563-HP-C619	1,771	B	195	✓
563-HP-C675	1,673	B	257	✓
563-HP-C681	1,669	B	77	✓
563-HP-C687	1,974	C	170	✓
563-JA-60495	1,499	A	78	
563-JA-65396	1,536	B	297	
563-JA-66096	1,495	A	88	
563-JA-77798	1,461	A	284	
563-JA-79698	1,462	A	176	
563-JA-80498	1,591	B	252	
563-JA-83899	1,342	A	155	
563-JFD-15-1493-1	1,493	A	232	
563-JFD-20-17921	1,792	B	172	
563-JV-1268A	1,268	A	311	
563-JV-1273B	1,273	A	272	
563-JV-1297-A	1,297	A	133	
563-JV-1379-A-SJ	1,379	A	32	
563-JV-1735A	1,735	B	122	✓
563-MG-9538	1,404	E	72	
563-MG-97086	1,277	E	215	
563-MG-97099	1,093	AA	200	
563-N006	1,209	A	279	✓
563-N010	624	AAA	91	✓
563-N015	1,275	A	167	✓
563-N020	1,836	C	322	✓
563-N026	1,106	AA	280	✓
563-N042	1,280	A	57	✓
563-N048	1,272	A	227	✓
563-N049	1,391	A	137	✓
563-N057	1,211	A	138	✓
563-N061	1,224	A	339	✓
563-N063	1,299	A	149	✓
563-N064	1,176	AA	131	✓
563-N065	1,750	B	66	✓
563-N084	2,652	E	326	✓
563-N085	1,316	A	252	✓
563-N087	784	AAA	83	✓
563-N089	1,160	AA	176	✓
563-N107	1,680	B	205	✓
563-N109	1,806	C	62	✓
563-N114	792	AAA	229	✓
563-N118	527	AAA	45	✓
563-N119	1,200	A	273	✓
563-N131	733	AAA	139	✓
563-N142	1,354	A	263	✓
563-N145	618	AAA	30	✓
563-N147	865	AAA	37	✓
563-N149	1,280	A	101	✓
563-NDG-113-1	1,525	B	161	✓
563-NDG-414	1,397	A	177	✓
563-NDG-415	1,544	B	258	✓
563-NDG-418	1,472	A	152	✓
563-NDG-623	1,294	A	24	✓
563-RDD-1374-9	1,374	A	114	
563-RDD-1429-9	1,429	A	264	
563-RDD-1791-9	1,791	B	266	
563-RDD-1815-8	1,815	C	121	
563-RJ-A1068V	1,053	AA	135	
563-RJ-A1079	1,021	AA	74	
563-RJ-A1175	1,192	AA	131	
563-RJ-A1283	1,214	A	327	
563-RJ-A1293	1,253	A	262	
563-RJ-A1369A	1,398	A	304	
563-RJ-A1467	1,475	A	336	
563-RJ-A1485	1,436	A	294	
563-RJ-A1491	1,482	A	272	
563-RJ-B123	1,270	A	54	
563-RJ-B1416	1,455	A	158	
563-S-106	960	AA	333	✓
563-SH-SEA-001	1,735	B	156	
563-SH-SEA-008	1,073	AA	255	✓
563-SH-SEA-226	1,543	B	171	
563-SH-SEA-242	1,408	A	184	
563-SH-SEA-285	1,795	B	295	
563-SH-SEA-298	1,405	A	35	
563-SH-SEA-310	1,108	AA	299	
563-SH-SEA-400	1,568	B	231	
563-SRD-150	1,508	B	237	
563-SRD-214	1,856	C	271	
563-SRD-244	1,593	B	190	
563-SRD-279	1,611	B	180	
563-SRD-335	1,544	B	130	
563-SRD-352	1,509	B	309	
563-VL947	947	AA	288	✓
563-VL1267	1,267	A	41	✓
563-VL-1372	1,372	A	334	
563-VL-1458	1,458	A	288	

Other Helpful Building Aids...

Your Blueprint Package will contain the necessary construction information to build your home. We also offer the following products and services to save you time and money in the building process.

Express Delivery - Most orders are processed within 24 hours of receipt. Please allow 7-10 working days for delivery. If you need to place a rush order, please call us by 11:00 a.m. CST and ask for express service (allow 1-2 business days).

Technical Assistance - If you have questions, call our technical support line at 1-314-770-2228 between 8:00 a.m. and 5:00 p.m. CST. Whether it involves design modifications or field assistance, our designers are extremely familiar with all of our designs and will be happy to help you. We want your home to be everything you expect it to be.

Material List - Material lists are available for many of our plans. Each list gives you the quantity, dimensions and description of the building materials necessary to construct your home. You'll get faster and more accurate bids from your contractor and material suppliers, and you'll save money by paying for only the materials you need. Refer to the Home Plan Index for availability.

What Kind Of Plan Package Do You Need?

Once you find the home plan you've been looking for, here are some suggestions on how to make your Dream Home a reality. To get started, order the type of plans that fit your particular situation.

Your Choices:

The One-set package - We offer a 1-set plan package so you can study your home in detail. This one set is considered a study set and is marked "not for construction". It is a copyright violation to reproduce blueprints.

The Minimum 5-set package - If you're ready to start the construction process, this 5-set package is the minimum number of blueprint sets you will need. It will require keeping close track of each set so they can be used by multiple subcontractors and tradespeople.

The Standard 8-set package - For best results in terms of cost, schedule and quality of construction, we recommend you order eight (or more) sets of blueprints. Besides one set for yourself, additional sets of blueprints will be required by your mortgage lender, local building department, general contractor and all subcontractors working on foundation, electrical, plumbing, heating/air conditioning, carpentry work, etc.

Reproducible Masters - If you wish to make some minor design changes, you'll want to order reproducible masters. These drawings contain the same information as the blueprints but are printed on erasable and reproducible paper which clearly indicates your right to copy or reproduce. This will allow your builder or a local design professional to make the necessary drawing changes without the major expense of redrawing the plans. This package also allows you to print copies of the modified plans as needed. The right of building only one structure from these plans is licensed exclusively to the buyer. You may not use this design to build a second or multiple dwelling(s) without purchasing another blueprint. Each violation of the Copyright Law is punishable in a fine.

Mirror Reverse Sets - Plans can be printed in mirror reverse. These plans are useful when the house would fit your site better if all the rooms were on the opposite side than shown. They are simply a mirror image of the original drawings causing the lettering and dimensions to read backwards. Therefore, when ordering mirror reverse drawings, you must purchase at least one set of right reading plans.

OTHER GREAT PRODUCTS TO HELP YOU BUILD YOUR DREAM HOME

It sounds like lots of fun and just might be the biggest purchase you will ever make. But the process of building a home can be a tricky one. This program walks you through the process step-by-step. Compiled by consumers who have built new homes and learned the hard way. This is not a "how-to" video, but a visual checklist to open your eyes to issues you would never think about until you have lived in your home for years. *Available in VHS or DVD.*

$19.97 VHS   **$26.97** DVD

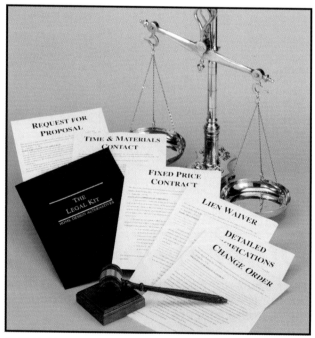

THE LEGAL KIT
Avoid many legal pitfalls and build your home with confidence using the forms and contracts featured in this kit. Included are request for proposal documents, various fixed price and cost plus contracts, instructions on how and when to use each form, warranty statements and more. Save time and money before you break ground on your new home or start a remodeling project. All forms are reproducible. The kit is ideal for homebuilders and contractors.
Cost: $35.00

- **Exchange Policies -** Since blueprints are printed in response to your order, we cannot honor requests for refunds. However, if for some reason you find that the plan you have purchased does not meet your requirements, you may exchange that plan for another plan in our collection. At the time of the exchange, you will be charged a processing fee of 25% of your original plan package price, plus the difference in price between the plan packages (if applicable) and the cost to ship the new plans to you.

  Please note: Reproducible drawings can only be exchanged if the package is unopened, and exchanges are allowed only within 90 days of purchase.

- **Building Codes & Requirements -** At the time the construction drawings were prepared, every effort was made to ensure that these plans and specifications meet nationally recognized codes. Our plans conform to most national building codes. Because building codes vary from area to area, some drawing modifications and/or the assistance of a professional designer or architect may be necessary to comply with your local codes or to accommodate specific building site conditions. We advise you to consult with your local building official for information regarding codes governing your area.

Questions? Call Our Customer Service Number
314-770-2228

BLUEPRINT PRICE SCHEDULE
BEST VALUE

Price Code	1-Set	SAVE $110 5-Sets	SAVE $200 8-Sets	Material List*	Reproducible Masters
AAA	$225	$295	$340	$50	$440
AA	$275	$345	$390	$55	$490
A	$325	$395	$440	$60	$540
B	$375	$445	$490	$60	$590
C	$425	$495	$540	$65	$640
D	$475	$545	$590	$65	$690
E	$525	$595	$640	$70	$740
F	$575	$645	$690	$70	$790
G	$650	$720	$765	$75	$865
H	$755	$825	$870	$80	$970

Plan prices guaranteed through June 30, 2004.
Please note that plans are not refundable.

- **Additional Sets* -** Additional sets of the plan ordered are available for $45.00 each. Five-set, eight-set, and reproducible packages offer considerable savings.

- **Mirror Reverse Plans* -** Available for an additional $5.00 per set, these plans are simply a mirror image of the original drawings causing the dimensions & lettering to read backwards. Therefore, when ordering mirror reverse plans, you must purchase at least one set of right reading plans.

- **One-Set Study Package -** We offer a one-set plan package so you can study your home in detail. This one set is considered a study set and is marked "not for construction". It is a copyright violation to reproduce blueprints.

*Available only within 90 days after purchase of plan package or reproducible masters of same plan.

SHIPPING & HANDLING CHARGES

U.S. SHIPPING	1-4 Sets	5-7 Sets	8 Sets or Reproducibles
Regular *(allow 7-10 business days)*	$15.00	$17.50	$25.00
Priority *(allow 3-5 business days)*	$25.00	$30.00	$35.00
Express* *(allow 1-2 business days)*	$35.00	$40.00	$45.00

CANADA SHIPPING (to/from) - Plans with suffix DR & SH	1-4 Sets	5-7 Sets	8 Sets or Reproducibles
Standard *(allow 8-12 business days)*	$25.00	$30.00	$35.00
Express* *(allow 3-5 business days)*	$40.00	$40.00	$45.00

Overseas Shipping/International - Call, fax, or e-mail (plans@hdainc.com) for shipping costs.

* For express delivery please call us by 11:00 a.m. CST

How To Order

For fastest service, Call Toll-Free
1-800-DREAM HOME
(1-800-373-2646) day or night

Three Easy Ways To Order

1. CALL toll free 1-800-373-2646 for credit card orders. MasterCard, Visa, Discover and American Express are accepted.

2. FAX your order to 1-314-770-2226.

3. MAIL the Order Form to:

   HDA, Inc.
   4390 Green Ash Drive
   St. Louis, MO 63045

ORDER FORM

Please send me -
   PLAN NUMBER 563- _____
      PRICE CODE _____ (see Plan Index)
   (for plans on pgs. 10-339)

Specify Foundation Type - see plan page for availability
   ☐ Slab   ☐ Crawl space   ☐ Pier
   ☐ Basement   ☐ Walk-out basement

☐ Reproducible Masters	$ _____
☐ Eight-Set Plan Package	$ _____
☐ Five-Set Plan Package	$ _____
☐ One-Set Study Package (no mirror reverse)	$ _____
☐ Additional Plan Sets	
_____ (Qty.) at $45.00 each	$ _____
☐ Print in Mirror Reverse	
_____ (Qty.) add $5.00 per set	$ _____
☐ Material List (see chart at left)	$ _____
☐ Legal Kit (see page 8)	$ _____
Building Smart: (see page 8)	
☐ VHS $19.97 #FP00001 ☐ DVD $26.97 #FP00002	$ _____
SUBTOTAL	$ _____
SALES TAX (MO residents add 6%)	$ _____
☐ Shipping / Handling (see chart at left)	$ _____
TOTAL ENCLOSED (US funds only)	$ _____
(Sorry no CODs)	

I hereby authorize HDA, Inc. to charge this purchase to my credit card account (check one):

☐ MasterCard   ☐ VISA   ☐ DISCOVER NOVUS   ☐ AMERICAN EXPRESS Cards

Credit Card number _____

Expiration date _____

Signature _____

Name _____
            (Please print or type)

Street Address _____
            (Please **do not** use PO Box)

City _____

State _____ Zip _____

Daytime phone number (____) - _____

I'm a ☐ Builder/Contractor   I ☐ have
      ☐ Homeowner   ☐ have not
      ☐ Renter   selected my
                                 general contractor

Thank you for your order!

9

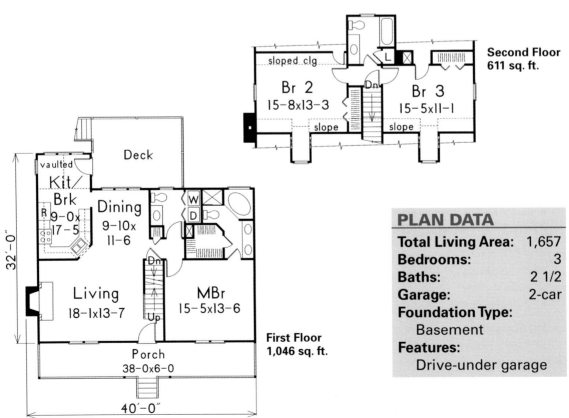

Second Floor
611 sq. ft.

sloped clg

Br 2
15-8x13-3

Br 3
15-5x11-1

slope   slope

Deck

vaulted

Kit/
Brk
9-0x
17-5

Dining
9-10x
11-6

W
D

Living
18-1x13-7

MBr
15-5x13-6

Up

Dn

32'-0"

First Floor
1,046 sq. ft.

Porch
38-0x6-0

40'-0"

PLAN DATA

Total Living Area:	1,657
Bedrooms:	3
Baths:	2 1/2
Garage:	2-car
Foundation Type:	
Basement	
Features:	
Drive-under garage	

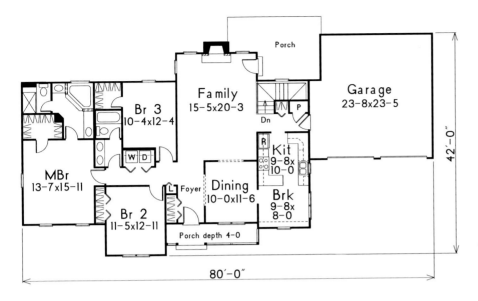

PLAN DATA

Total Living Area:	1,708
Bedrooms:	3
Baths:	2
Garage:	2-car
Foundation Types:	
Basement standard	
Crawl space	

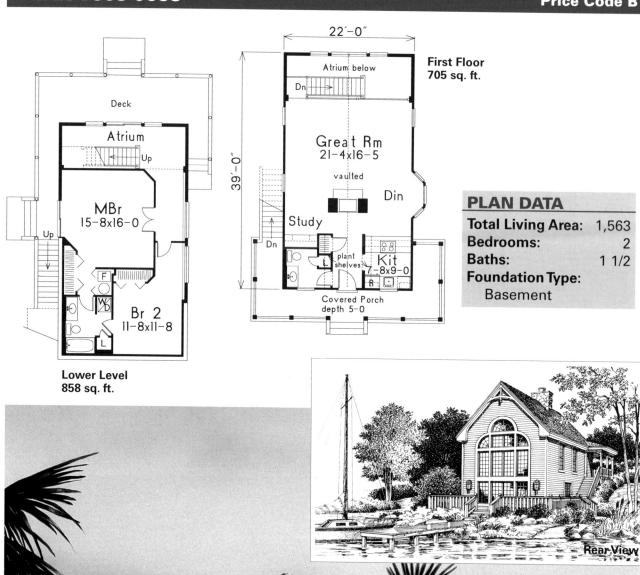

Deck

Atrium

MBr
15-8x16-0

Up

Up

F

W/D
L

Br 2
11-8x11-8

Lower Level
858 sq. ft.

22'-0"

Atrium below

Dn

39'-0"

Great Rm
21-4x16-5

vaulted

Din

Study

Dn

plant
shelves

L

Kit
7-8x9-0

R

Covered Porch
depth 5-0

First Floor
705 sq. ft.

PLAN DATA

Total Living Area: 1,563
Bedrooms: 2
Baths: 1 1/2
Foundation Type:
Basement

Rear View

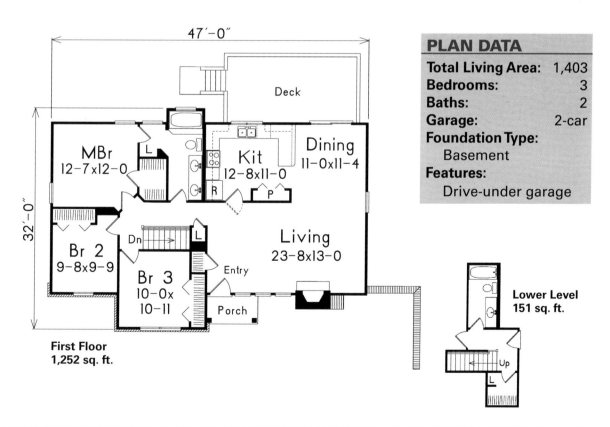

47'-0"

Deck

MBr
12-7x12-0

L

Kit
12-8x11-0

Dining
11-0x11-4

R

P

32'-0"

Br 2
9-8x9-9

Dn

L

Living
23-8x13-0

Entry

Br 3
10-0x
10-11

Porch

**First Floor
1,252 sq. ft.**

Up

L

**Lower Level
151 sq. ft.**

PLAN DATA

Total Living Area:	1,403
Bedrooms:	3
Baths:	2
Garage:	2-car
Foundation Type:	
Basement	
Features:	
Drive-under garage	

PLAN DATA

Total Living Area: 1,769
Bedrooms: 3
Baths: 2
Foundation Types:
  Basement standard
  Crawl space
  Slab

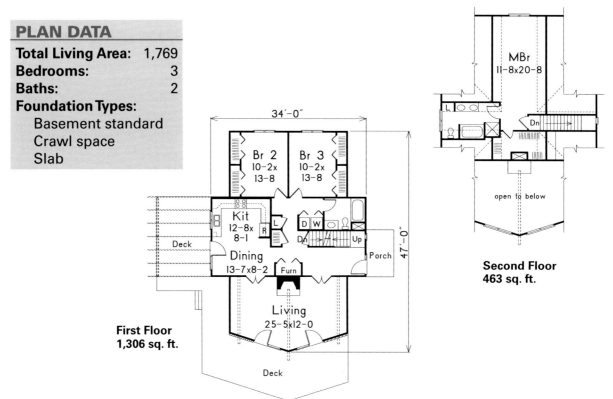

First Floor
1,306 sq. ft.

Second Floor
463 sq. ft.

PLAN DATA

Total Living Area: 1,721
Bedrooms: 3
Baths: 2
Garage: 3-car
Foundation Types:
  Walk-out basement -
  standard
  Crawl space
  Slab

Rear View

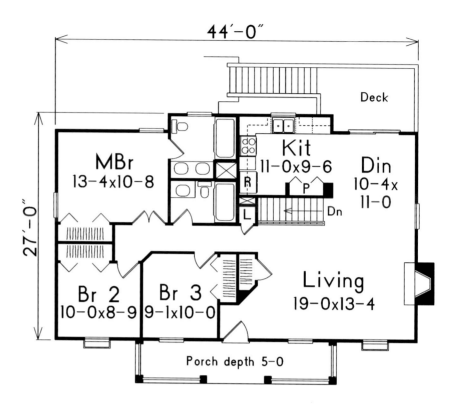

44'-0"

27'-0"

Deck

MBr
13-4x10-8

Kit
11-0x9-6

Din
10-4x
11-0

R

P

L

Dn

Br 2
10-0x8-9

Br 3
9-1x10-0

Living
19-0x13-4

Porch depth 5-0

PLAN DATA

Total Living Area:	1,140
Bedrooms:	3
Baths:	2
Garage:	2-car
Foundation Type:	
Basement	
Features:	
Drive-under garage	

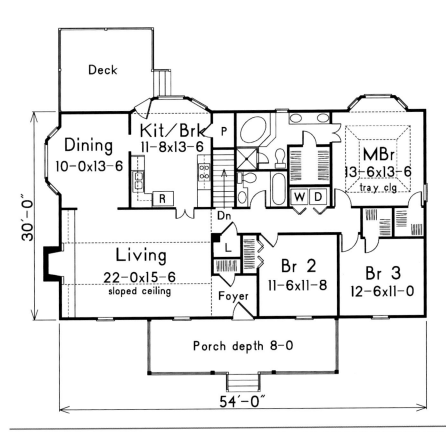

Deck

Dining
10-0x13-6

Kit/Brk
11-8x13-6

P

MBr
13-6x13-6
tray clg

W D

Dn

30'-0"

Living
22-0x15-6
sloped ceiling

L

Br 2
11-6x11-8

Br 3
12-6x11-0

Foyer

Porch depth 8-0

54'-0"

PLAN DATA

Total Living Area:	1,668
Bedrooms:	3
Baths:	2
Garage:	2-car
Foundation Type:	
Basement	
Features:	
Drive-under garage	

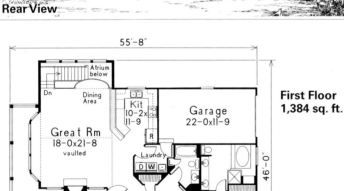

Rear View

PLAN DATA

Total Living Area:	1,384
Bedrooms:	2
Baths:	2
Garage:	1-car

Foundation Type:
Walk-out basement

Features:
Atrium open to 611 square feet of optional living area below

55'-8"

Atrium below

Dn

Dining Area

Kit 10-2x 11-9

Great Rm 18-0x21-8 vaulted

Garage 22-0x11-9

46'-0"

Laundry

DW

R

Cover porch depth 6-0

Br 2 11-4x12-6

MBr 12-8x15-0

First Floor 1,384 sq. ft.

Lower Level

Up

Patio

Family Rm 25-0x21-4

Unexcavated

Unfinished Basement

© HOME DESIGN SERVICES, INC.

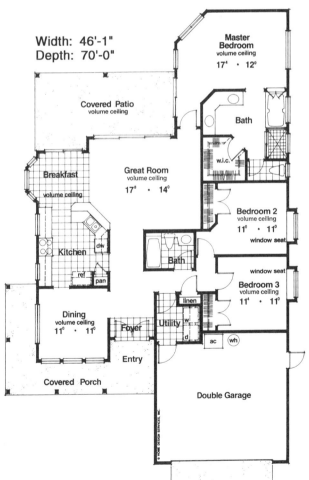

Width: 46'-1"
Depth: 70'-0"

Covered Patio
volume ceiling

Master Bedroom
volume ceiling
17⁴ · 12⁰

Bath

Breakfast
volume ceiling

Great Room
volume ceiling
17⁸ · 14⁰

w.i.c.

Bedroom 2
volume ceiling
11⁰ · 11⁰
window seat

Kitchen

dw

ref   pan

Bath

window seat

Bedroom 3
volume ceiling
11⁴ · 11⁰

Dining
volume ceiling
11⁰ · 11⁰

Foyer   Utility

linen

w
d

ac   wh

Entry

Covered Porch

Double Garage

PLAN DATA

Total Living Area:	1,627
Bedrooms:	3
Baths:	2
Garage:	2-car
Foundation Type:	
Slab	

PLAN DATA

Total Living Area: 1,705
Bedrooms: 4
Baths: 2
Foundation Types:
   Crawl space standard
   Basement
   Slab

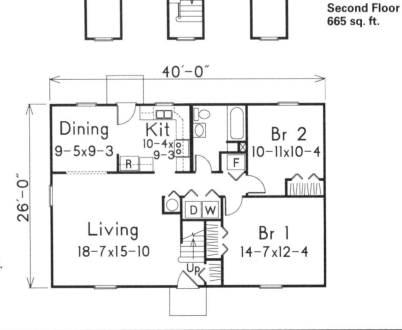

Second Floor
665 sq. ft.

Br 3
12-9x16-4

Br 4
10-11x16-4

Dn

Stor.

40'-0"

26'-0"

Dining
9-5x9-3

Kit
10-4x9-3

R

Br 2
10-11x10-4

F

Living
18-7x15-10

D W

Br 1
14-7x12-4

Up

First Floor
1,040 sq. ft.

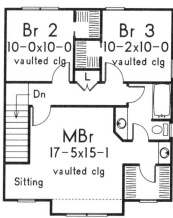

Second Floor
667 sq. ft.

Br 2
10-0x10-0
vaulted clg

Br 3
10-2x10-0
vaulted clg

Dn

L

MBr
17-5x15-1
vaulted clg

Sitting

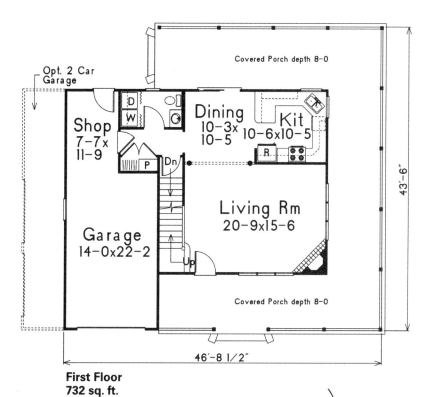

Opt. 2 Car Garage

Covered Porch depth 8-0

D
W

Shop
7-7 x
11-9

Dining
10-3x
10-5

Kit
10-6x10-5

P   Dn

R

Living Rm
20-9x15-6

Garage
14-0x22-2

Up

43'-6"

Covered Porch depth 8-0

46'-8 1/2"

First Floor
732 sq. ft.

PLAN DATA

Total Living Area:	1,399
Bedrooms:	3
Baths:	1 1/2
Garage:	1-car
Foundation Types:	

Basement standard
Crawl space
Slab

PLAN DATA

Total Living Area: 1,978
Bedrooms: 3
Baths: 2 1/2
Garage: 2-car
Foundation Type:
  Walk-out basement
Features:
  Drive-under garage

Second Floor
872 sq. ft.

First Floor
1,106 sq. ft.

Lower Level

PLAN DATA

Total Living Area: 1,107
Bedrooms: 3
Baths: 2
Foundation Type:
   Basement

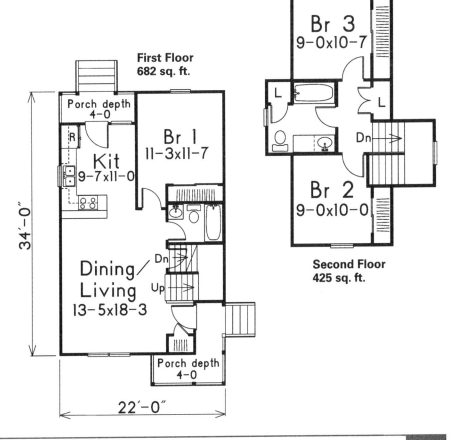

First Floor
682 sq. ft.

Porch depth
4-0

Kit
9-7x11-0

Br 1
11-3x11-7

Dining
Living
13-5x18-3

Dn

Up

Porch depth
4-0

34'-0"

22'-0"

Br 3
9-0x10-7

L

L

Dn

Br 2
9-0x10-0

Second Floor
425 sq. ft.

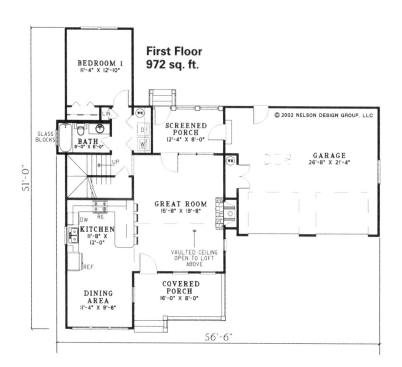

First Floor
972 sq. ft.

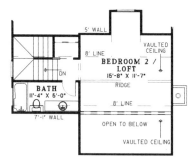

Second Floor
322 sq. ft.

PLAN DATA

Total Living Area:	1,294
Bedrooms:	2
Baths:	2
Garage:	2-car
Foundation Types:	
Crawl space	
Slab	

Please specify when ordering

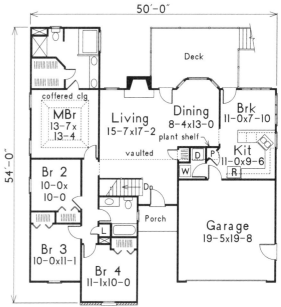

50'-0"

54'-0"

Deck

coffered clg

MBr
13-7 x
13-4

Living
15-7x17-2
vaulted

Dining
8-4x13-0
plant shelf

Brk
11-0x7-10

Kit
11-0x9-6

Br 2
10-0x
10-0

Porch

Garage
19-5x19-8

Br 3
10-0x11-1

Br 4
11-1x10-0

PLAN DATA

Total Living Area:	1,609
Bedrooms:	4
Baths:	2
Garage:	2-car
Foundation Type:	
Basement	

71' - 4"

35' - 10"

Terrace

Kit/Brk
14-8x10-0

MBr
12-4x15-2

sloped clg

skylt

Living
13-0x18-6

Garage
21-0x19-6

Dressing

Dining
11-4x10-0

Stor.

Br 2
11-0x10-0
vaulted

Br 3
10-6x
10-0

Porch depth 7-6

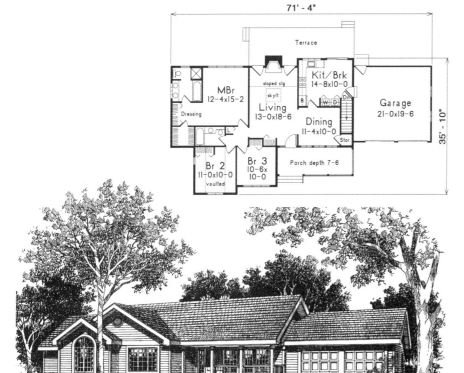

PLAN DATA

Total Living Area:	1,367
Bedrooms:	3
Baths:	2
Garage:	2-car
Foundation Types:	
Basement standard	
Slab	

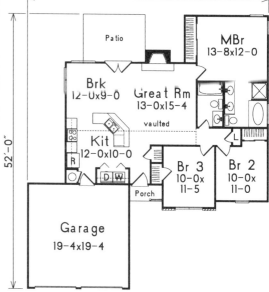

PLAN DATA

Total Living Area:	1,170
Bedrooms:	3
Baths:	2
Garage:	2-car
Foundation Type:	
Slab	

PLAN #563-0687

Price Code B

PLAN DATA

Total Living Area:	1,596
Bedrooms:	3
Baths:	2
Foundation Type:	
Slab	

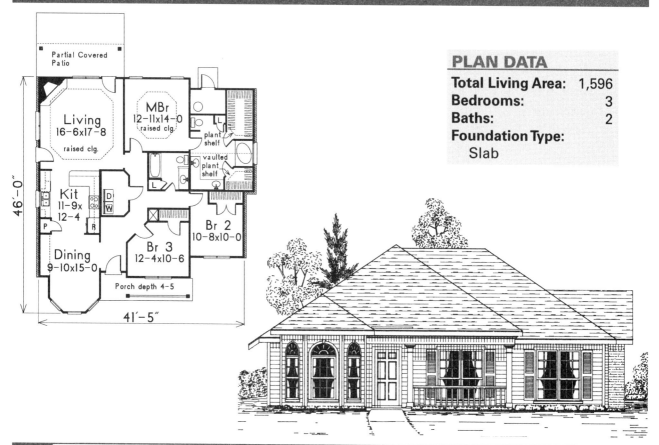

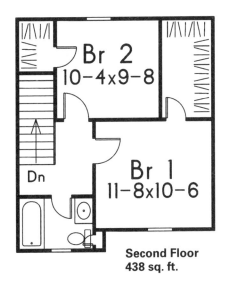

Br 2
10-4x9-8

Br 1
11-8x10-6

Dn

Second Floor
438 sq. ft.

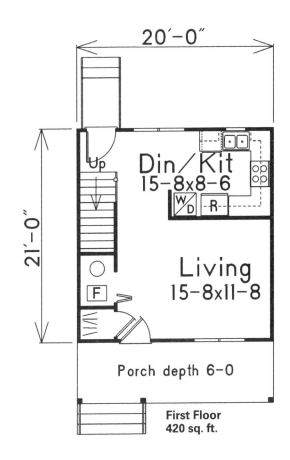

20'-0"

21'-0"

Up

Din/Kit
15-8x8-6

W/D   R

Living
15-8x11-8

F

Porch depth 6-0

First Floor
420 sq. ft.

PLAN DATA

Total Living Area:	858
Bedrooms:	2
Baths:	1
Foundation Type:	
Crawl space	

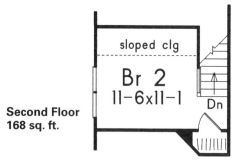

**Second Floor
168 sq. ft.**

sloped clg

Br 2
11-6x11-1

Dn

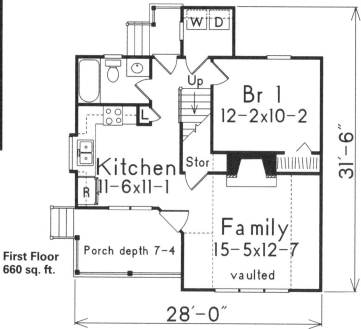

W D

Up

Br 1
12-2x10-2

Stor

L

Kitchen
11-6x11-1

R

**First Floor
660 sq. ft.**

Porch depth 7-4

Family
15-5x12-7

vaulted

31'-6"

28'-0"

PLAN DATA

Total Living Area:	828
Bedrooms:	2
Baths:	1

Foundation Type:
  Crawl space
Features:
  Vaulted ceiling in
  living area

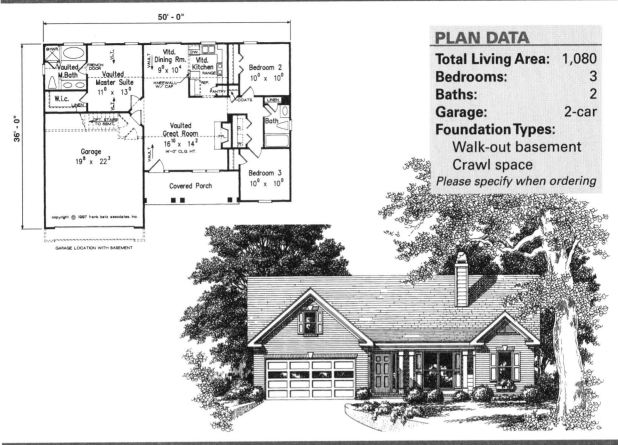

50' - 0"

36' - 0"

SH·WR.
Vaulted M.Bath
FRENCH DOOR
Vaulted Master Suite 11⁰ x 13⁰
W.i.c.
LINEN
OPT. STAIRS TO BSMT.
Garage 19⁸ x 22³

Vltd. Dining Rm. 9⁰ x 10⁴
KNEEWALL W/ CAP
Vltd. Kitchen
D.W.
RANGE
REF.
PANTRY

Bedroom 2 10⁰ x 10⁰

COATS
LINEN
Bath

Vaulted Great Room 16¹⁰ x 14² 14'-0" CLG. HT.
FPL.

Bedroom 3 10⁰ x 10⁰

Covered Porch

copyright © 1997 frank betz associates, inc.

GARAGE LOCATION WITH BASEMENT

PLAN DATA

Total Living Area:	1,080
Bedrooms:	3
Baths:	2
Garage:	2-car
Foundation Types:	
Walk-out basement	
Crawl space	
Please specify when ordering	

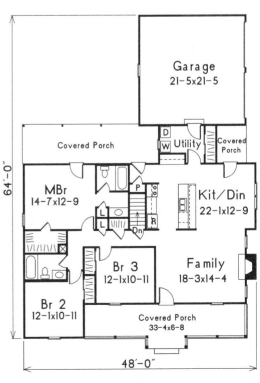

Garage 21-5x21-5

Covered Porch

D
W
Utility
Covered Porch

64'-0"

MBr 14-7x12-9

P

Kit/Din 22-1x12-9

L
L
R
Dn

Br 3 12-1x10-11

Family 18-3x14-4

Br 2 12-1x10-11

Covered Porch 33-4x6-8

48'-0"

PLAN DATA

Total Living Area:	1,501
Bedrooms:	3
Baths:	2
Garage:	2-car
Foundation Type:	
Basement standard	
Crawl space	
Slab	

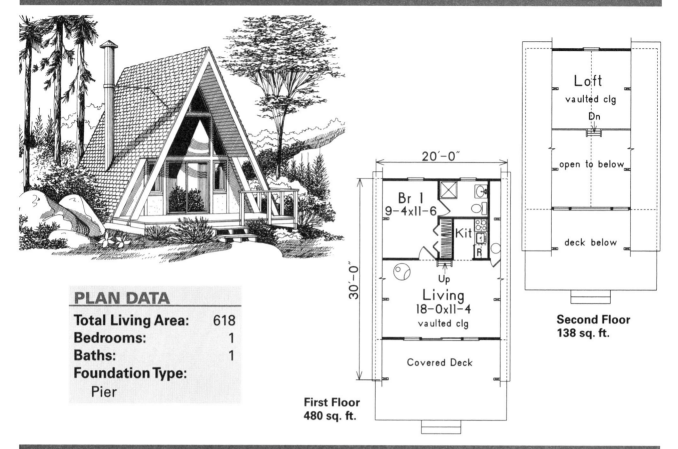

PLAN DATA

Total Living Area: 618
Bedrooms: 1
Baths: 1
Foundation Type:
   Pier

20'-0"

30'-0"

Br 1
9-4x11-6

Kit

Living
18-0x11-4
vaulted clg

Up

Covered Deck

**First Floor
480 sq. ft.**

Loft
vaulted clg

Dn

open to below

deck below

**Second Floor
138 sq. ft.**

PLAN DATA

Total Living Area: 1,600
Bedrooms: 3
Baths: 2
Garage: 2-car
Foundation Types:
   Slab standard
   Crawl space
   Basement
Features:
- 16' ceiling in living room
- 2" x 6" exterior walls

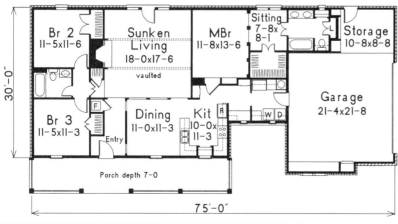

Br 2
11-5x11-6

Sunken
Living
18-0x17-6
vaulted

MBr
11-8x13-6

Sitting
7-8x
8-1

Storage
10-8x8-8

30'-0"

Br 3
11-5x11-3

Entry

Dining
11-0x11-3

Kit
10-0x
11-3

W D

Garage
21-4x21-8

Porch depth 7-0

75'-0"

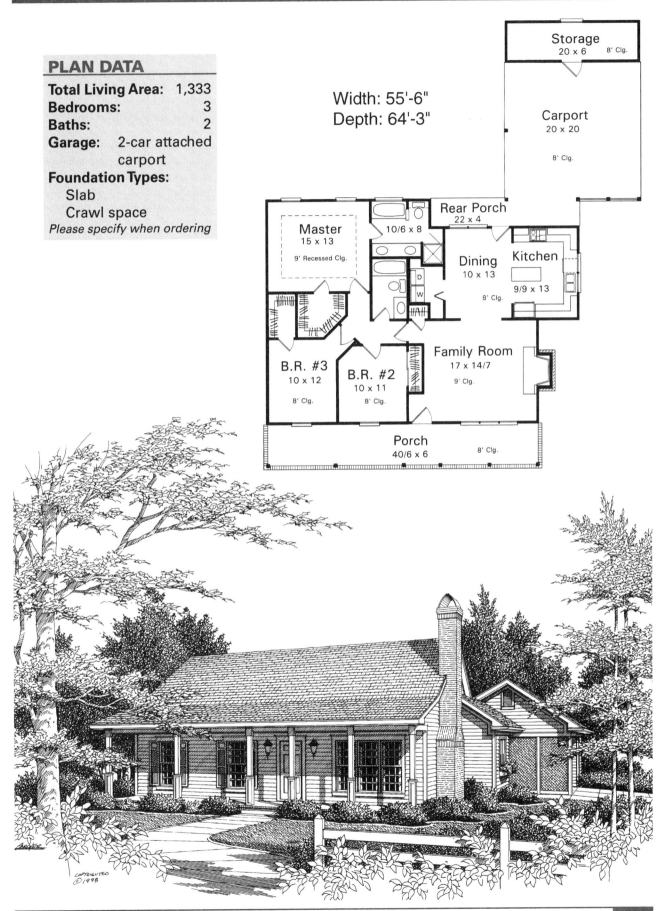

PLAN DATA

Total Living Area: 1,333
Bedrooms: 3
Baths: 2
Garage: 2-car attached carport
Foundation Types:
  Slab
  Crawl space
Please specify when ordering

Width: 55'-6"
Depth: 64'-3"

Storage
20 x 6   8' Clg.

Carport
20 x 20

8' Clg.

Master
15 x 13

9' Recessed Clg.

10/6 x 8

Rear Porch
22 x 4

Dining
10 x 13

Kitchen
9/9 x 13

8' Clg.

D
W

B.R. #3
10 x 12

8' Clg.

B.R. #2
10 x 11

8' Clg.

Family Room
17 x 14/7

9' Clg.

Porch
40/6 x 6   8' Clg.

COPYRIGHTED
© 1998

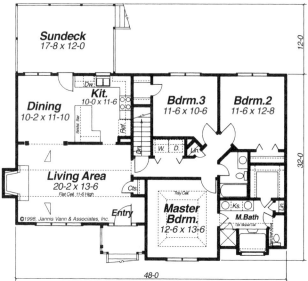

PLAN DATA

Total Living Area: 1,379
Bedrooms: 3
Baths: 2
Garage: 2-car
Foundation Type:
  Basement
Features:
  Drive-under garage

Sundeck
17-8 x 12-0

Dining
10-2 x 11-10

Kit.
10-0 x 11-6

Bdrm.3
11-6 x 10-6

Bdrm.2
11-6 x 12-8

Living Area
20-2 x 13-6

©1998, Jannis Vann & Associates, Inc.

Entry

Master Bdrm.
12-6 x 13-6

M.Bath

48-0

12-0

32-0

PLAN DATA

Total Living Area: 1,344
Bedrooms: 3
Baths: 2
Foundation Types:
  Crawl space standard
  Basement
  Slab

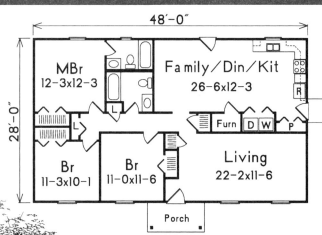

48'-0"

28'-0"

MBr
12-3x12-3

Family/Din/Kit
26-6x12-3

Br
11-3x10-1

Br
11-0x11-6

Living
22-2x11-6

Furn

Porch

PLAN DATA

Total Living Area: 1,360
Bedrooms: 3
Baths: 2
Garage: 2-car
Foundation Type:
  Basement

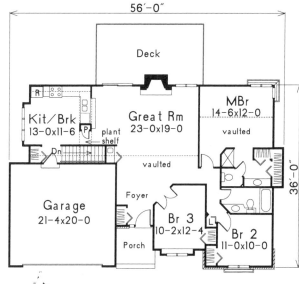

PLAN DATA

Total Living Area: 1,084
Bedrooms: 2
Baths: 2
Foundation Type:
  Basement

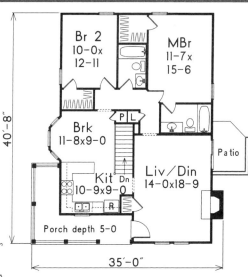

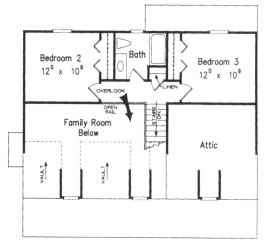

Second Floor
430 sq. ft.

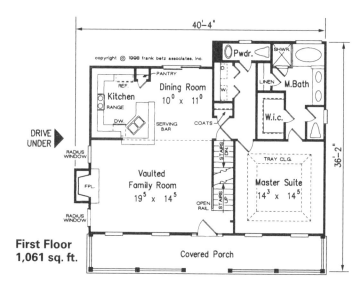

First Floor
1,061 sq. ft.

PLAN DATA

Total Living Area: 1,491
Bedrooms: 3
Baths: 2 1/2
Garage: 2-car
Foundation Type:
   Walk-out basement
Features:
   Drive-under garage

PLAN DATA

Total Living Area: 1,405
Bedrooms: 3
Baths: 2
Foundation Types:
  Basement
  Crawl space
Please specify when ordering

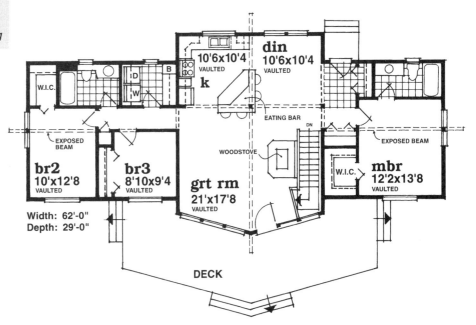

din
10'6x10'4
VAULTED

10'6x10'4
VAULTED

k

W.I.C.

D
W

B

EATING BAR

DN

EXPOSED
BEAM

EXPOSED
BEAM

br2
10'x12'8
VAULTED

br3
8'10x9'4
VAULTED

WOODSTOVE

W.I.C.

mbr
12'2x13'8
VAULTED

grt rm
21'x17'8
VAULTED

Width: 62'-0"
Depth: 29'-0"

DECK

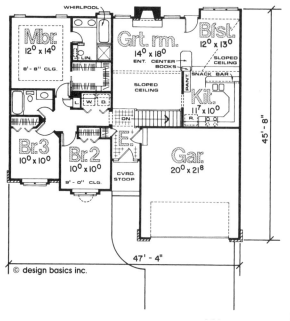

© design basics inc.

PLAN DATA

Total Living Area: 1,341
Bedrooms: 3
Baths: 2
Garage: 2-car
Foundation Type:
   Basement

PLAN #563-0268

Price Code AA

PLAN DATA

Total Living Area: 1,135
Bedrooms: 3
Baths: 2
Garage: 2-car
Foundation Types:
   Basement standard
   Crawl space
Features:
   2" x 6" exterior walls

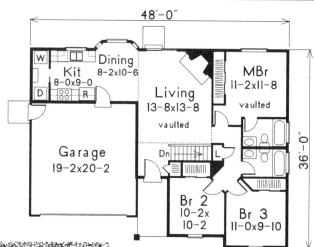

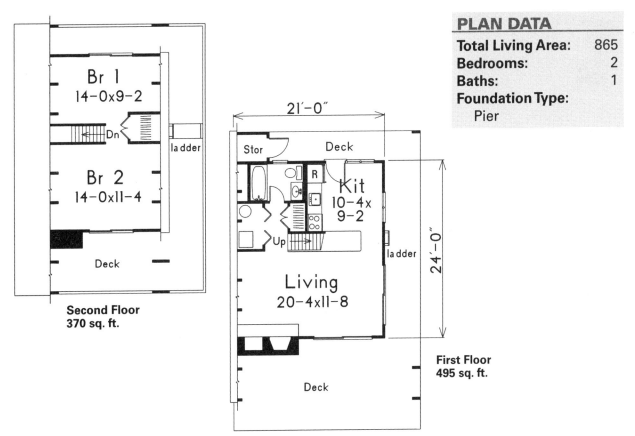

PLAN DATA

Total Living Area:	865
Bedrooms:	2
Baths:	1
Foundation Type:	
Pier	

Br 1
14-0x9-2

Dn

ladder

Br 2
14-0x11-4

Deck

**Second Floor
370 sq. ft.**

21'-0"

Stor

Deck

R

Kit
10-4x
9-2

24'-0"

Up

ladder

Living
20-4x11-8

Deck

**First Floor
495 sq. ft.**

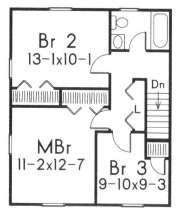

Second Floor
552 sq. ft.

Br 2
13-1x10-1

MBr
11-2x12-7

Br 3
9-10x9-3

Dn
L

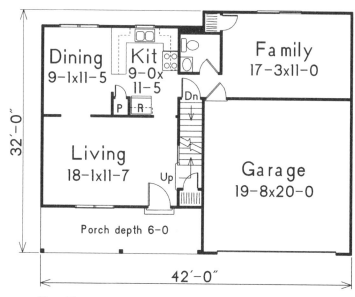

Dining
9-1x11-5

Kit
9-0x
11-5

P R

Family
17-3x11-0

Dn

Living
18-1x11-7

Up

Garage
19-8x20-0

32'-0"

Porch depth 6-0

42'-0"

First Floor
762 sq. ft.

PLAN DATA

Total Living Area: 1,314
Bedrooms: 3
Baths: 1 1/2
Garage: 2-car
Foundation Types:
  Basement standard
  Crawl space

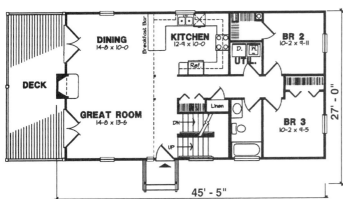

DINING 14-8 x 10-0

KITCHEN 12-4 x 10-0

Breakfast Bar

BR 2 10-2 x 9-11

Ref.

D. UTIL.

DECK

GREAT ROOM 14-8 x 13-6

Linen

DN

UP

BR 3 10-2 x 9-5

27' - 0"

45' - 5"

First Floor
1,062 sq. ft.

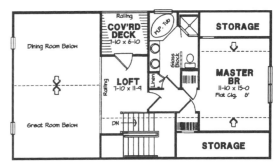

Railing

COV'RD DECK 7-10 x 6-10

STORAGE

Dining Room Below

Railing

Glass Block

LOFT 7-10 x 11-4

Linen

MASTER BR 11-10 x 15-0
Flat Clg. 8'

Great Room Below

DN

STORAGE

Second Floor
500 sq. ft.

PLAN DATA

Total Living Area: 1,562
Bedrooms: 3
Baths: 2
Foundation Type:
  Basement
Features:
  Optional lower level
  has an addtional 678
  square feet of living
  area

Ref. W F.

WET BAR 12-5 x 10-1

PATIO

OPTIONAL REC ROOM 18-8 x 23-5

UNFINISHED BASEMENT 15-8 x 23-5

storage

UP

Optional Lower Level

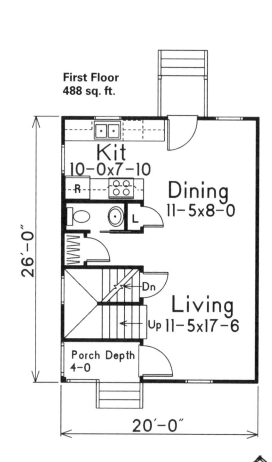

First Floor
488 sq. ft.

Kit
10-0x7-10

Dining
11-5x8-0

26'-0"

Dn

Living
Up 11-5x17-6

Porch Depth
4-0

20'-0"

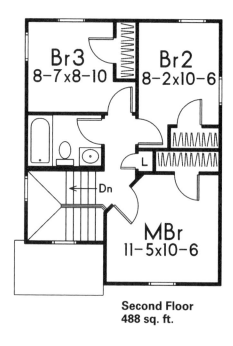

Br3
8-7x8-10

Br2
8-2x10-6

L

Dn

MBr
11-5x10-6

Second Floor
488 sq. ft.

PLAN DATA

Total Living Area:	976
Bedrooms:	3
Baths:	1 1/2
Foundation Type:	
Basement	

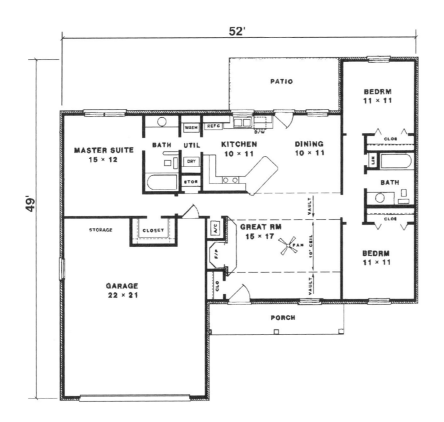

PLAN DATA

Total Living Area: 1,267
Bedrooms: 3
Baths: 2
Garage: 2-car
Foundation Types:
  Slab
  Crawl space
Please specify when ordering

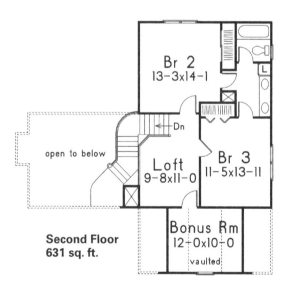

**Second Floor
631 sq. ft.**

Br 2
13-3x14-1

Dn

open to below

Loft
9-8x11-0

Br 3
11-5x13-11

Bonus Rm
12-0x10-0
vaulted

PLAN DATA

Total Living Area:	1,889
Bedrooms:	3
Baths:	2 1/2
Garage:	2-car
Foundation Type:	
Basement	

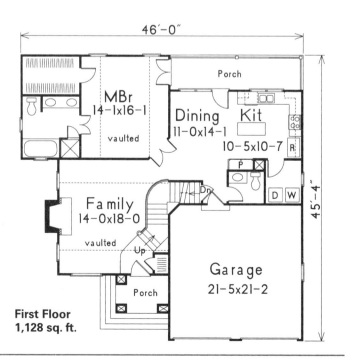

46'-0"

Porch

MBr
14-1x16-1
vaulted

Dining
11-0x14-1

Kit
10-5x10-7

R

45'-4"

P

D W

Family
14-0x18-0
vaulted

Dn

Up

Garage
21-5x21-2

Porch

**First Floor
1,128 sq. ft.**

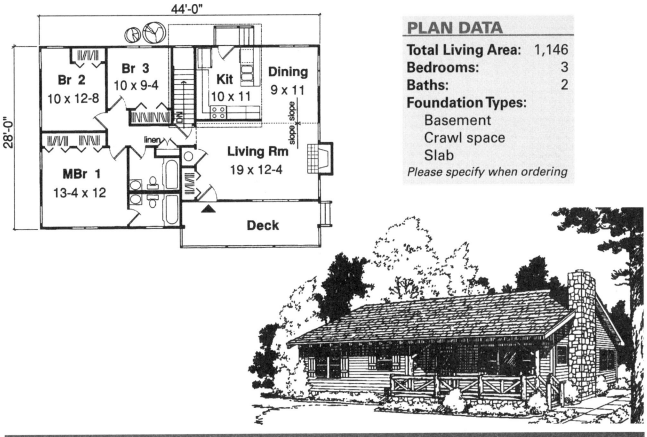

44'-0"

28'-0"

| Br 2 10 x 12-8 | Br 3 10 x 9-4 | Kit 10 x 11 | Dining 9 x 11 |

linen

MBr 1 13-4 x 12

slope slope

Living Rm 19 x 12-4

Deck

PLAN DATA
Total Living Area: 1,146
Bedrooms: 3
Baths: 2
Foundation Types:
   Basement
   Crawl space
   Slab
Please specify when ordering

PLAN DATA
Total Living Area: 1,104
Bedrooms: 3
Baths: 2
Foundation Types:
   Crawl space standard
   Basement
   Slab

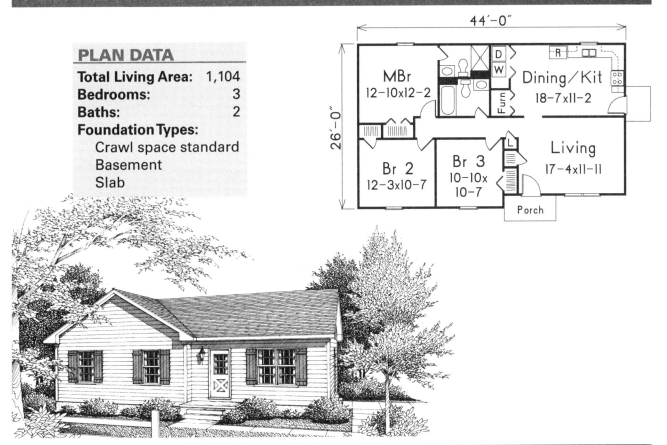

44'-0"

26'-0"

| MBr 12-10x12-2 | Dining/Kit 18-7x11-2 |

Furn

| Br 2 12-3x10-7 | Br 3 10-10x 10-7 | Living 17-4x11-11 |

Porch

PLAN DATA

Total Living Area:	581
Bedrooms:	1
Baths:	1
Foundation Type:	
Slab	

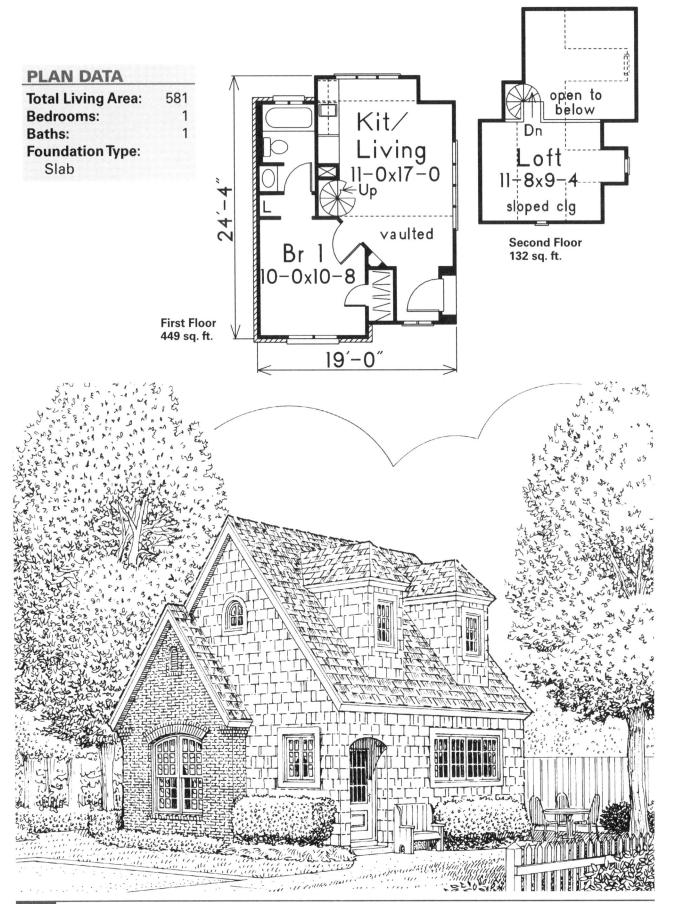

Kit/
Living
11-0x17-0
Up
vaulted

Br 1
10-0x10-8

24'-4"

19'-0"

First Floor
449 sq. ft.

open to
below

Dn

Loft
11-8x9-4

sloped clg

Second Floor
132 sq. ft.

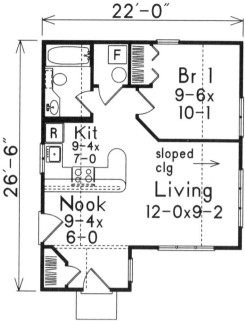

22'-0"

26'-6"

Br 1
9-6x
10-1

sloped clg

Living
12-0x9-2

F

R

Kit
9-4x
7-0

Nook
9-4x
6-0

PLAN DATA

Total Living Area:	527
Bedrooms:	1
Baths:	1
Foundation Type:	
Crawl space	

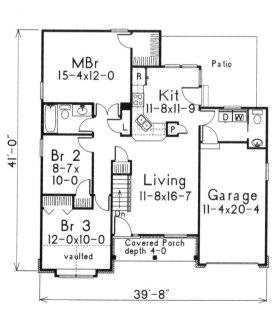

41'-0"

39'-8"

MBr
15-4x12-0

R

Patio

Kit
11-8x11-9

L

P

D W

Br 2
8-7x
10-0

Living
11-8x16-7

Garage
11-4x20-4

Dn

Br 3
12-0x10-0
vaulted

Covered Porch
depth 4-0

PLAN DATA

Total Living Area:	1,092
Bedrooms:	3
Baths:	1 1/2
Garage:	1-car
Foundation Type:	
Basement	

PLAN DATA

Total Living Area: 1,921
Bedrooms: 3
Baths: 2 1/2
Garage: 2-car
Foundation Type:
  Basement
Features:
  2" x 6" exterior walls

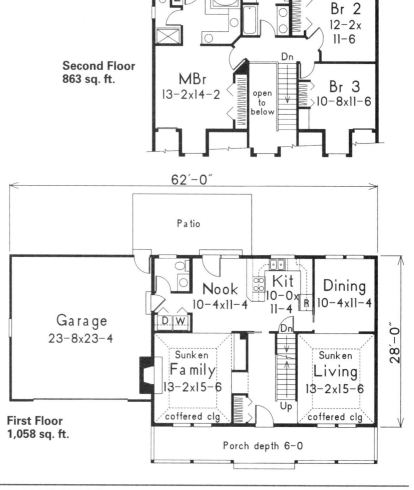

Second Floor
863 sq. ft.

Deck

Br 2
12-2x
11-6

MBr
13-2x14-2

Dn

open
to
below

Br 3
10-8x11-6

62'-0"

Patio

Nook
10-4x11-4

Kit
10-0x
11-4

Dining
10-4x11-4

Garage
23-8x23-4

D W

R

Sunken
Family
13-2x15-6

Dn

Sunken
Living
13-2x15-6

coffered clg

Up

coffered clg

28'-0"

First Floor
1,058 sq. ft.

Porch depth 6-0

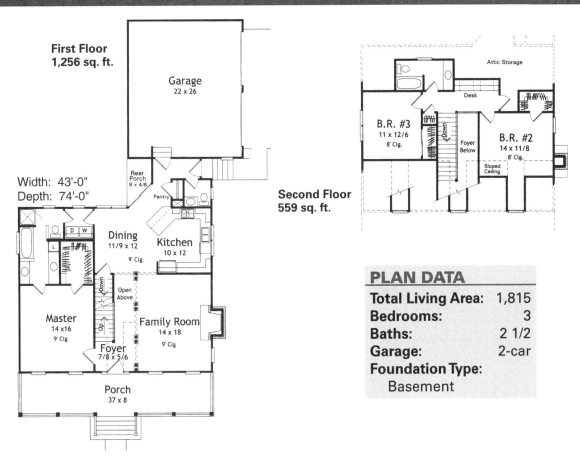

First Floor
1,256 sq. ft.

Garage
22 x 26

Width: 43'-0"
Depth: 74'-0"

Rear
Porch
9 x 4/6

Pantry

Dining
11/9 x 12
9' Clg.

Kitchen
10 x 12

D W

L

Open
Above

Down

Master
14 x16
9' Clg

Up

Foyer
7/8 x 5/6

Family Room
14 x 18
9' Clg

Porch
37 x 8

Second Floor
559 sq. ft.

Attic Storage

Desk

B.R. #3
11 x 12/6
8' Clg.

Down

Foyer
Below

B.R. #2
14 x 11/8
8' Clg.

Sloped
Ceiling

PLAN DATA

Total Living Area: 1,815
Bedrooms: 3
Baths: 2 1/2
Garage: 2-car
Foundation Type:
Basement

GARAGE
22' x 21'

DISAPPEARING STAIRS

STORAGE
11' x 5'

UTILITY
11' x 5'

WASH

DRY

W H

PATIO

BATH

DRESS.

RANGE
SINK
REFRIGERATOR

DISHWASHER PANTRY

BROOMS

KITCHEN
12' x 10'

DINING
12' x 12'

BEAM

MASTER
BEDROOM
16' x 12'

LIVING
18' x 16'

SLOPE CEILING

FLAT CEILING

BEDROOM
12' x 10'

HEAT
IN AC

LINEN

BATH

BEDROOM
12' x 10'

59'-0"

PORCH
42' x 5'

44'-6"

PLAN DATA
Total Living Area: 1,191
Bedrooms: 3
Baths: 2
Garage: 2-car
Foundation Types:
  Crawl space
  Slab
Please specify when ordering
Features:
  2" x 6" exterior walls

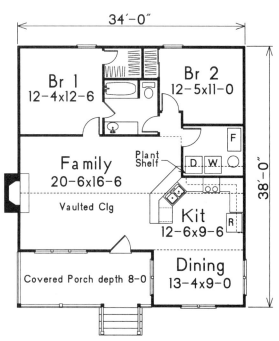

34'-0"

Br 1
12-4x12-6

Br 2
12-5x11-0

F

Family
20-6x16-6

Plant Shelf

D. W.

Vaulted Clg

Kit
12-6x9-6

R

38'-0"

Covered Porch depth 8-0

Dining
13-4x9-0

PLAN DATA
Total Living Area: 1,143
Bedrooms: 2
Baths: 1
Foundation Type:
  Crawl space

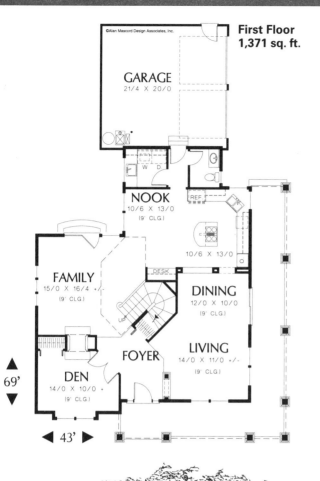

First Floor
1,371 sq. ft.

©Alan Mascord Design Associates, Inc.

GARAGE
21/4 X 20/0

NOOK
10/6 X 13/0
(9' CLG.)

W D

REF.

10/6 X 13/0

FAMILY
15/0 X 16/4 +/-
(9' CLG.)

DESK

DINING
12/0 X 10/0
(9' CLG.)

UP

FOYER

LIVING
14/0 X 11/0 +/-
(9' CLG.)

DEN
14/0 X 10/0 +
(9' CLG.)

▲ 69' ▼

◀ 43' ▶

BR. 3
10/6 X 13/0

PLANT SHELF

FAMILY BELOW

©Alan Mascord Design Associates, Inc.

DN

LINEN

BR. 2
12/4 X 11/0

VAULTED
MASTER
12/0 X 15/0 +

Second Floor
916 sq. ft.

PLAN DATA

Total Living Area:	2,287
Bedrooms:	4
Baths:	2 1/2
Garage:	2-car
Foundation Type:	
Crawl space	

PLAN DATA

Total Living Area: 1,668
Bedrooms: 3
Baths: 2
Garage: 2-car
Foundation Types:
   Partial basement/
   crawl space -
   standard
   Crawl space
   Slab

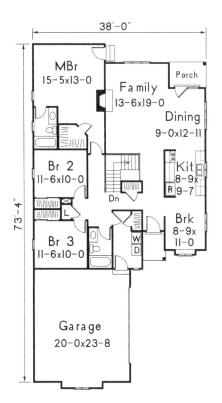

PLAN DATA

Total Living Area: 1,624
Bedrooms: 3
Baths: 2
Garage: 2-car
Foundation Types:
   Basement standard
   Crawl space
   Slab

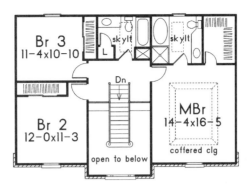

Second Floor
859 sq. ft.

PLAN DATA

Total Living Area: 1,996
Bedrooms: 3
Baths: 2 1/2
Garage: 2-car
Foundation Types:
  Basement standard
  Crawl space
  Slab
Features:
  9' ceilings on first
  floor

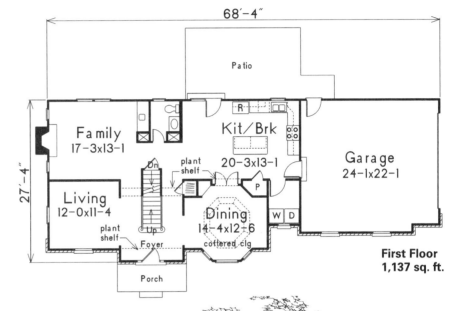

First Floor
1,137 sq. ft.

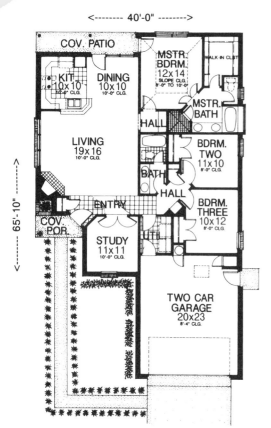

COV. PATIO

KIT
10 x 10
8'-0" CLG.

DINING
10 x 10
10'-0" CLG.

MSTR.
BDRM.
12 x 14
SLOPE CLG.
8'-0" TO 10'-0"

WALK-IN CLST.

MSTR.
BATH

HALL

LIVING
19 x 16
10'-0" CLG.

BATH

BDRM.
TWO
11 x 10
8'-0" CLG.

HALL

ENTRY

BDRM.
THREE
10 x 12
8'-0" CLG.

COV.
POR.

STUDY
11 x 11
10'-0" CLG.

UTIL.

TWO CAR
GARAGE
20 x 23
8'-4" CLG.

40'-0"

65'-10"

PLAN DATA

Total Living Area: 1,604
Bedrooms: 3
Baths: 2
Garage: 2-car
Foundation Type:
  Slab

PLAN DATA

Total Living Area: 1,496
Bedrooms: 3
Baths: 2
Garage: 2-car
Foundation Type:
  Basement
Features:
  Drive-under garage

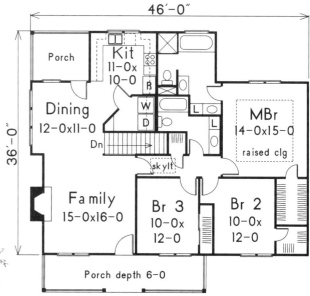

46'-0"

36'-0"

Porch

Kit
11-0x
10-0

R

W
D

Dn

sk ylt

Dining
12-0x11-0

MBr
14-0x15-0
raised clg

L

L

Family
15-0x16-0

Br 3
10-0x
12-0

Br 2
10-0x
12-0

Porch depth 6-0

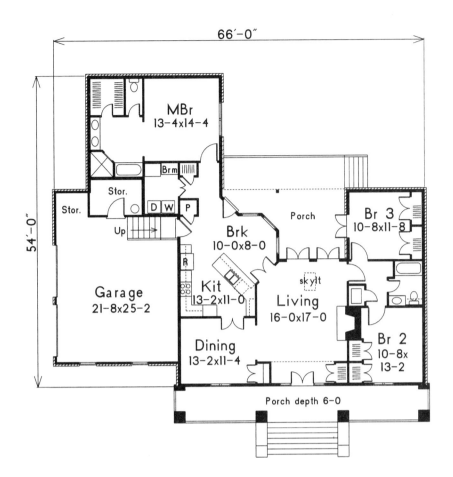

66'-0"

54'-0"

MBr
13-4x14-4

Brm

Stor.

Stor.

Up

Garage
21-8x25-2

R

Kit
13-2x11-0

Brk
10-0x8-0

Porch

Living
16-0x17-0

sky lt

Br 3
10-8x11-8

Br 2
10-8x
13-2

Dining
13-2x11-4

Porch depth 6-0

D W P

PLAN DATA

Total Living Area: 1,800
Bedrooms: 3
Baths: 2
Garage: 2-car
Foundation Types:
  Crawl space standard
  Slab
Features:
  - 2" x 6" exterior walls
  - 12' ceilings in
    kitchen, eating area,
    bedroom #2, dining
    and living rooms

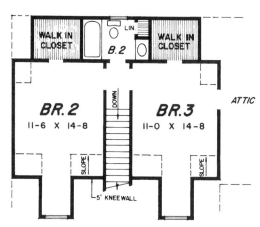

**Second Floor
548 sq. ft.**

WALK IN CLOSET

LIN

B.2

WALK IN CLOSET

BR.2
11-6 X 14-8

DOWN

BR.3
11-0 X 14-8

ATTIC

SLOPE

SLOPE

5' KNEE WALL

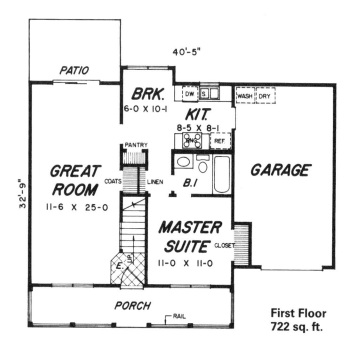

40'-5"

PATIO

BRK.
6-0 X 10-1

DW S

WASH DRY

KIT.
8-5 X 8-1

RNG REF.

PANTRY

GREAT
ROOM
11-6 X 25-0

COATS LINEN

B.1

GARAGE

32'-9"

MASTER
SUITE
11-0 X 11-0

CLOSET

E. UP

PORCH

RAIL

**First Floor
722 sq. ft.**

PLAN DATA
Total Living Area: 1,270
Bedrooms: 3
Baths: 2
Garage: 1-car
Foundation Types:
 Crawl space
 Slab
Please specify when ordering

PLAN #563-0503

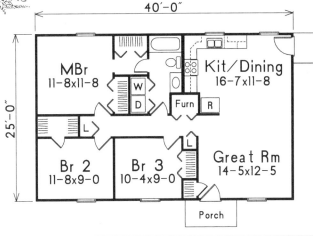

40'-0"

25'-0"

MBr
11-8x11-8

Kit/Dining
16-7x11-8

W
D

Furn R

L

L

Br 2
11-8x9-0

Br 3
10-4x9-0

Great Rm
14-5x12-5

Porch

PLAN DATA

Total Living Area: 1,000
Bedrooms: 3
Baths: 1
Foundation Types:
  Crawl space standard
  Basement
  Slab

PLAN #563-FB-3484

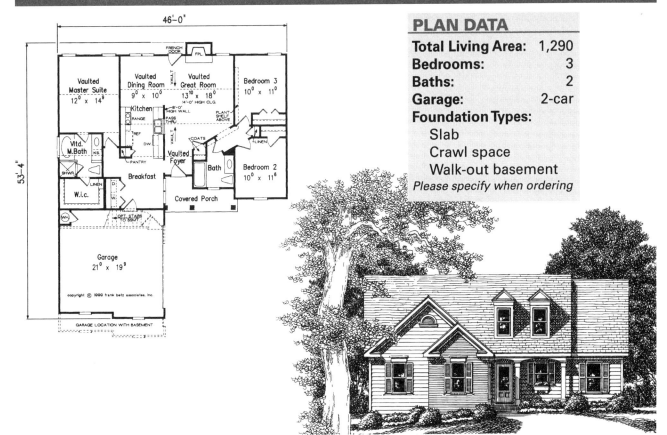

46'-0"

53'-4"

FRENCH DOOR   FPL

Vaulted
Master Suite
12⁰ x 14⁹

Vaulted
Dining Room
9⁰ x 10⁰

Vaulted
Great Room
13¹⁰ x 18⁰
14'-0" HIGH CLG.

VAULT

8'-0"
HIGH WALL

PASS
THRU

PLANT
SHELF
ABOVE

Bedroom 3
10⁰ x 11⁰

Kitchen
RANGE

REF

DW

VAULT

Vtd.
M.Bath
KS.

PANTRY

COATS

Vaulted
Foyer

LINEN

Bath

Bedroom 2
10⁰ x 11⁶

SHWR.

LINEN

W.i.c.

D.
W.

Breakfast

Covered Porch

W.H.

OPT STAIRS
TO BSMT.

Garage
21⁰ x 19⁹

copyright © 1999 frank betz associates, inc.

GARAGE LOCATION WITH BASEMENT

PLAN DATA

Total Living Area: 1,290
Bedrooms: 3
Baths: 2
Garage: 2-car
Foundation Types:
  Slab
  Crawl space
  Walk-out basement
Please specify when ordering

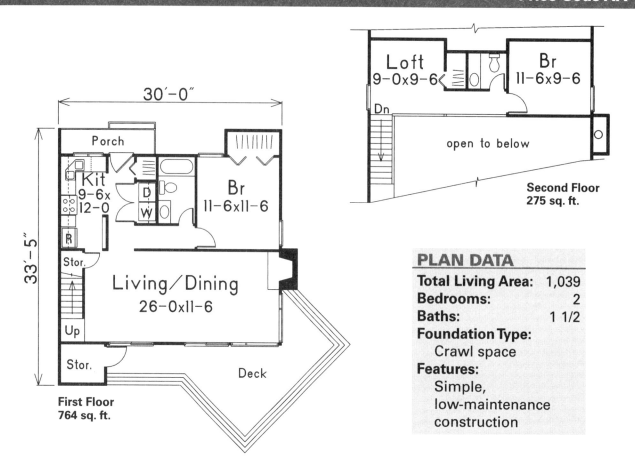

Porch

Kit
9-6x
12-0

Br
11-6x11-6

D
W

Stor.

Living/Dining
26-0x11-6

Up

Stor.

Deck

30'-0"

33'-5"

**First Floor
764 sq. ft.**

Loft
9-0x9-6

Br
11-6x9-6

Dn

open to below

**Second Floor
275 sq. ft.**

PLAN DATA

Total Living Area: 1,039
Bedrooms: 2
Baths: 1 1/2
Foundation Type:
 Crawl space
Features:
 Simple,
 low-maintenance
 construction

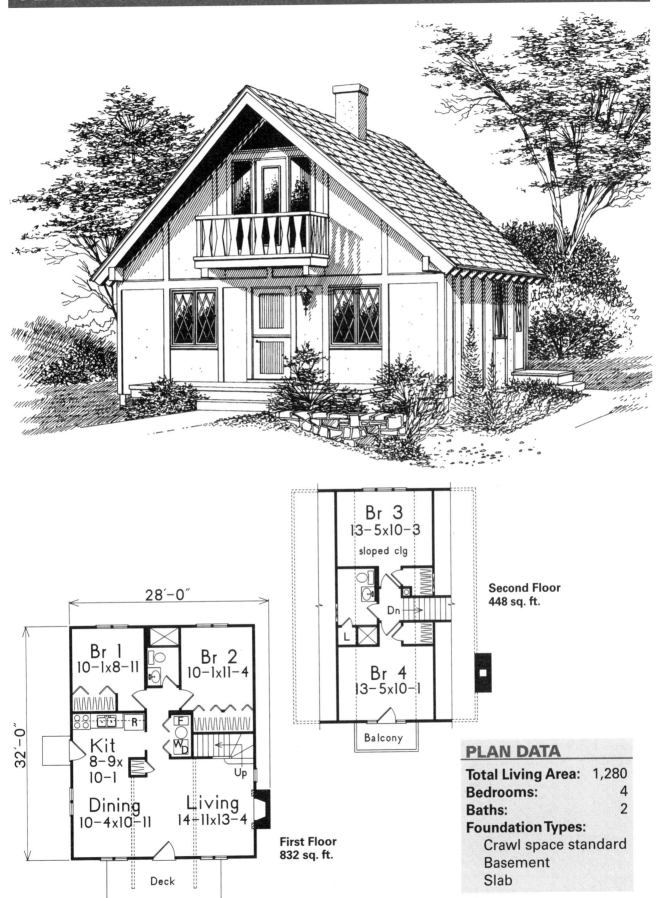

28'-0"

32'-0"

Br 1
10-1x8-11

Br 2
10-1x11-4

Kit
8-9x 10-1

Dining
10-4x10-11

Living
14-11x13-4

Up

Deck

First Floor
832 sq. ft.

Br 3
13-5x10-3
sloped clg

Dn

L

Br 4
13-5x10-1

Balcony

Second Floor
448 sq. ft.

PLAN DATA

Total Living Area: 1,280
Bedrooms: 4
Baths: 2
Foundation Types:
Crawl space standard
Basement
Slab

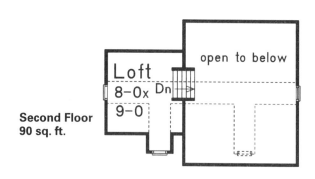

Loft
8-0x
9-0

Dn

open to below

Second Floor
90 sq. ft.

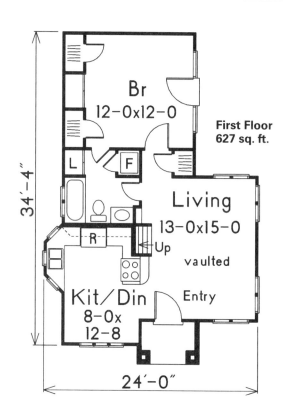

Br
12-0x12-0

First Floor
627 sq. ft.

L   F

Living
13-0x15-0

vaulted

R

Up

Entry

Kit/Din
8-0x
12-8

34'-4"

24'-0"

PLAN DATA

Total Living Area:	717
Bedrooms:	1
Baths:	1
Foundation Type:	
Slab	

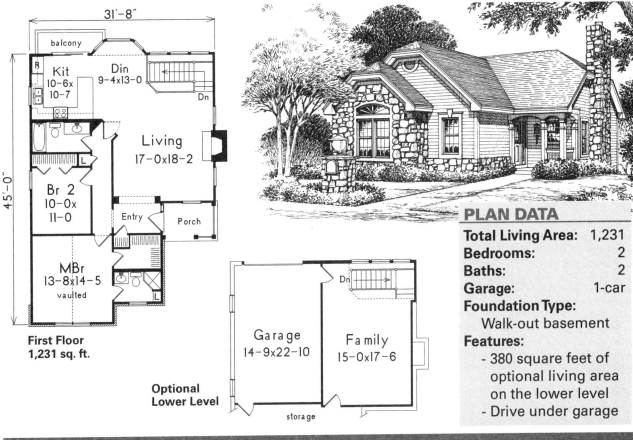

31'-8"

balcony

Kit
10-6x
10-7

Din
9-4x13-0

Dn

Living
17-0x18-2

45'-0"

Br 2
10-0x
11-0

Entry

Porch

MBr
13-8x14-5
vaulted

First Floor
1,231 sq. ft.

Dn

Garage
14-9x22-10

Family
15-0x17-6

Optional
Lower Level

storage

PLAN DATA

Total Living Area:	1,231
Bedrooms:	2
Baths:	2
Garage:	1-car

Foundation Type:
Walk-out basement

Features:
- 380 square feet of optional living area on the lower level
- Drive under garage

PLAN DATA

Total Living Area:	1,103
Bedrooms:	2
Baths:	1
Garage:	1-car

Foundation Type:
Basement

12'-4" X 13'-0"
2,70 X 3,90

10'-0" X 12'-8"
3,00 X 3,80

11'-4" X 10'-0"
3,40 X 3,00

12'-0" X 10'-0"
3,60 X 3,00

48'-0"
14,4 m

13'-0" X 14'-4"
3,90 X 4,30

12'-0" X 20'-4"
3,60 X 6,10

30'-8"
9,2 m

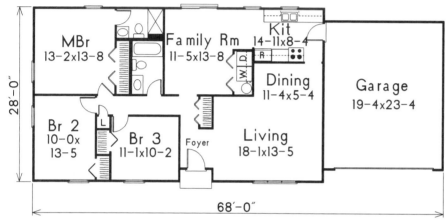

MBr 13-2x13-8	Family Rm 11-5x13-8	Kit 14-11x8-4	
Br 2 10-0x 13-5	Br 3 11-1x10-2	Dining 11-4x5-4	Garage 19-4x23-4
	Foyer	Living 18-1x13-5	

28'-0"

68'-0"

PLAN DATA

Total Living Area:	1,343
Bedrooms:	3
Baths:	2
Garage:	2-car
Foundation Types:	
Crawl space standard	
Basement	

PLAN DATA

Total Living Area:	1,393
Bedrooms:	3
Baths:	2
Garage:	detached 2-car
Foundation Types:	
Crawl space standard	
Slab	

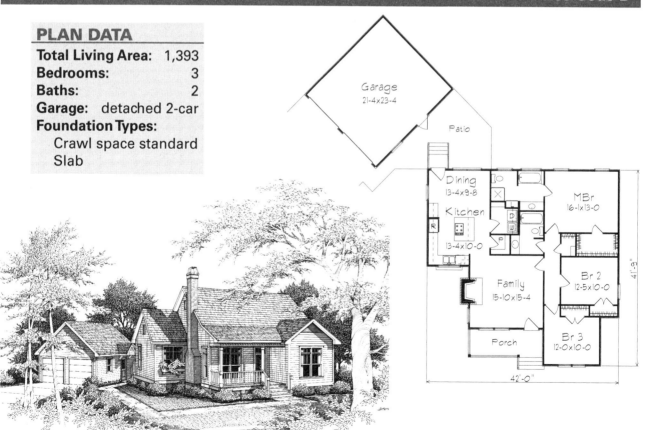

Garage 21-4x23-4

Patio

Dining 13-4x9-8

Kitchen 13-4x10-0

MBr 16-1x13-0

Family 15-10x15-4

Br 2 12-5x10-0

Porch

Br 3 12-0x10-0

41'-9"

42'-0"

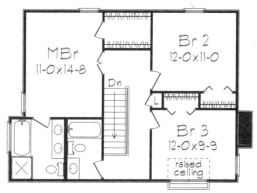

Second Floor
732 sq. ft.

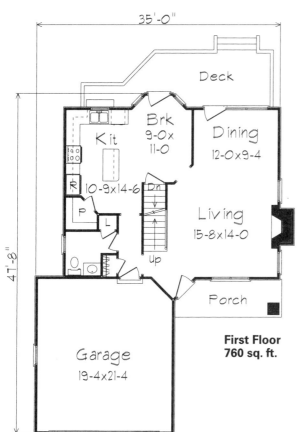

First Floor
760 sq. ft.

PLAN DATA

Total Living Area:	1,492
Bedrooms:	3
Baths:	2 1/2
Garage:	2-car
Foundation Type:	
Basement	

PLAN DATA

Total Living Area: 1,806
Bedrooms: 3
Baths: 2
Foundation Type:
  Basement

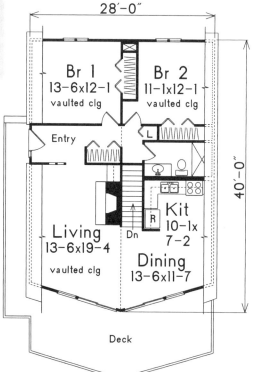

28'-0"

Br 1
13-6x12-1
vaulted clg

Br 2
11-1x12-1
vaulted clg

Entry

L

40'-0"

Living
13-6x19-4

vaulted clg

Dn

Kit
10-1x
7-2

R

Dining
13-6x11-7

**First Floor
1,064 sq. ft.**

Deck

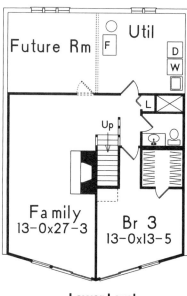

Future Rm

Util

F

D

W

L

Up

Family
13-0x27-3

Br 3
13-0x13-5

**Lower Level
742 sq. ft.**

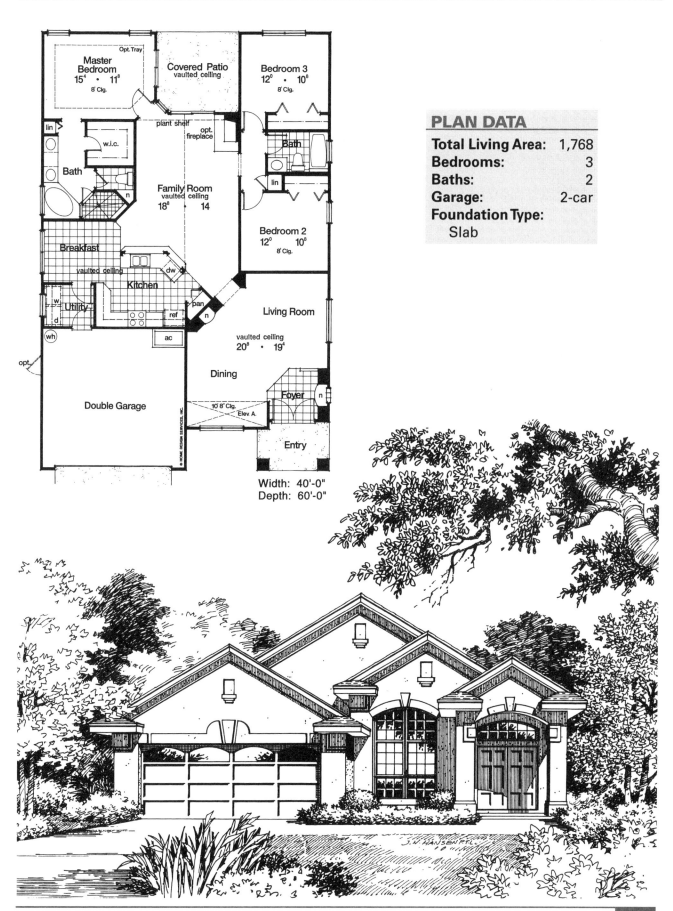

Master Bedroom
15⁴ · 11⁸
8' Clg.
Opt. Tray

Covered Patio
vaulted ceiling

Bedroom 3
12⁰ · 10⁸
8' Clg.

lin

w.i.c.

Bath

plant shelf

opt. fireplace

Bath

lin

Family Room
vaulted ceiling
18⁸   14

n

Bedroom 2
12⁰ · 10⁸
8' Clg.

Breakfast
vaulted ceiling

dw

Kitchen

pan

ref

n

Living Room
vaulted ceiling
20⁸ · 19⁴

w
Utility
d

wh

ac

opt.

Dining

10' 8" Clg.
Elev. A.

Foyer

n

Double Garage

Entry

Width: 40'-0"
Depth: 60'-0"

PLAN DATA

Total Living Area:	1,768
Bedrooms:	3
Baths:	2
Garage:	2-car
Foundation Type:	
Slab	

J.N. HANSEN PTL.

PLAN DATA

Total Living Area: 1,453
Bedrooms: 3
Baths: 2
Garage: 2-car
Foundation Types:
  Basement standard
  Crawl space
Features:
  2" x 6" exterior walls

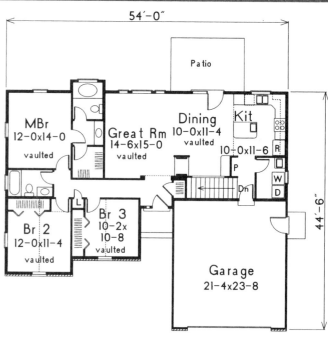

PLAN DATA

Total Living Area: 1,429
Bedrooms: 3
Baths: 2
Garage: 2-car
Foundation Type:
  Slab

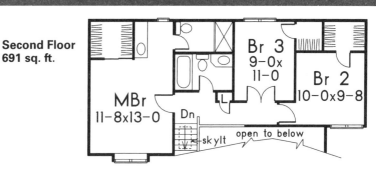

Second Floor
691 sq. ft.

MBr
11-8x13-0

Br 3
9-0x
11-0

Br 2
10-0x9-8

Dn

skylt

open to below

PLAN DATA

Total Living Area: 1,359
Bedrooms: 3
Baths: 2 1/2
Garage: 2-car
Foundation Type:
 Basement

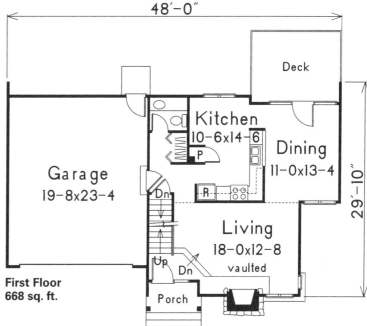

48'-0"

29'-10"

Deck

Kitchen
10-6x14-6

Dining
11-0x13-4

Garage
19-8x23-4

P

Dn

R

Living
18-0x12-8
vaulted

Up

Dn

Porch

First Floor
668 sq. ft.

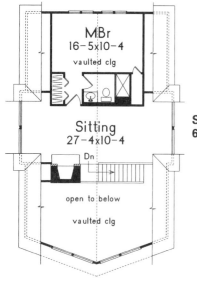

Second Floor
624 sq. ft.

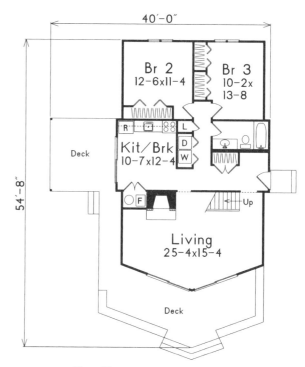

First Floor
1,126 sq. ft.

PLAN DATA

Total Living Area: 1,750
Bedrooms: 3
Baths: 2
Foundation Types:
   Basement standard
   Crawl space
   Slab

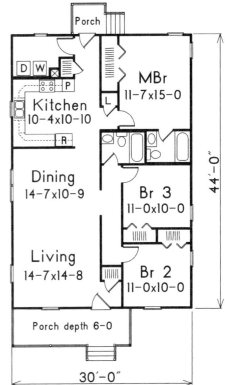

Porch

MBr
11-7x15-0

D W

Kitchen
10-4x10-10

L

Dining
14-7x10-9

Br 3
11-0x10-0

Living
14-7x14-8

Br 2
11-0x10-0

Porch depth 6-0

44'-0"

30'-0"

PLAN DATA

Total Living Area: 1,320
Bedrooms: 3
Baths: 2
Foundation Type:
Crawl space

PLAN DATA

Total Living Area: 1,712
Bedrooms: 3
Baths: 2 1/2
Garage: 2-car
Foundation Type:
Crawl space
Features:
9' wide patio doors in great room

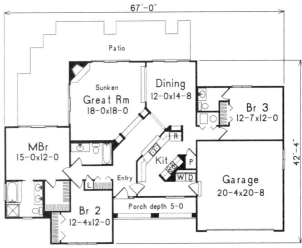

67'-0"

Patio

Sunken
Great Rm
18-0x18-0

Dining
12-0x14-8

Br 3
12-7x12-0

MBr
15-0x12-0

Kit

Entry

Garage
20-4x20-8

L

Br 2
12-4x12-0

Porch depth 5-0

42'-4"

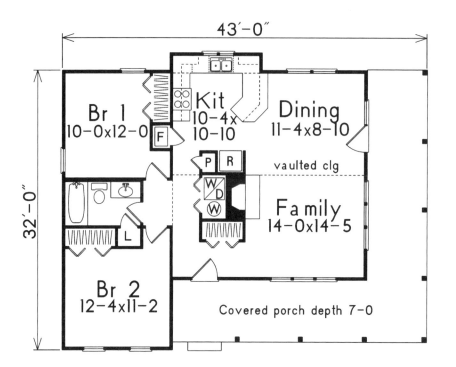

43'-0"

32'-0"

Br 1
10-0x12-0

Kit
10-4x
10-10

Dining
11-4x8-10

F

vaulted clg

P R

W
D

W

Family
14-0x14-5

L

Br 2
12-4x11-2

Covered porch depth 7-0

PLAN DATA

Total Living Area:	990
Bedrooms:	2
Baths:	1
Foundation Type:	
Crawl space	

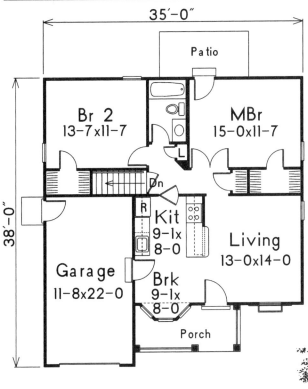

35'-0"

38'-0"

Patio

Br 2
13-7x11-7

MBr
15-0x11-7

Dn

Kit
9-1x
8-0

Living
13-0x14-0

Garage
11-8x22-0

Brk
9-1x
8-0

Porch

PLAN DATA

Total Living Area:	888
Bedrooms:	2
Baths:	1
Garage:	1-car
Foundation Type:	
Basement	

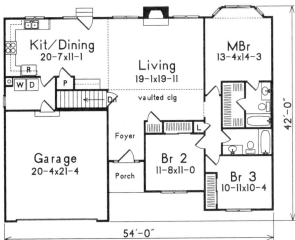

Kit/Dining
20-7x11-1

Living
19-1x19-11

vaulted clg

MBr
13-4x14-3

Foyer

Dn

Garage
20-4x21-4

Porch

Br 2
11-8x11-0

Br 3
10-11x10-4

42'-0"

54'-0"

PLAN DATA

Total Living Area:	1,558
Bedrooms:	3
Baths:	2
Garage:	2-car
Foundation Type:	
Basement	

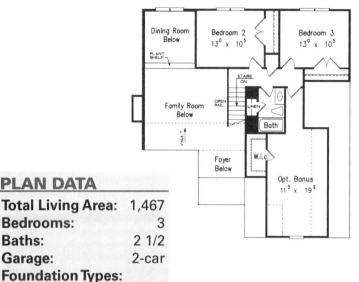

Second Floor
466 sq. ft.

First Floor
1,001 sq. ft.

PLAN DATA

Total Living Area: 1,467
Bedrooms: 3
Baths: 2 1/2
Garage: 2-car
Foundation Types:
   Walk-out basement
   Crawl space
Please specify when ordering
Features:
  - 9' ceiling throughout
  - 292 square feet of
    additional living
    area over garage

PLAN #563-0271

Price Code A

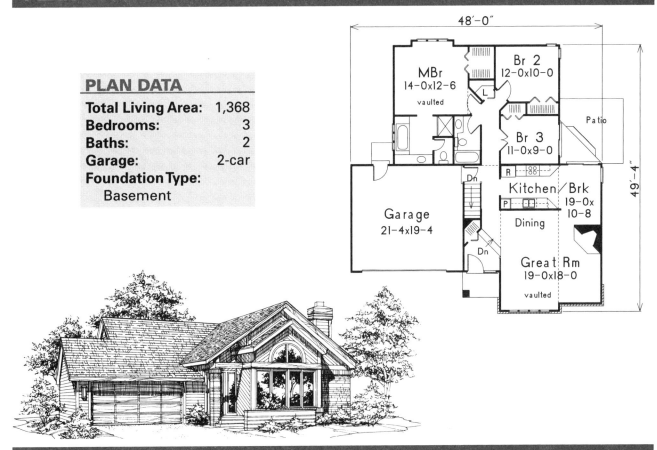

PLAN DATA

Total Living Area:	1,368
Bedrooms:	3
Baths:	2
Garage:	2-car
Foundation Type:	
Basement	

PLAN #563-1248

Price Code B

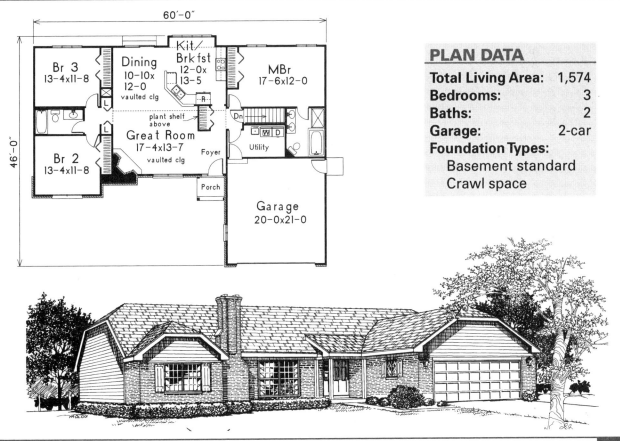

PLAN DATA

Total Living Area:	1,574
Bedrooms:	3
Baths:	2
Garage:	2-car
Foundation Types:	
Basement standard	
Crawl space	

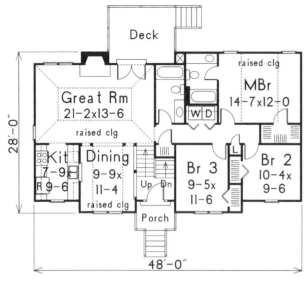

PLAN DATA

Total Living Area:	1,261
Bedrooms:	3
Baths:	2
Garage:	2-car
Foundation Type:	
Basement	
Features:	
Drive-under garage	

PLAN DATA

Total Living Area:	1,404
Bedrooms:	3
Baths:	2 1/2
Garage:	2-car
Foundation Type:	
Slab	

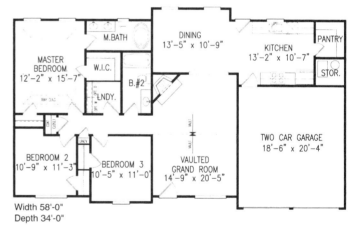

Width 58'-0"
Depth 34'-0"

© 2003, Garrell Associates, Inc.

PLAN #563-0510

PLAN DATA

Total Living Area:	1,400
Bedrooms:	3
Baths:	2
Garage:	2-car

Foundation Types:
Crawl space standard
Basement
Slab

74'-0"

28'-0"

MBr
12-3x13-6

Kit
8-1x
13-6

Dining
18-1x13-6

Garage
23-8x23-5

Br 2
12-3x10-3

Br 3
12-1x10-3

Great Rm
22-1x13-7

Porch
28-0x5-0

D W L P R Furn L

PLAN #563-0273

38'-0"

46'-0"

MBr
14-0x12-6

Deck

Kit/Din
13-0x11-4
vaulted

Br 2
12-0x10-0

Dn

Great Rm
17-8x13-8
vaulted

Garage
20-0x20-0

P R L

PLAN DATA

Total Living Area:	988
Bedrooms:	2
Baths:	1
Garage:	2-car

Foundation Type:
Basement

PLAN #563-RJ-A1079

Price Code AA

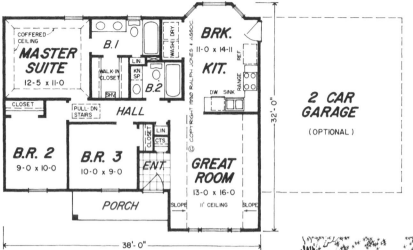

PLAN DATA

Total Living Area: 1,021
Bedrooms: 3
Baths: 2
Garage: optional 2-car
Foundation Types:
  Crawl space
  Slab
Please specify when ordering
Features:
  11' ceiling in great
  room

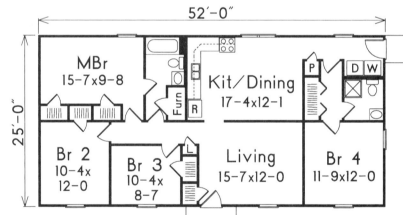

PLAN #563-0584

Price Code A

PLAN DATA

Total Living Area: 1,300
Bedrooms: 4
Baths: 2
Foundation Types:
  Crawl space standard
  Basement
  Slab

28'-0"

32'-0"

Kit. 11 x 8

linen

bar

Dining
12 x 8

DN

UP

Br 1
11-8 x 11

loft above

fireplace

Living
15 x 15

Deck

First Floor
728 sq. ft.

Second Floor
573 sq. ft.

Loft /Br 3
11-9 x 16-4

railing

clerestory windows

open to below

DN

Mbr
11-8 x 14

Lndry

D

W

furn.

w.h.

bar

Garage
11-8 x 19-4

Recreation
14-9 x 16-9

whirlpool tub

UP

Lower Level
409 sq. ft.

PLAN DATA

Total Living Area: 1,710
Bedrooms: 3
Baths: 2
Garage: 1-car
Foundation Type:
   Basement
Features:
   Drive-under garage

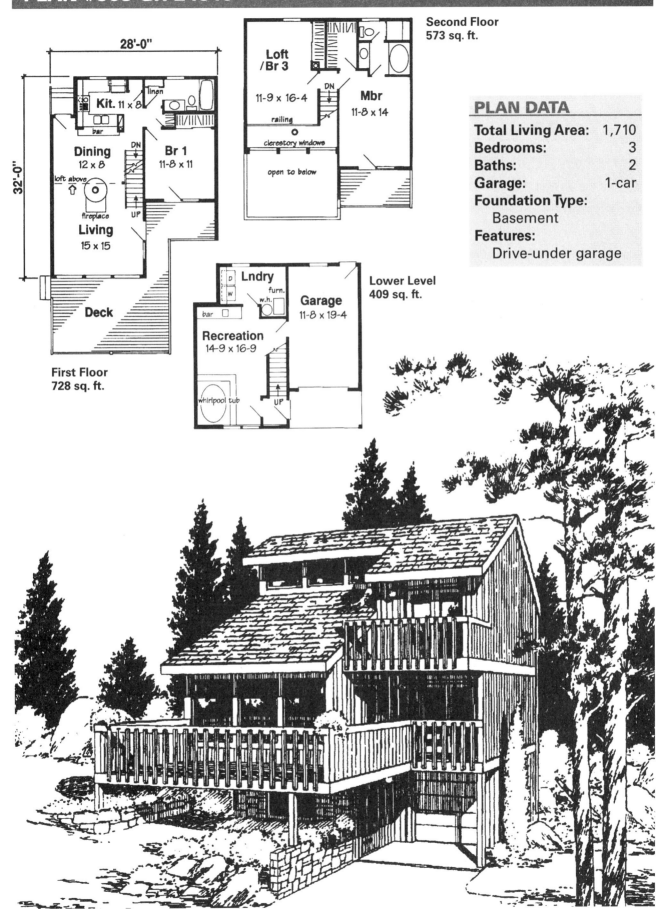

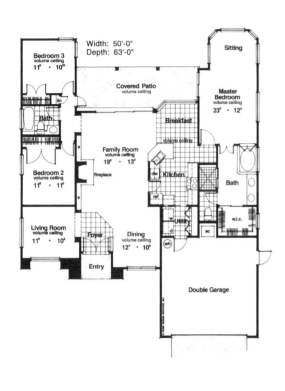

Width: 50'-0"
Depth: 63'-0"

Bedroom 3
volume ceiling
11⁰ · 10¹⁰

Sitting

Covered Patio
volume ceiling

Master Bedroom
volume ceiling
23⁰ · 12⁴

Bath

lin

Breakfast
volume ceiling

Bedroom 2
volume ceiling
11⁰ · 11⁰

Family Room
volume ceiling
19⁰ · 13⁰

fireplace

dw

Kitchen

ref

Bath

Living Room
volume ceiling
11⁰ · 10⁴

Foyer

Dining
volume ceiling
12⁴ · 10⁰

Utility

d

w.i.c.

ac

wh

Entry

Double Garage

PLAN DATA

Total Living Area:	1,817
Bedrooms:	3
Baths:	2
Garage:	2-car
Foundation Type: Slab	

PLAN DATA

Total Living Area:	1,960
Bedrooms:	3
Baths:	2
Garage:	2-car
Foundation Type: Slab	

Width: 50'-0"
Depth: 60'-8"

MASTER

CLOSET

B.R.-2

PORCH

BATH

FAMILY RM.

KITCH.

NOOK

B.R.-3

DINING

GARAGE

LIVING

POR.

© David C. Lutz

Second Floor
576 sq. ft.

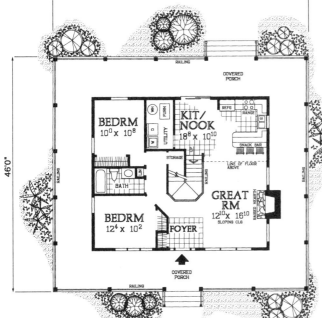

52'0"

46'0"

First Floor
1,093 sq. ft.

PLAN DATA

Total Living Area:	1,669
Bedrooms:	3
Baths:	2
Foundation Type:	
Crawl space	

PLAN DATA

Total Living Area:	1,742
Bedrooms:	3
Baths:	2
Garage:	2-car
Foundation Types:	
Slab standard	
Crawl space	

PLAN DATA

Total Living Area:	1,499
Bedrooms:	3
Baths:	2
Garage:	2-car
Foundation Type:	
Basement	
Features:	
Vaulted and cathedral ceilings throughout	

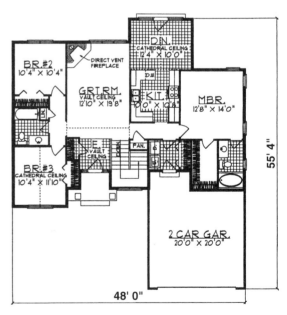

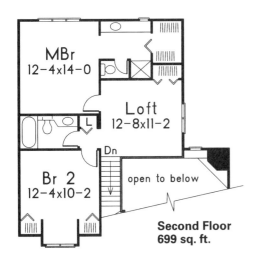

MBr
12-4x14-0

Loft
12-8x11-2

Br 2
12-4x10-2

Dn

open to below

**Second Floor
699 sq. ft.**

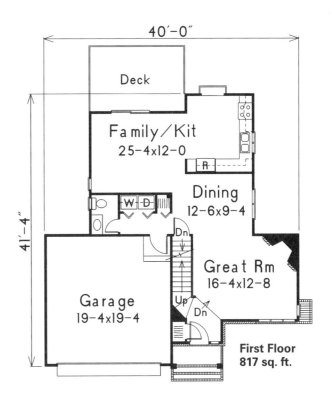

40'-0"

Deck

Family/Kit
25-4x12-0

R

Dining
12-6x9-4

41'-4"

W D

Dn

Garage
19-4x19-4

Up

Dn

Great Rm
16-4x12-8

**First Floor
817 sq. ft.**

PLAN DATA

Total Living Area:	1,516
Bedrooms:	3
Baths:	2 1/2
Garage:	2-car
Foundation Type:	
Basement	

Width: 34'-0"   Depth: 46'-0"

First Floor
1,174 sq. ft.

Second Floor
1,028 sq. ft.

PLAN DATA

Total Living Area: 2,202
Bedrooms: 5
Baths: 4 full, 2 half
Garage: 2-car
Foundation Types:
    Basement
    Walk-out basement
Please specify when ordering
Features:
    - 9' ceiling on first
      floor
    - Drive-under garage

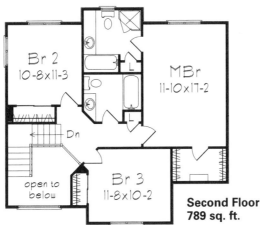

Br 2
10-8x11-3

MBr
11-10x17-2

Dn

Br 3
11-8x10-2

open to
below

**Second Floor
789 sq. ft.**

PLAN DATA

Total Living Area:	1,859
Bedrooms:	3
Baths:	2 1/2
Garage:	2-car
Foundation Type:	
Basement	

63'-4"

Brk
9-8x
11-6

Kit
10-0x13-8

Great Rm
15-2x19-0

P

R

D

36'-0"

**First Floor
1,070 sq. ft.**

vaulted

Up

Foyer

Dn

Dining
11-8x11-2

Garage
21-8x21-8

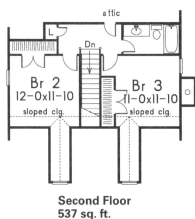

**Second Floor
537 sq. ft.**

Br 2
12-0x11-10
sloped clg.

Br 3
11-0x11-10
sloped clg.

attic

L

Dn

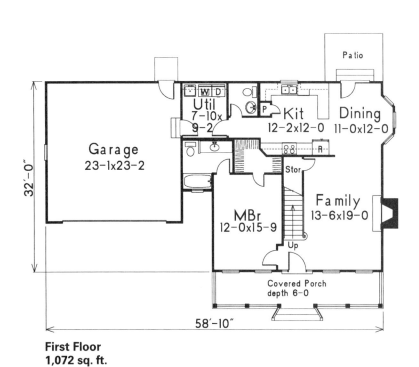

**First Floor
1,072 sq. ft.**

Garage
23-1x23-2

32'-0"

58'-10"

Util
7-10x
9-2

W D

Kit
12-2x12-0

Dining
11-0x12-0

Patio

Stor

MBr
12-0x15-9

Family
13-6x19-0

Up

P

R

Covered Porch
depth 6-0

PLAN DATA
Total Living Area: 1,609
Bedrooms: 3
Baths: 2 1/2
Garage: 2-car
Foundation Type:
Slab

PLAN DATA

Total Living Area:	784
Bedrooms:	3
Baths:	1
Foundation Type:	
Pier	

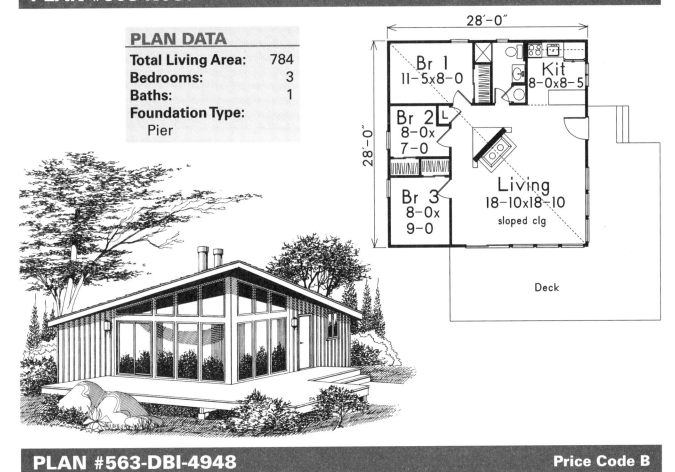

28'-0"

28'-0"

Br 1
11-5x8-0

Kit
8-0x8-5

Br 2
8-0x
7-0

L

Living
18-10x18-10
sloped clg

Br 3
8-0x
9-0

Deck

PLAN #563-DBI-4948

Price Code B

PLAN DATA

Total Living Area:	1,758
Bedrooms:	3
Baths:	2
Garage:	2-car
Foundation Type:	
Basement	

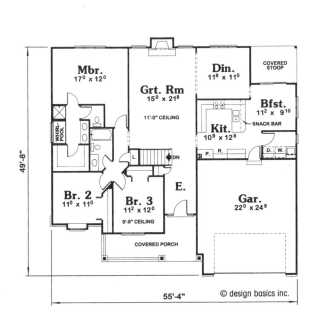

Mbr.
17⁰ x 12⁰

WHIRL-
POOL

Din.
11⁸ x 11⁰

COVERED
STOOP

Grt. Rm
15⁰ x 21⁸

11'-0" CEILING

Bfst.
11² x 9¹⁰

Kit.
10⁹ x 12⁸

SNACK BAR

L

DN

P. R.

D. W.

Br. 2
11⁰ x 11⁰

Br. 3
11² x 12⁰

9'-8" CEILING

E.

Gar.
22⁰ x 24⁸

49'-8"

COVERED PORCH

55'-4"

© design basics inc.

Second Floor
871 sq. ft.

Br 3
12-4x12-5

Br 2
11-0x12-5

Dn

open to below

Br 4
11-4x13-3

PLAN DATA

Total Living Area:	1,985
Bedrooms:	4
Baths:	3 1/2
Garage:	2-car
Foundation Type:	
Basement	

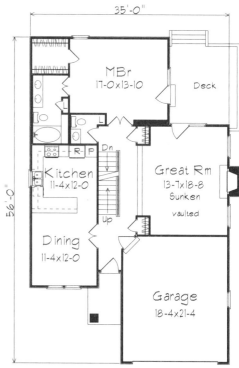

35'-0"

MBr
17-0x13-10

Deck

Kitchen
11-4x12-0

Dn

Great Rm
13-7x18-8
Sunken
vaulted

56'-0"

Dining
11-4x12-0

Up

Garage
18-4x21-4

First Floor
1,114 sq. ft.

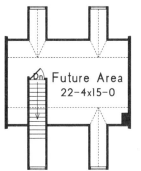

**Optional
Second Floor**

Future Area
22-4x15-0

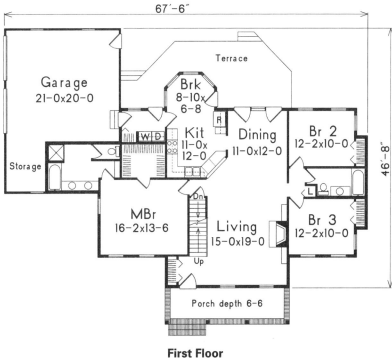

PLAN DATA

Total Living Area: 1,567
Bedrooms: 3
Baths: 2
Garage: 2-car
Foundation Types:
  Basement standard
  Slab
Features:
  Optional second floor
  has an additional 338
  square feet of living
  area

67'-6"

Terrace

Garage
21-0x20-0

Brk
8-10x
6-8

Kit
11-0x
12-0

Dining
11-0x12-0

Br 2
12-2x10-0

Storage

46'-8"

MBr
16-2x13-6

Living
15-0x19-0

Br 3
12-2x10-0

Up

Dn

Porch depth 6-6

**First Floor
1,567 sq. ft.**

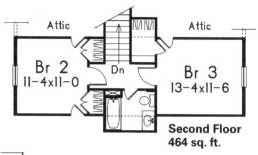

Attic

Br 2
11-4x11-0

Dn

Attic

Br 3
13-4x11-6

Second Floor
464 sq. ft.

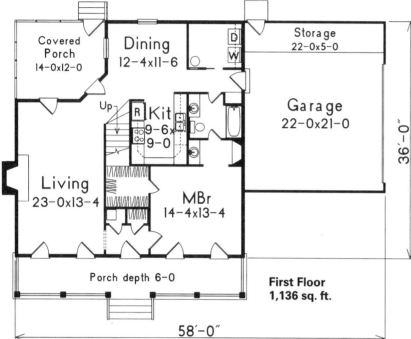

Covered Porch
14-0x12-0

Dining
12-4x11-6

D
W

Storage
22-0x5-0

Up

R **Kit**
9-6x
9-0

Garage
22-0x21-0

Living
23-0x13-4

MBr
14-4x13-4

36'-0"

Porch depth 6-0

First Floor
1,136 sq. ft.

58'-0"

PLAN DATA

Total Living Area: 1,600
Bedrooms: 3
Baths: 2
Garage: 2-car
Foundation Types:
  Crawl space standard
  Slab
Features:
  2" x 6" exterior walls

PLAN #563-0195

Price Code AA

PLAN DATA

Total Living Area: 988
Bedrooms: 3
Baths: 1
Garage: 1-car
Foundation Types:
 Basement standard
 Crawl space

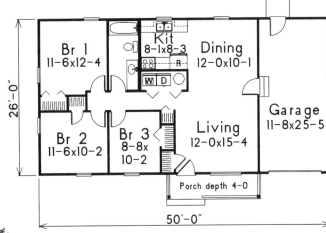

Br 1
11-6x12-4

Kit
8-1x8-3

Dining
12-0x10-1

W D

Garage
11-8x25-5

Br 2
11-6x10-2

Br 3
8-8x
10-2

Living
12-0x15-4

26'-0"

Porch depth 4-0

50'-0"

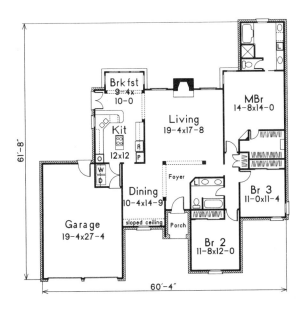

PLAN #563-0215

Price Code C

Brk fst
9-4x
10-0

MBr
14-8x14-0

Kit
12x12

Living
19-4x17-8

R
P

W
D

Foyer

Dining
10-4x14-9

Br 3
11-0x11-4

sloped ceiling

Porch

Garage
19-4x27-4

Br 2
11-8x12-0

61'-8"

60'-4"

PLAN DATA

Total Living Area: 1,846
Bedrooms: 3
Baths: 2
Garage: 2-car
Foundation Type:
 Slab

PLAN DATA

Total Living Area: 1,073
Bedrooms: 2
Baths: 1
Foundation Type:
Crawl space

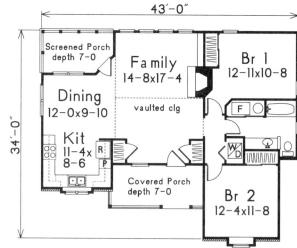

PLAN #563-JA-66096

Price Code A

PLAN DATA

Total Living Area: 1,495
Bedrooms: 3
Baths: 2
Garage: 2-car
Foundation Type:
Basement

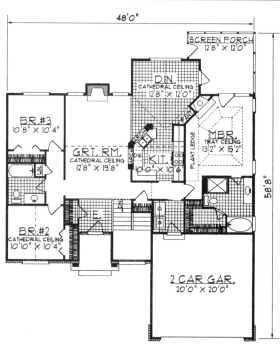

TRAY CEILING

MASTER BDRM
16'-4" x 15'-0"

D W

DN ►

BEDROOM 2
12'-0" x 12'-8"

BEDROOM 3
12'-8" x 12'-0"

WINDOW SEAT

**Second Floor
976 sq. ft.**

**First Floor
1,009 sq. ft.**

DECK
30'-6" x 11'-7"

BRKFST

PNTRY

KITCHEN
15'-0" x 17'-0"

DINING
14'-8" x 12'-8"

UP ►

ENTRY
7'-11" x 15'-6"

FAMILY
18'-8" x 16'-0"

COATS

PORCH
30'-6" x 7'-7"

◄ 31'-2" ►

◄ 42'-0" ►

PLAN DATA

Total Living Area:	1,985
Bedrooms:	3
Baths:	2 1/2

Foundation Types:
  Basement
  Crawl space
Please specify when ordering

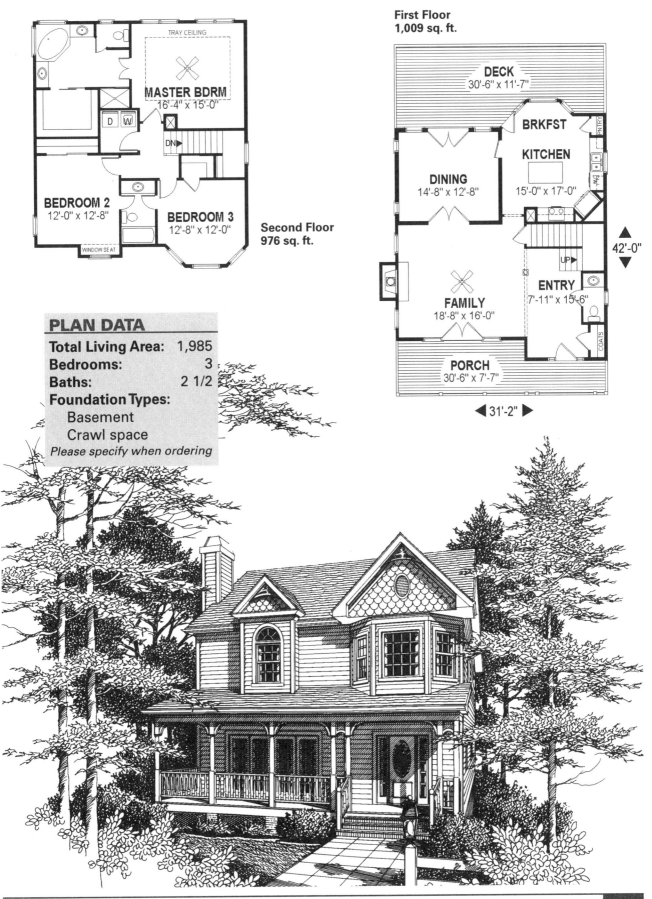

50-0 WIDE X 42-0 DEEP
(INCLUDING COVERED PORCH)

PLAN DATA

Total Living Area:	1,700
Bedrooms:	3
Baths:	2
Foundation Type:	
Crawl space	

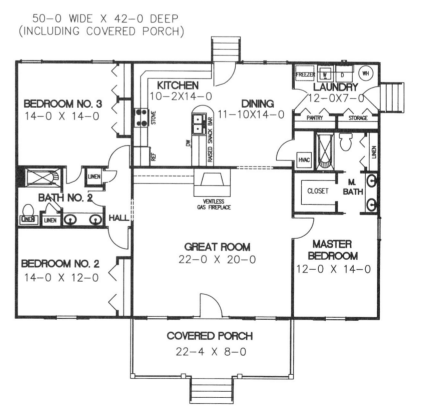

BEDROOM NO. 3
14-0 X 14-0

KITCHEN
10-2X14-0

DINING
11-10X14-0

FREEZER

LAUNDRY
12-0X7-0

STOVE

REF

DW

RAISED SNACK BAR

PANTRY

STORAGE

LINEN

HVAC

LINEN

BATH NO. 2

CLOSET

M. BATH

LINEN LINEN

HALL

VENTLESS GAS FIREPLACE

BEDROOM NO. 2
14-0 X 12-0

GREAT ROOM
22-0 X 20-0

MASTER BEDROOM
12-0 X 14-0

COVERED PORCH
22-4 X 8-0

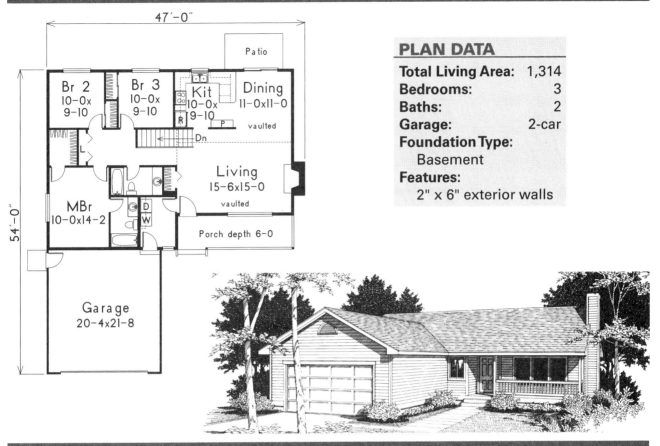

47'-0"

54'-0"

Patio

Br 2
10-0x
9-10

Br 3
10-0x
9-10

Kit
10-0x
9-10

Dining
11-0x11-0
vaulted

Dn

Living
15-6x15-0
vaulted

MBr
10-0x14-2

D
W

Porch depth 6-0

Garage
20-4x21-8

PLAN DATA

Total Living Area: 1,314
Bedrooms: 3
Baths: 2
Garage: 2-car
Foundation Type:
  Basement
Features:
  2" x 6" exterior walls

PLAN DATA

Total Living Area: 624
Bedrooms: 2
Baths: 1
Foundation Type:
  Pier

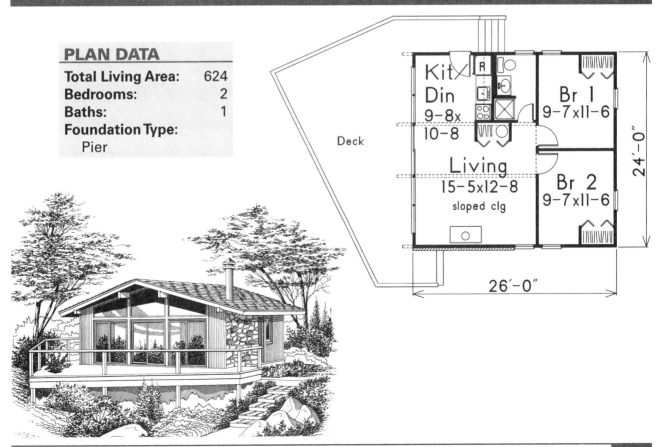

Kit
Din
9-8x
10-8

Br 1
9-7x11-6

Deck

Living
15-5x12-8
sloped clg

Br 2
9-7x11-6

24'-0"

26'-0"

PLAN DATA

Total Living Area: 1,720
Bedrooms: 3
Baths: 1 full, 2 half
Garage: 2-car
Foundation Type:
  Basement
Features:
  Drive-under garage

**First Floor
1,218 sq. ft.**

Deck

28'-0"

MBr
13-0x12-8

Kit
11-7x
12-8

Dining
9-10x
13-0

L

Br 2
10-6x9-8

Br 3
10-7x8-8

Up Dn

Living
14-11x14-5

Stoop

44'-0"

26'-0"

Garage
20-11x24-9

D
W

Furn

Up

Family
14-7x24-9

**Lower Level
502 sq. ft.**

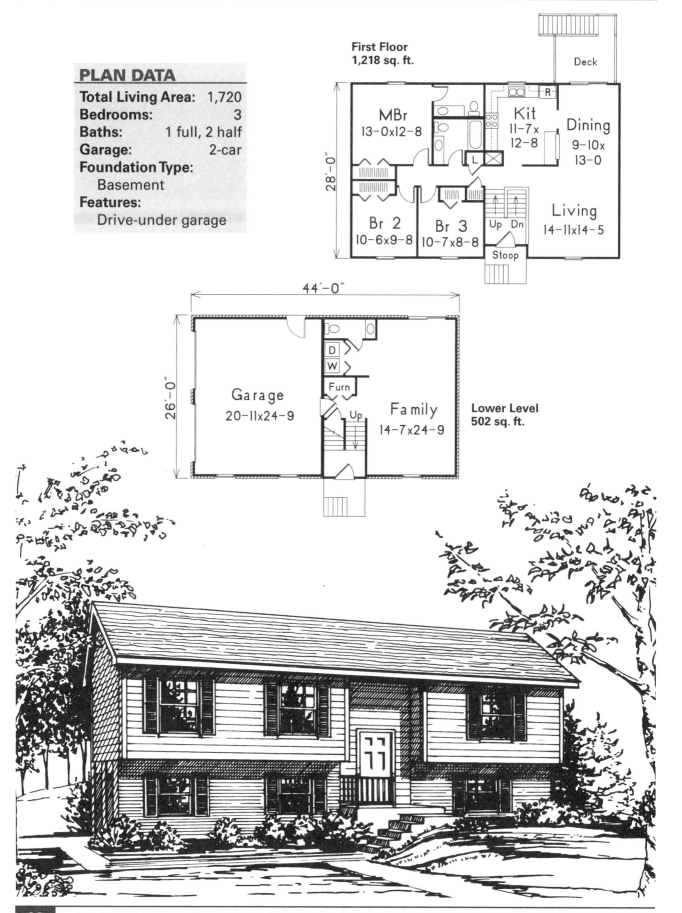

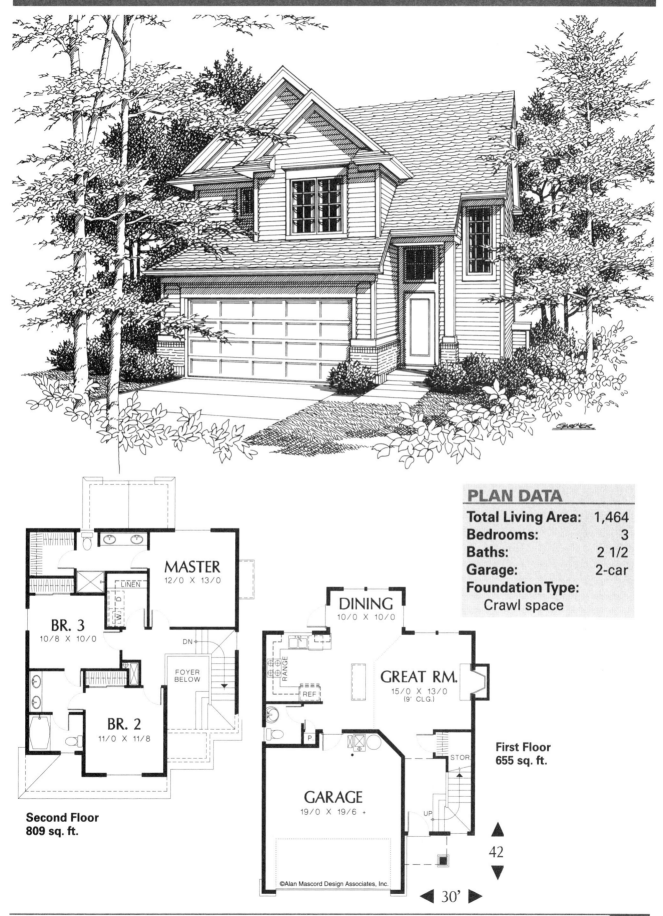

PLAN DATA

Total Living Area:	1,464
Bedrooms:	3
Baths:	2 1/2
Garage:	2-car
Foundation Type:	
Crawl space	

MASTER
12/0 X 13/0

LINEN

BR. 3
10/8 X 10/0

W D

DN

FOYER
BELOW

BR. 2
11/0 X 11/8

**Second Floor
809 sq. ft.**

DINING
10/0 X 10/0

RANGE

REF

GREAT RM.
15/0 X 13/0
(9' CLG.)

P

STOR.

**First Floor
655 sq. ft.**

GARAGE
19/0 X 19/6 +

UP

©Alan Mascord Design Associates, Inc.

42

30'

PLAN DATA

Total Living Area: 1,377
Bedrooms: 3
Baths: 1
Foundation Types:
  Crawl space
  Slab
Please specify when ordering
Features:
  Optional second floor
  has an additional
  349 square feet of
  living area

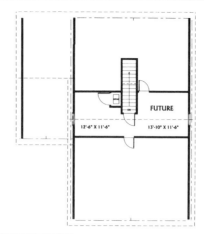

Optional
Second Floor

FUTURE

12'-6" X 11'-6"   13'-10" X 11'-6"

44'-0"

PORCH 2
30'-0" X 6'X6"

SCREENED
PORCH
13'-10" X 14'-0"

DINING

BEDROOM 2
12'-4" X 12'-0"

KITCHEN
9'-0" X 12'-0"

MASTER
BEDROOM
13'-10" X 16'-6"

BATH

51'-0"

HALL

GREAT
ROOM
17'-10" X 18'-6"

BEDROOM 3
12'-6" X 10'-6"

PORCH 1
30'-0" X 6'X6"

First Floor
1,377 sq. ft.

52'-0"

Dining
13-0x11-0
vaulted

Porch

MBr
13-4x15-0

Kit
13-0x11-0

Living
14-4x20-4

58-4"

Foyer

Garage
19-8x22-4

Porch

Br 2
11-0x12-0

Br 3
10-0x12-0

PLAN DATA

Total Living Area: 1,661
Bedrooms: 3
Baths: 2
Garage: 2-car
Foundation Type:
  Slab

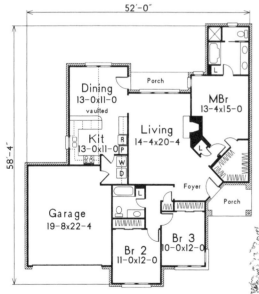

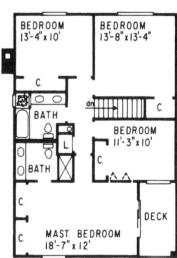

**Second Floor
1,042 sq. ft.**

BEDROOM
13'-4" x 10'

BEDROOM
13'-8" x 13'-4"

C.

BATH

dn

C.

BEDROOM
11'-3" x 10'

C.

BATH

L

C.

C.

DECK

C.

MAST. BEDROOM
18'-7" x 12'

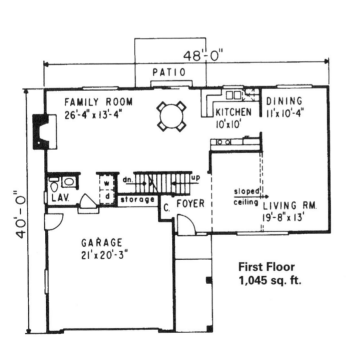

48'-0"

PATIO

FAMILY ROOM
26'-4" x 13'-4"

KITCHEN
10'x10'

DINING
11'x10'-4"

40'-0"

LAV.

w
d

dn.

storage

up

C.

FOYER

sloped
ceiling

LIVING RM.
19'-8" x 13'

GARAGE
21'x 20'-3"

**First Floor
1,045 sq. ft.**

PLAN DATA

Total Living Area: 2,087
Bedrooms: 4
Baths: 2 1/2
Garage: 2-car
Foundation Types:
  Basement standard
  Crawl space
  Slab

PLAN #563-0583

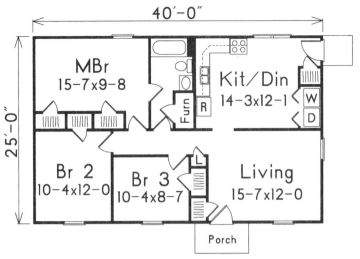

40´-0"

25´-0"

MBr
15-7x9-8

Kit/Din
14-3x12-1

Fun
R

W
D

Br 2
10-4x12-0

Br 3
10-4x8-7

L

Living
15-7x12-0

Porch

PLAN DATA

Total Living Area: 1,000
Bedrooms: 3
Baths: 1
Foundation Types:
  Crawl space standard
  Basement
  Slab

PLAN #563-0192

PLAN DATA

Total Living Area: 1,266
Bedrooms: 3
Baths: 2
Garage: 2-car
Foundation Types:
  Crawl space standard
  Slab
Features:
  2" x 6" exterior walls

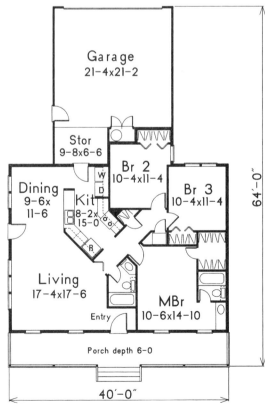

Garage
21-4x21-2

Stor
9-8x6-6

Br 2
10-4x11-4

Br 3
10-4x11-4

Dining
9-6x
11-6

Kit
8-2x
15-0

W
D

64´-0"

Living
17-4x17-6

MBr
10-6x14-10

Entry

Porch depth 6-0

40´-0"

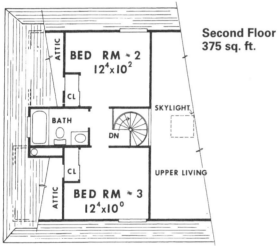

**Second Floor
375 sq. ft.**

BED RM ≠ 2
12⁴x10²

ATTIC

CL

BATH

DN

SKYLIGHT

CL

UPPER LIVING

ATTIC

BED RM ≠ 3
12⁴x10⁰

PLAN DATA

Total Living Area:	1,303
Bedrooms:	3
Baths:	2

Foundation Types:
Basement
Crawl space
Slab
Please specify when ordering

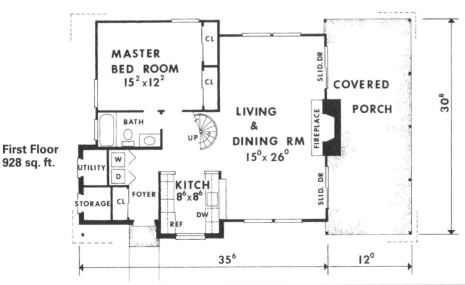

**First Floor
928 sq. ft.**

MASTER
BED ROOM
15²x12²

CL

CL

SLID. DR

COVERED
PORCH

BATH

UP

LIVING
&
DINING RM
15⁰x26⁰

FIREPLACE

30⁸

UTILITY

W

D

STORAGE

CL

FOYER

KITCH
8⁶x8⁶

DW

REF

SLID. DR

35⁶

12⁰

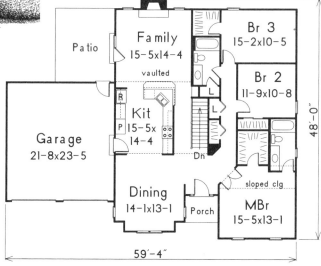

PLAN DATA

Total Living Area: 1,642
Bedrooms: 3
Baths: 2
Garage: 2-car
Foundation Types:
   Basement standard
   Crawl space
   Slab

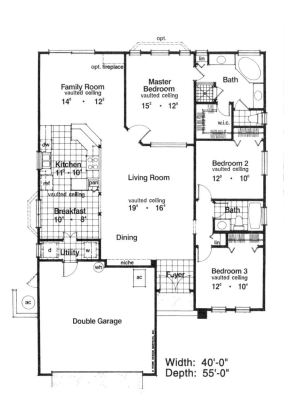

Width: 40'-0"
Depth: 55'-0"

PLAN DATA

Total Living Area: 1,565
Bedrooms: 3
Baths: 2
Garage: 2-car
Foundation Type:
   Slab
Features:
   Vaulted ceilings
   throughout

PLAN #563-CHP-1332A

Price Code A

PLAN DATA

Total Living Area: 1,363
Bedrooms: 3
Baths: 2
Foundation Type:
  Slab
Features:
  Optional 1-car carport

Master Bath

Patio 16'x 6'

Future Storage

Porch 16'x 6'

Master Bedroom 13'4"x 13'

Future Carport 12'x 20'

Living 15'8"x 14'

Walk-In Closet

Bedroom 11'x 9'11"

Width: 30'-0"
Depth: 60'-0"

Kitchen 11'x 11'

Bath

Dining 11'x 12'

Foyer

Bedroom 11'x 10'

Porch 30'x 6'

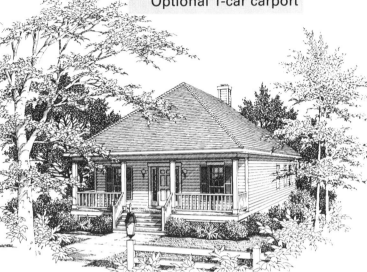

PLAN #563-0587

Price Code AA

PLAN DATA

Total Living Area: 1,120
Bedrooms: 3
Baths: 1 1/2
Foundation Types:
  Crawl space standard
  Slab
  Basement

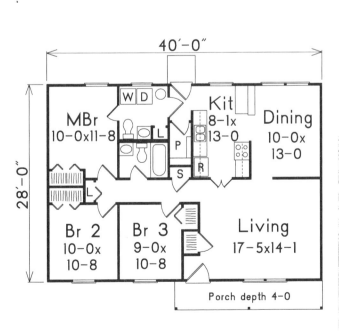

40'-0"

28'-0"

W D

Kit 8-1x 13-0

Dining 10-0x 13-0

MBr 10-0x11-8

P

L

S

R

Br 2 10-0x 10-8

Br 3 9-0x 10-8

Living 17-5x14-1

Porch depth 4-0

BEDR'M 10'-0" X 10'-0"

BRK (VAULTED)

GREAT ROOM 13'-0" X 17'-0" (VAULTED)

MASTER BATH

W.I.C.

F/P

CL

PANT

LIN

BATH

MASTER SUITE

7' HIGH WALL WITH PLANT LEDGE

KIT

REF

BEDR'M 10'-0" X 10'-0"

40'-4"

FOYER

DINING 11'-0" X 10'-0"

W D

CL

48'-10"

DOUBLE GARAGE 19'-0" X 20'-0"

PLAN DATA

Total Living Area: 1,379
Bedrooms: 3
Baths: 2
Garage: 2-car
Foundation Type: Slab

Second Floor
448 sq. ft.

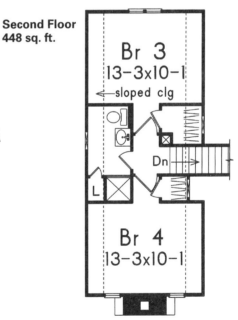

Br 3
13-3x10-1
←sloped clg

Dn

L

Br 4
13-3x10-1

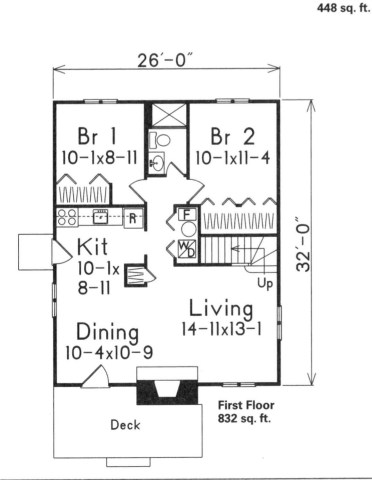

26'-0"

Br 1
10-1x8-11

Br 2
10-1x11-4

F

R

W
D

Kit
10-1x
8-11

Up

Living
14-11x13-1

32'-0"

Dining
10-4x10-9

Deck

First Floor
832 sq. ft.

PLAN DATA
Total Living Area: 1,280
Bedrooms: 4
Baths: 2
Foundation Types:
  Basement standard
  Crawl space
  Slab

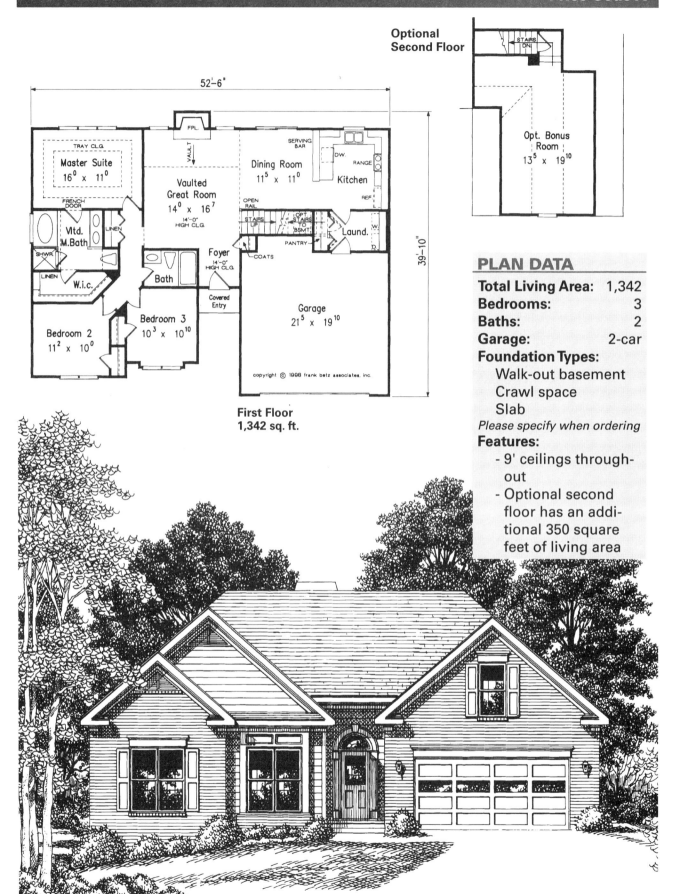

**Optional
Second Floor**

STAIRS DN.

Opt. Bonus
Room
13⁵ x 19¹⁰

52'–6"

TRAY CLG.

Master Suite
16⁰ x 11⁰

FPL.

VAULT

Vaulted
Great Room
14⁰ x 16⁷
14'–0"
HIGH CLG.

SERVING BAR

Dining Room
11⁵ x 11⁰

DW.

RANGE

Kitchen

REF.

FRENCH DOOR

Vtd.
M.Bath

LINEN

OPEN RAIL

STAIRS UP

OPT. STAIRS TO BSMT.

Laund.

W.

D.

SHWR.

LINEN

W.i.c.

Bath

PANTRY

Foyer
14'–0"
HIGH CLG.

COATS

Covered
Entry

Bedroom 2
11² x 10⁰

Bedroom 3
10³ x 10¹⁰

Garage
21⁵ x 19¹⁰

copyright © 1998 frank betz associates, inc.

39'–10"

**First Floor
1,342 sq. ft.**

PLAN DATA

Total Living Area: 1,342
Bedrooms: 3
Baths: 2
Garage: 2-car
Foundation Types:
  Walk-out basement
  Crawl space
  Slab
Please specify when ordering
Features:
  - 9' ceilings through-
    out
  - Optional second
    floor has an addi-
    tional 350 square
    feet of living area

38' 0"

52' 0"

SITTING
12'x9'

BATH

BEDROOM
12'-6"x12'-0"

PORCH

HEAT & AC

W H

BEDROOM
11'x11'

LINEN

HALL

STOR.
6'x5'

BATH

UTIL

LIVING
17'x14'

GARAGE
21'x21'

DINING
11'x8'

GLASS SHELVES

ENTRY

BAR

PORCH

KITCHEN
12'x10'

REF

PLAN DATA

Total Living Area:	1,150
Bedrooms:	2
Baths:	2
Garage:	2-car

Foundation Types:
Crawl space
Slab
Please specify when ordering

PLAN DATA

Total Living Area:	1,127
Bedrooms:	2
Baths:	2
Garage:	2-car

Foundation Type:
Basement

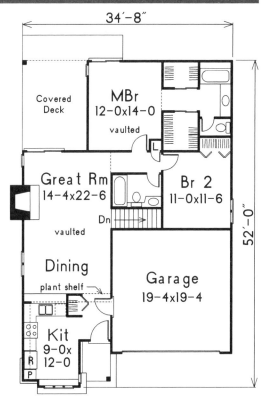

34'-8"

52'-0"

Covered
Deck

MBr
12-0x14-0
vaulted

Great Rm
14-4x22-6
vaulted

Br 2
11-0x11-6

Dn

Dining
plant shelf

Garage
19-4x19-4

Kit
9-0x
12-0

R

P

PLAN #563-DL-16053L1

PLAN DATA

Total Living Area: 1,605
Bedrooms: 3
Baths: 2
Garage: 2-car
Foundation Type:
Slab

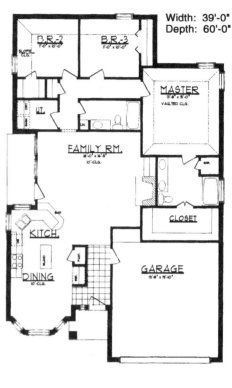

Width: 39'-0"
Depth: 60'-0"

PLAN #563-BF-1314

PLAN DATA

Total Living Area: 1,375
Bedrooms: 3
Baths: 2
Garage: 2-car carport
Foundation Type:
Slab

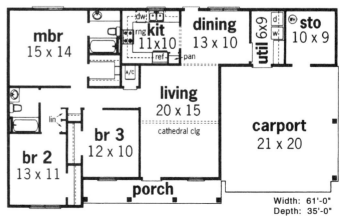

Width: 61'-0"
Depth: 35'-0"

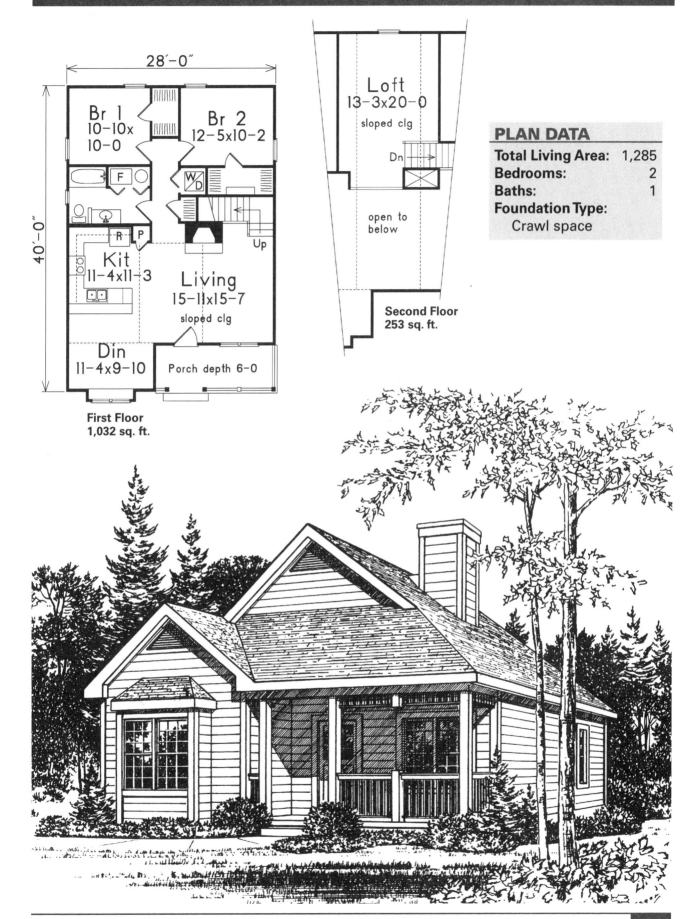

28'-0"

Br 1
10-10x
10-0

Br 2
12-5x10-2

F

W/D

40'-0"

R   P

Kit
11-4x11-3

Living
15-11x15-7

sloped clg

Up

Din
11-4x9-10

Porch depth 6-0

First Floor
1,032 sq. ft.

Loft
13-3x20-0

sloped clg

Dn

open to
below

Second Floor
253 sq. ft.

PLAN DATA
Total Living Area: 1,285
Bedrooms: 2
Baths: 1
Foundation Type:
  Crawl space

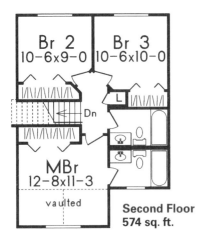

Br 2
10-6x9-0

Br 3
10-6x10-0

Dn

L

MBr
12-8x11-3

vaulted

**Second Floor
574 sq. ft.**

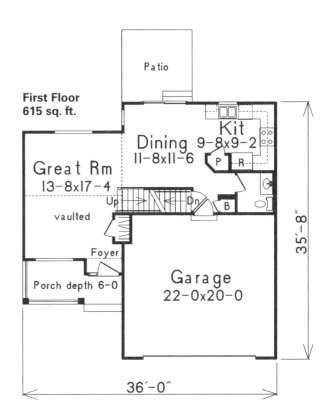

**First Floor
615 sq. ft.**

Patio

Kit
9-8x9-2

Dining
11-8x11-6

P   R

Great Rm
13-8x17-4

vaulted

Up   Dn

B

Foyer

Porch depth 6-0

Garage
22-0x20-0

35'-8"

36'-0"

PLAN DATA

Total Living Area:	1,189
Bedrooms:	3
Baths:	2 1/2
Garage:	2-car
Foundation Type:	
Basement	

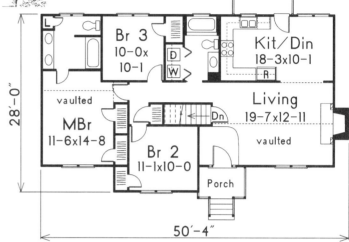

Deck

Br 3
10-0x
10-1

Kit/Din
18-3x10-1

28'-0"

vaulted

MBr
11-6x14-8

Living
19-7x12-11

vaulted

Br 2
11-1x10-0

Porch

50'-4"

PLAN DATA

Total Living Area: 1,220
Bedrooms: 3
Baths: 2
Garage: 2-car
Foundation Type:
  Basement
Features:
  Drive-under garage

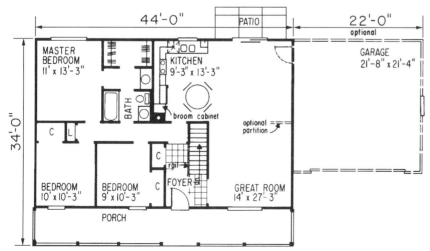

44'-0"

PATIO

22'-0"
optional

MASTER
BEDROOM
11' x 13'-3"

KITCHEN
9'-3" x 13'-3"

GARAGE
21'-8" x 21'-4"

34'-0"

broom cabinet

optional
partition

C   L

BATH

BEDROOM
10' x 10'-3"

BEDROOM
9' x 10'-3"

C

C
rail

FOYER

GREAT ROOM
14' x 27'-3"

PORCH

PLAN DATA

Total Living Area: 1,232
Bedrooms: 3
Baths: 1
Garage: optional 2-car
Foundation Types:
  Basement standard
  Crawl space
  Slab

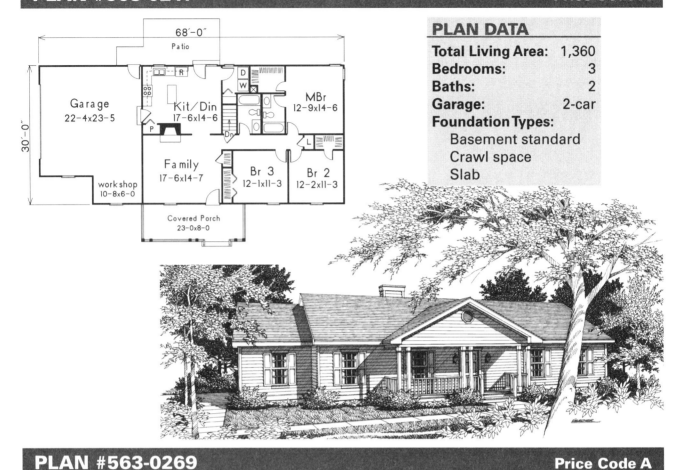

PLAN DATA

Total Living Area:	1,360
Bedrooms:	3
Baths:	2
Garage:	2-car

Foundation Types:
- Basement standard
- Crawl space
- Slab

PLAN DATA

Total Living Area:	1,428
Bedrooms:	3
Baths:	2
Garage:	2-car

Foundation Types:
- Basement standard
- Crawl space

Features:
- 10' ceiling in entry and hallway
- 2" x 6" exterior walls

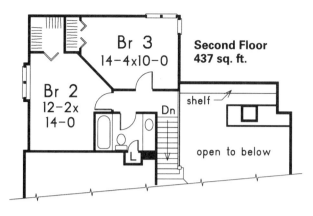

Br 3
14-4x10-0

**Second Floor
437 sq. ft.**

Br 2
12-2x
14-0

shelf

Dn

open to below

L

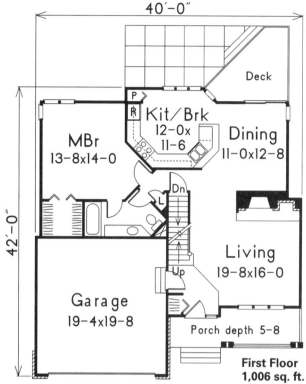

40'-0"

Deck

P R

Kit/Brk
12-0x
11-6

MBr
13-8x14-0

Dining
11-0x12-8

42'-0"

Dn

L

Living
19-8x16-0

Up

Garage
19-4x19-8

Porch depth 5-8

**First Floor
1,006 sq. ft.**

PLAN DATA

Total Living Area:	1,443
Bedrooms:	3
Baths:	2
Garage:	2-car
Foundation Type:	
Basement	

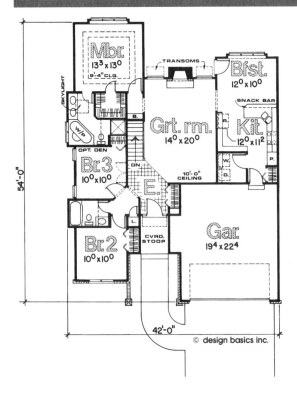

PLAN DATA
Total Living Area: 1,347
Bedrooms: 3
Baths: 2
Garage: 2-car
Foundation Type:
  Basement

PLAN #563-1117

Price Code A

PLAN DATA
Total Living Area: 1,440
Bedrooms: 3
Baths: 2
Garage: 2-car
Foundation Types:
  Basement standard
  Crawl space
  Slab

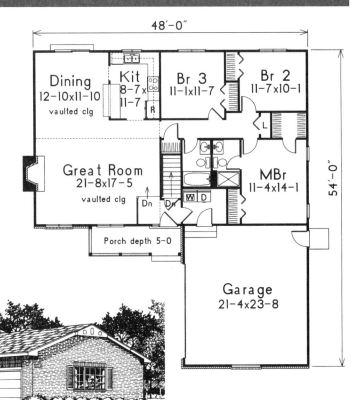

PLAN DATA

Total Living Area: 977
Bedrooms: 2
Baths: 1 1/2
Garage: 1-car
Foundation Type:
Basement

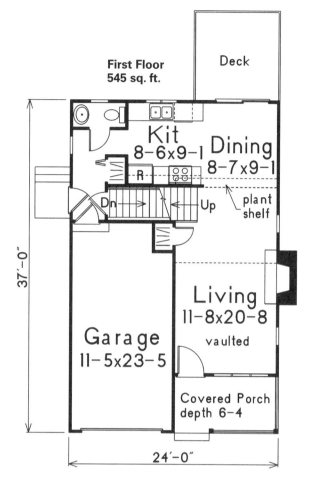

First Floor
545 sq. ft.

Deck

Kit
8-6x9-1

Dining
8-7x9-1

R

plant shelf

Dn   Up

Living
11-8x20-8
vaulted

Garage
11-5x23-5

Covered Porch
depth 6-4

37'-0"

24'-0"

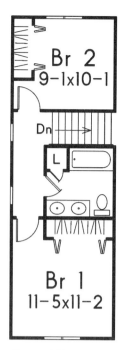

Br 2
9-1x10-1

Dn

L

Br 1
11-5x11-2

Second Floor
432 sq. ft.

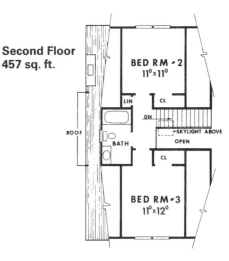

Second Floor
457 sq. ft.

BED RM #2
11⁰ × 11⁰

ROOF

LIN CL

BATH

DN

SKYLIGHT ABOVE

OPEN

CL

BED RM #3
11⁰ × 12⁰

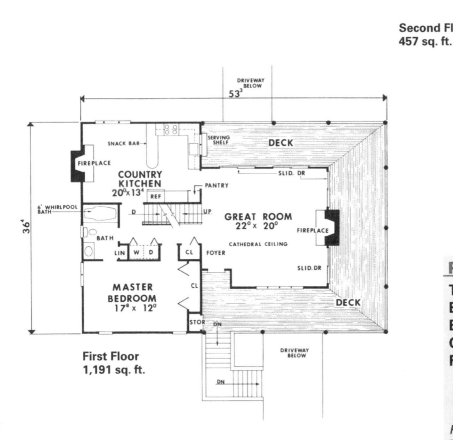

DRIVEWAY BELOW
53³

DECK

SNACK BAR

SERVING SHELF

FIREPLACE

COUNTRY KITCHEN
20⁰ × 13⁴

SLID. DR

PANTRY

REF

6' WHIRLPOOL BATH

D

UP

GREAT ROOM
22⁰ × 20⁰

FIREPLACE

36⁴

BATH

CATHEDRAL CEILING

LIN W D

CL FOYER

SLID. DR

MASTER BEDROOM
17⁸ × 12⁰

CL

DECK

STOR

DN

DRIVEWAY BELOW

DN

First Floor
1,191 sq. ft.

PLAN DATA

Total Living Area: 1,648
Bedrooms: 3
Baths: 2
Garage: 2-car
Foundation Types:
 Basement
 Crawl space
 Slab
Please specify when ordering
Features:
 Drive-under garage

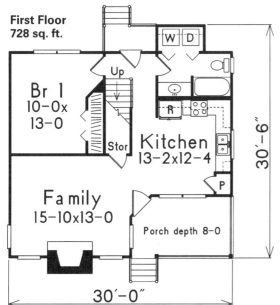

First Floor
728 sq. ft.

W D

Up

Br 1
10-0x
13-0

Stor

Kitchen
13-2x12-4

R

P

Family
15-10x13-0

Porch depth 8-0

30'-6"

30'-0"

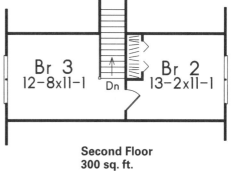

Br 3
12-8x11-1

Dn

Br 2
13-2x11-1

Second Floor
300 sq. ft.

PLAN DATA

Total Living Area: 1,028
Bedrooms: 3
Baths: 1
Foundation Type:
Crawl space

PLAN DATA

Total Living Area: 1,374
Bedrooms: 3
Baths: 2
Garage: 2-car
Foundation Types:
  Slab
  Crawl space
Please specify when ordering

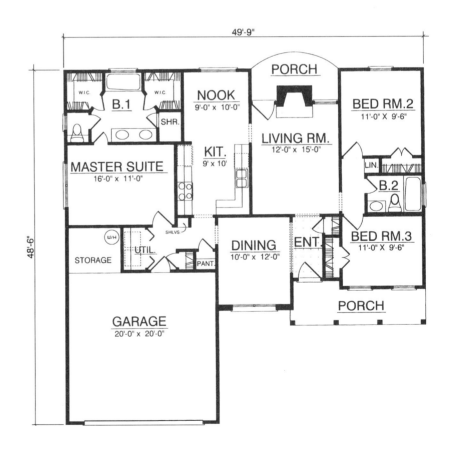

PLAN DATA

Total Living Area: 1,550
Bedrooms: 2
Baths: 2 1/2
Garage: 2-car
Foundation Type:
Basement

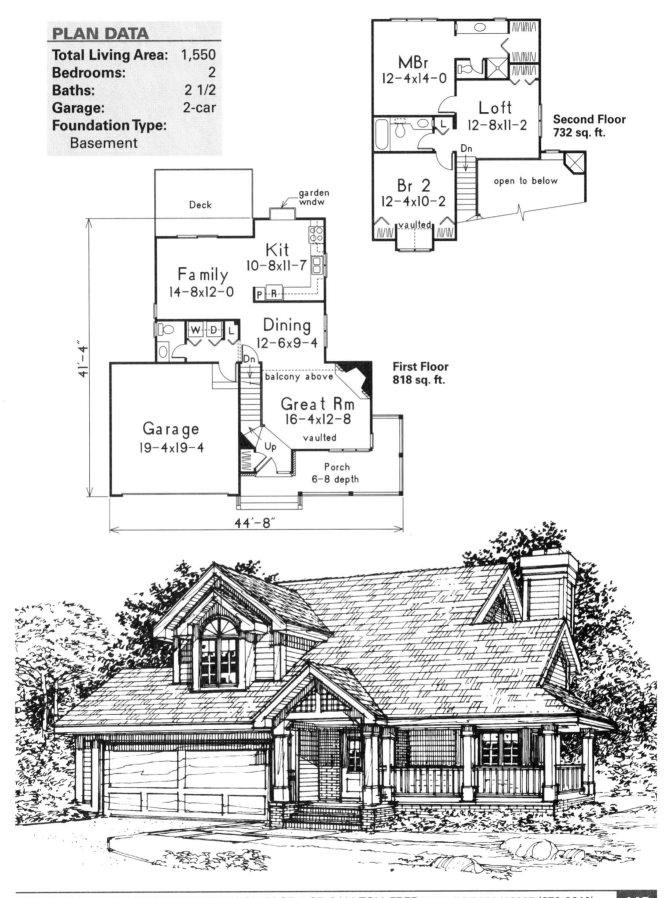

Second Floor
732 sq. ft.

MBr
12-4x14-0

Loft
12-8x11-2

Br 2
12-4x10-2

vaulted

Dn

open to below

L

Deck

garden wndw

Kit
10-8x11-7

Family
14-8x12-0

P R

Dining
12-6x9-4

W D L

Dn

balcony above

First Floor
818 sq. ft.

Great Rm
16-4x12-8
vaulted

Garage
19-4x19-4

Up

Porch
6-8 depth

41'-4"

44'-8"

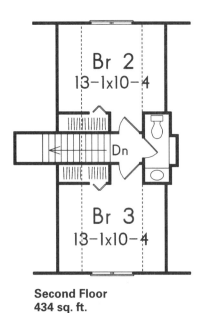

Second Floor
434 sq. ft.

First Floor
720 sq. ft.

PLAN DATA

Total Living Area: 1,154
Bedrooms: 3
Baths: 1 1/2
Foundation Types:
   Crawl space standard
   Slab

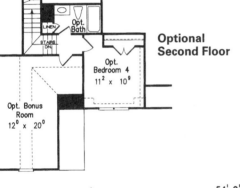

**Optional
Second Floor**

Opt.
Bath

LINEN

STAIRS
DN.

Opt.
Bedroom 4
11² x 10⁰

Opt. Bonus
Room
12⁰ x 20⁰

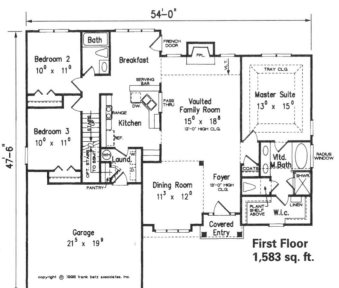

**First Floor
1,583 sq. ft.**

54'-0"

47'-6"

Bedroom 2
10⁰ x 11⁰

Bath

Breakfast

FRENCH
DOOR

FPL.

SERVING
BAR

DW.

PASS
THRU

Vaulted
Family Room
15⁰ x 18⁸
13'-0" HIGH CLG.

TRAY CLG.

Master Suite
13⁰ x 15⁰

VLT.

RANGE

Kitchen

REF.

Bedroom 3
10⁰ x 11⁰

STAIRS

OPT. STAIRS
TO BSMT.

WH

Laund.
W. D.

PANTRY

Dining Room
11³ x 12⁰

Foyer
13'-0" HIGH
CLG.

COATS

Vltd.
M.Bath

SHWR

RADIUS
WINDOW

Garage
21⁵ x 19⁹

Covered
Entry

PLANT
SHELF
ABOVE

W.i.c.

LINEN

copyright © 1998 frank betz associates, inc.

PLAN DATA

Total Living Area: 1,583
Bedrooms: 3
Baths: 2
Garage: 2-car
Foundation Types:
  Walk-out basement
  Crawl space
Please specify when ordering
Features:
- 9' ceilings through-out
- Optional second floor has an additional 532 square feet of living area

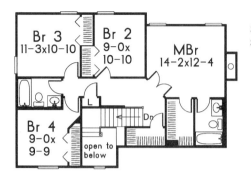

Second Floor
804 sq. ft.

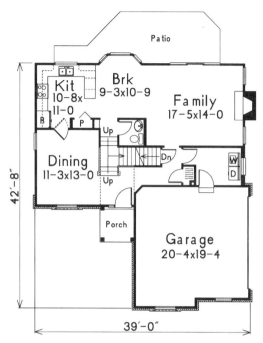

PLAN DATA

Total Living Area: 1,700
Bedrooms: 4
Baths: 2 1/2
Garage: 2-car
Foundation Type:
  Basement

First Floor
896 sq. ft.

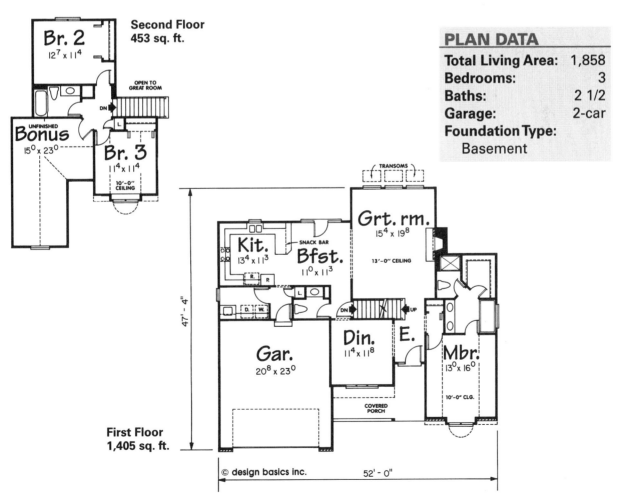

Second Floor
453 sq. ft.

Br. 2
12⁷ x 11⁴

OPEN TO
GREAT ROOM

DN

Bonus
UNFINISHED
15⁰ x 23⁰

Br. 3
11⁴ x 11⁴

10'-0"
CEILING

PLAN DATA

Total Living Area:	1,858
Bedrooms:	3
Baths:	2 1/2
Garage:	2-car
Foundation Type:	
Basement	

TRANSOMS

Grt. rm.
15⁴ x 19⁸

13'-0" CEILING

Kit.
13⁴ x 11³

SNACK BAR

Bfst.
11⁰ x 11³

47' - 4"

DN

UP

Gar.
20⁸ x 23⁰

Din.
11⁴ x 11⁸

E.

Mbr.
13⁰ x 16⁰

10'-0" CLG.

COVERED
PORCH

First Floor
1,405 sq. ft.

© design basics inc.

52' - 0"

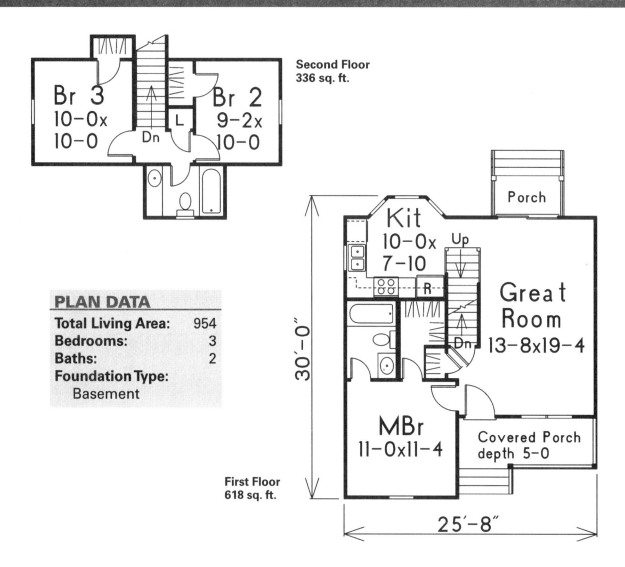

Second Floor
336 sq. ft.

Br 3
10-0x
10-0

Dn

L

Br 2
9-2x
10-0

Porch

Kit
10-0x
7-10

Up

R

Great
Room
13-8x19-4

Dn

MBr
11-0x11-4

Covered Porch
depth 5-0

30'-0"

25'-8"

First Floor
618 sq. ft.

PLAN DATA

Total Living Area:	954
Bedrooms:	3
Baths:	2
Foundation Type:	
Basement	

PLAN DATA

Total Living Area: 1,815
Bedrooms: 3
Baths: 2
Foundation Types:
Basement
Crawl space
Slab
Please specify when ordering

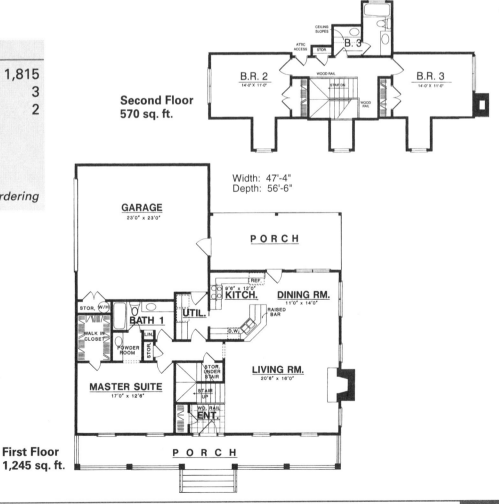

**Second Floor
570 sq. ft.**

Width: 47'-4"
Depth: 56'-6"

ATTIC ACCESS

CEILING SLOPES

STOR.

B. 3

B.R. 2
14'-0" X 11'-0"

WOOD RAIL

STAIR DN

WOOD RAIL

B.R. 3
14'-0" X 11'-0"

GARAGE
23'0" x 23'0"

PORCH

REF.

KITCH.
9'6" x 12'0"

DINING RM.
11'0" x 14'0"

STOR. W/H

BATH 1

UTIL.

RAISED BAR

D.W.

WALK IN CLOSET

POWDER ROOM

LIN.

STOR.

LIVING RM.
20'6" x 16'0"

STOR. UNDER STAIR

MASTER SUITE
17'0" x 12'6"

STAIR UP

WD. RAIL

ENT.

**First Floor
1,245 sq. ft.**

PORCH

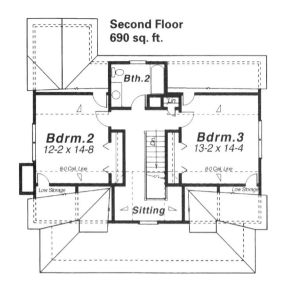

Second Floor
690 sq. ft.

Bth.2

Bdrm.2
12-2 x 14-8

Bdrm.3
13-2 x 14-4

Lin.

Dn

8-0 Ceil. Line

8-0 Ceil. Line

Low Storage

Low Storage

Sitting

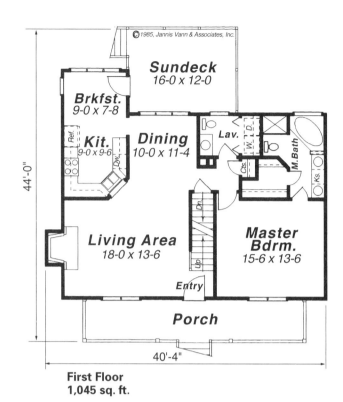

© 1985, Jannis Vann & Associates, Inc.

Sundeck
16-0 x 12-0

Brkfst.
9-0 x 7-8

Ref.

Kit.
9-0 x 9-6

DW

Dining
10-0 x 11-4

Lav.

W.D.

Cts.

M.Bath

Ks.

44'-0"

Living Area
18-0 x 13-6

Dn

Up

Master
Bdrm.
15-6 x 13-6

Entry

Porch

40'-4"

First Floor
1,045 sq. ft.

PLAN DATA

Total Living Area:	1,735
Bedrooms:	3
Baths:	2 1/2
Garage:	2-car
Foundation Type:	
Basement	
Features:	
Drive-under garage	

PLAN #563-0394

PLAN DATA

Total Living Area:	1,558
Bedrooms:	2
Baths:	2
Garage:	2-car
Foundation Type:	
Basement	

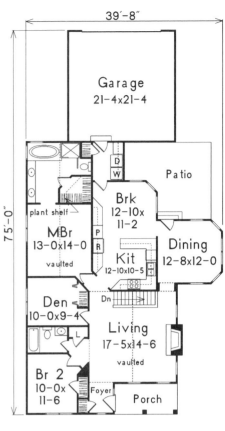

PLAN #563-AP-1205

Price Code B

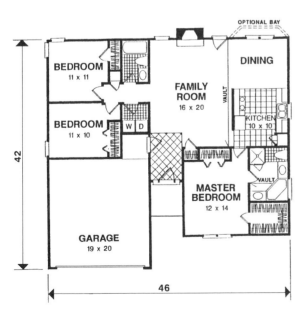

PLAN DATA

Total Living Area:	1,296
Bedrooms:	3
Baths:	2
Garage:	2-car
Foundation Type:	
Basement	
Crawl space	
Slab	

Please specify when ordering

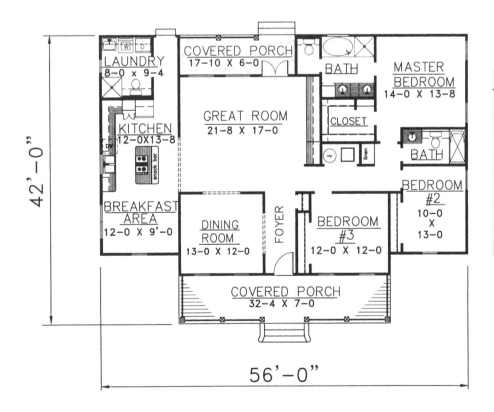

COVERED PORCH
17-10 X 6-0

LAUNDRY
8-0 X 9-4

BATH

MASTER
BEDROOM
14-0 X 13-8

GREAT ROOM
21-8 X 17-0

CLOSET

KITCHEN
12-0X13-8

snack bar

BATH

BREAKFAST
AREA
12-0 X 9'-0

DINING
ROOM
13-0 X 12-0

FOYER

BEDROOM
#3
12-0 X 12-0

BEDROOM
#2
10-0
X
13-0

42'-0"

COVERED PORCH
32-4 X 7-0

56'-0"

PLAN DATA
Total Living Area: 1,785
Bedrooms: 3
Baths: 3
Garage: detached 2-car
Foundation Types:
  Basement
  Crawl space
  Slab
Please specify when ordering

**Second Floor
909 sq. ft.**

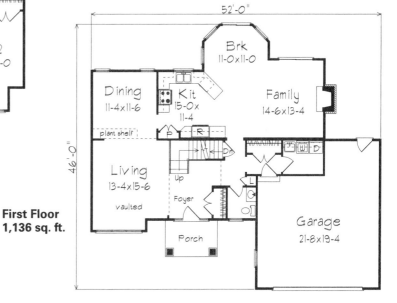

52'-0"

46'-0"

**First Floor
1,136 sq. ft.**

PLAN DATA

Total Living Area:	2,045
Bedrooms:	3
Baths:	2 1/2
Garage:	2-car
Foundation Type:	
Basement	

PLAN DATA

Total Living Area: 896
Bedrooms: 1
Baths: 1
Foundation Type:
  Slab
Features:
  Duplex has 448
  square feet of living
  space per unit

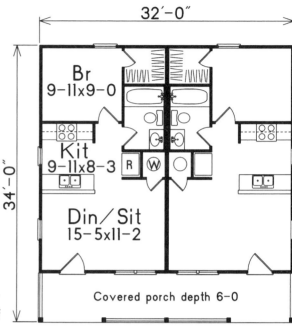

32'-0"

34'-0"

Br
9-11x9-0

Kit
9-11x8-3

Din/Sit
15-5x11-2

Covered porch depth 6-0

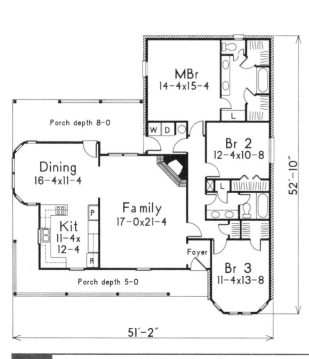

MBr
14-4x15-4

Porch depth 8-0

W D

Br 2
12-4x10-8

Dining
16-4x11-4

52'-10"

Family
17-0x21-4

Kit
11-4x
12-4

P

R

Foyer

Br 3
11-4x13-8

Porch depth 5-0

51'-2"

PLAN DATA

Total Living Area: 1,772
Bedrooms: 3
Baths: 2
Garage: detached 2-car
Foundation Types:
  Slab standard
  Crawl space

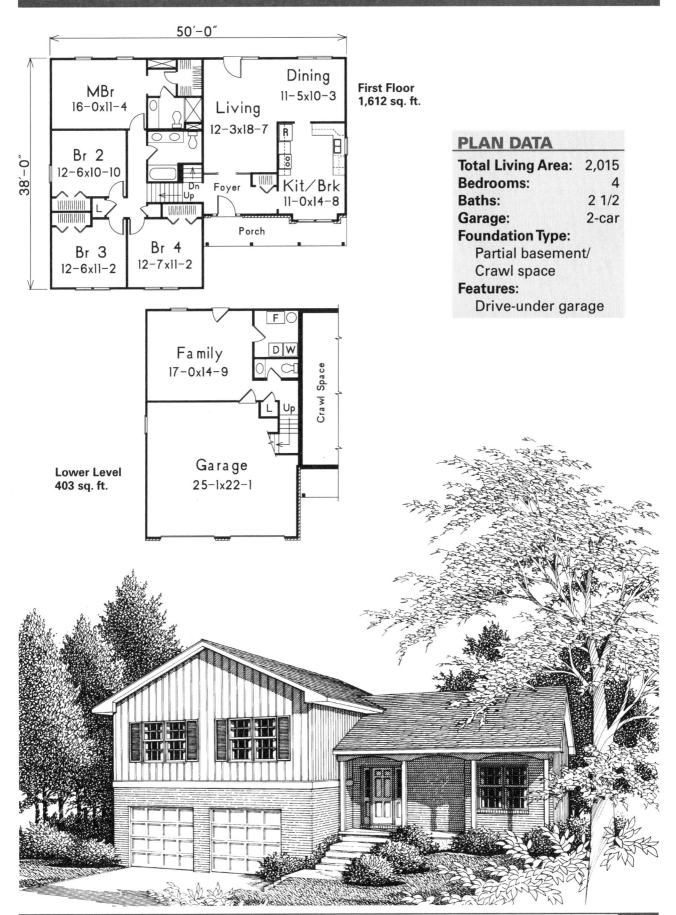

50'-0"

38'-0"

MBr
16-0x11-4

Br 2
12-6x10-10

Br 3
12-6x11-2

Br 4
12-7x11-2

Living
12-3x18-7

Dining
11-5x10-3

Kit/Brk
11-0x14-8

Foyer

Dn
Up

Porch

L

**First Floor
1,612 sq. ft.**

PLAN DATA

Total Living Area: 2,015
Bedrooms: 4
Baths: 2 1/2
Garage: 2-car
Foundation Type:
   Partial basement/
   Crawl space
Features:
   Drive-under garage

Family
17-0x14-9

Garage
25-1x22-1

Crawl Space

F

D W

L Up

**Lower Level
403 sq. ft.**

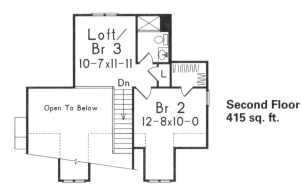

Loft/
Br 3
10-7x11-11

Dn

Open To Below

Br 2
12-8x10-0

L

Second Floor
415 sq. ft.

PLAN DATA

Total Living Area: 1,428
Bedrooms: 3
Baths: 2
Foundation Type:
  Basement

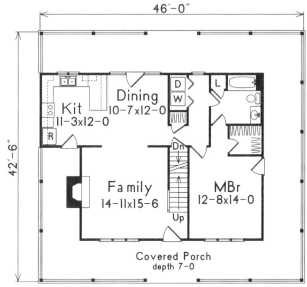

46'-0"

42'-6"

Kit
11-3x12-0

Dining
10-7x12-0

D
W

L

R

Dn

Family
14-11x15-6

Up

MBr
12-8x14-0

Covered Porch
depth 7-0

First Floor
1,013 sq. ft.

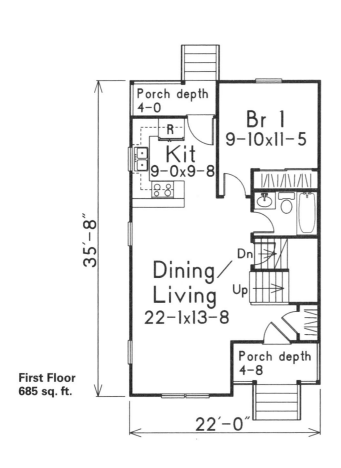

Porch depth
4-0

Br 1
9-10x11-5

Kit
9-0x9-8

R

35'-8"

Dn

Up

Dining / Living
22-1x13-8

Porch depth
4-8

First Floor
685 sq. ft.

22'-0"

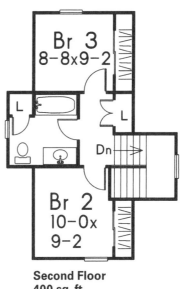

Br 3
8-8x9-2

L

L

Dn

Br 2
10-0x 9-2

Second Floor
400 sq. ft.

PLAN DATA	
Total Living Area:	1,085
Bedrooms:	3
Baths:	2
Foundation Type: Basement	

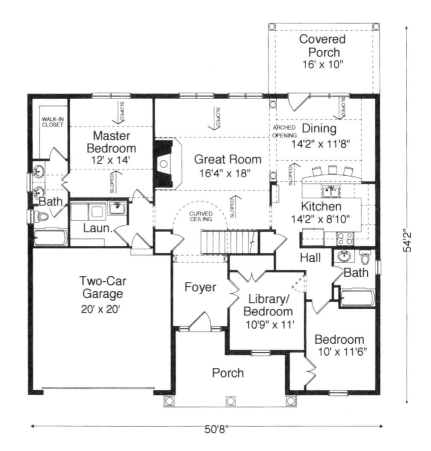

PLAN DATA

Total Living Area:	1,544
Bedrooms:	3
Baths:	2
Garage:	2-car
Foundation Type:	
Basement	

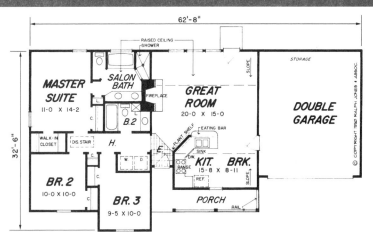

62'-8"

32'-6"

MASTER SUITE
11-0 X 14-2

SALON BATH

RAISED CEILING
SHOWER

B.2

FIREPLACE

GREAT ROOM
20-0 X 15-0

SLOPE

STORAGE

DOUBLE GARAGE

© COPYRIGHT 1990 RALPH JONES & ASSOC.

WALK-IN CLOSET

DIS STAIR

H.

PLANT SHELF

EATING BAR

SINK

E

KIT.
15-8 X

BRK.
8-11

DW.
RANGE

REF

SLOPE

BR. 2
10-0 X 10-0

W D

BR. 3
9-5 X 10-0

PORCH

RAIL

PLAN DATA

Total Living Area: 1,192
Bedrooms: 3
Baths: 2
Garage: 2-car
Foundation Types:
  Crawl space
  Slab
Please specify when ordering

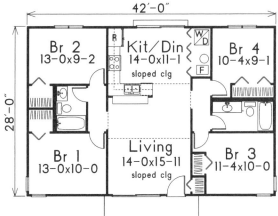

42'-0"

28'-0"

Br 2
13-0x9-2

Kit/Din
14-0x11-1
sloped clg

W D

Br 4
10-4x9-1

R

F

Br 1
13-0x10-0

Living
14-0x15-11
sloped clg

Br 3
11-4x10-0

PLAN DATA

Total Living Area: 1,176
Bedrooms: 4
Baths: 2
Foundation Types:
  Crawl space standard
  Slab

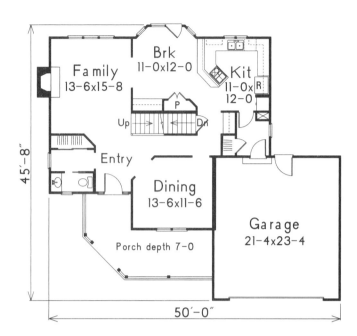

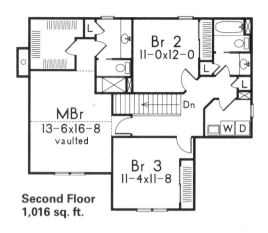

Brk
11-0x12-0

Family
13-6x15-8

Kit
11-0x
12-0

R

P

Up   Dn

Entry

Dining
13-6x11-6

Porch depth 7-0

Garage
21-4x23-4

45'-8"

50'-0"

First Floor
1,043 sq. ft.

Br 2
11-0x12-0

L

L

L

Dn

MBr
13-6x16-8
vaulted

Br 3
11-4x11-8

W D

Second Floor
1,016 sq. ft.

PLAN DATA

Total Living Area: 2,059
Bedrooms: 3
Baths: 2 1/2
Garage: 2-car
Foundation Type:
   Basement

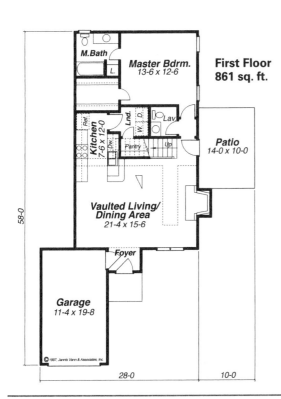

First Floor
861 sq. ft.

M.Bath

Master Bdrm.
13-6 x 12-6

Ref.

Kitchen
7-6 x 12-0

Lnd.

W. D.

Lav

Pantry

Up

Patio
14-0 x 10-0

Vaulted Living/
Dining Area
21-4 x 15-6

Foyer

Garage
11-4 x 19-8

© 1997, Jannis Vann & Associates, Inc.

58-0

28-0

10-0

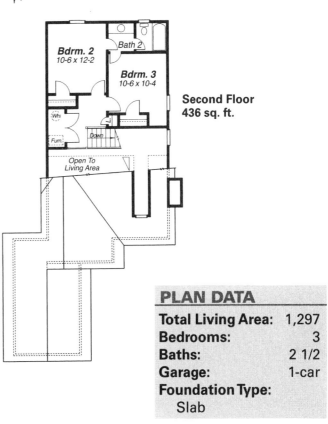

Bdrm. 2
10-6 x 12-2

Bath 2

Bdrm. 3
10-6 x 10-4

Second Floor
436 sq. ft.

Whi

Furn.

Down

Open To
Living Area

PLAN DATA

Total Living Area:	1,297
Bedrooms:	3
Baths:	2 1/2
Garage:	1-car
Foundation Type:	
Slab	

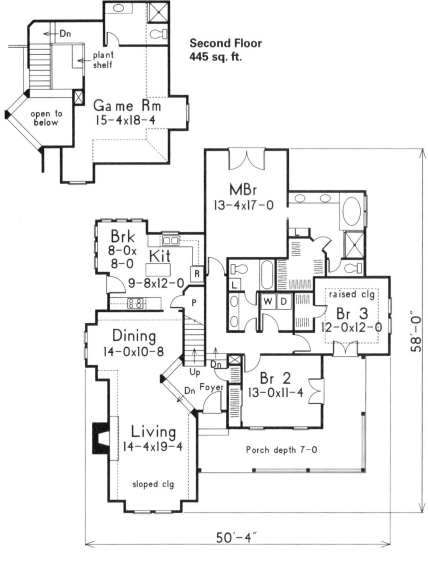

Second Floor
445 sq. ft.

Game Rm
15-4x18-4

open to below

plant shelf

Dn

PLAN DATA

Total Living Area: 2,282
Bedrooms: 3
Baths: 3
Garage: detached 2-car
Foundation Types:
 Slab standard
 Crawl space

MBr
13-4x17-0

Brk
8-0x 8-0

Kit
9-8x12-0

Dining
14-0x10-8

Br 3
12-0x12-0

raised clg

Living
14-4x19-4

sloped clg

Br 2
13-0x11-4

Foyer

Up

Dn

Porch depth 7-0

58'-0"

50'-4"

First Floor
1,837 sq. ft.

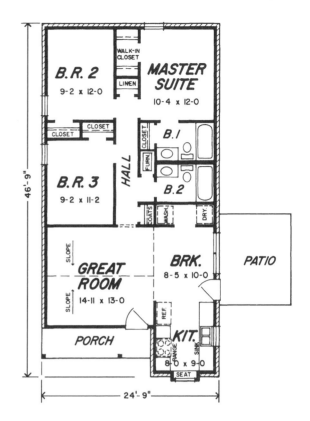

PLAN DATA

Total Living Area: 1,053
Bedrooms: 3
Baths: 2
Foundation Types:
  Crawl space
  Slab
Please specify when ordering

PLAN #563-0500

Price Code AA

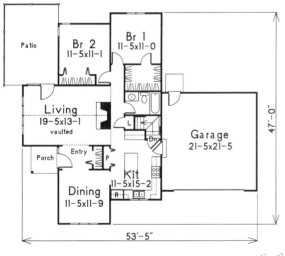

PLAN DATA

Total Living Area: 1,134
Bedrooms: 2
Baths: 1
Garage: 2-car
Foundation Type:
  Basement

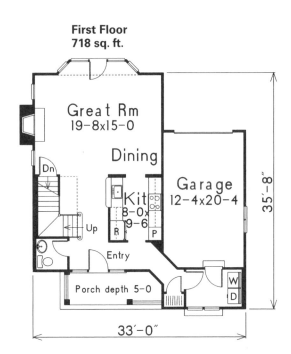

First Floor
718 sq. ft.

Great Rm
19-8x15-0

Dining

Kit
8-0x
9-6

Garage
12-4x20-4

Dn

Up

R

P

Entry

Porch depth 5-0

W
D

35'-8"

33'-0"

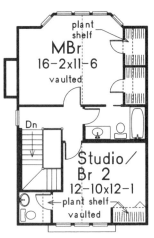

Second Floor
576 sq. ft.

plant
shelf

MBr
16-2x11-6
vaulted

Dn

Studio/
Br 2
12-10x12-1
plant shelf
vaulted

PLAN DATA

Total Living Area:	1,294
Bedrooms:	2
Baths:	1 full, 2 half
Garage:	1-car
Foundation Type:	
Basement	

PLAN DATA

Total Living Area: 1,391
Bedrooms: 2
Baths: 1
Foundation Types:
  Pier standard
  Crawl space

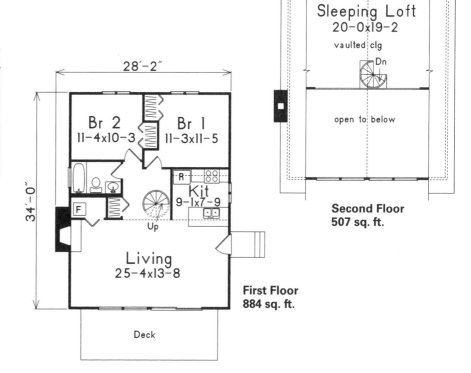

Sleeping Loft
20-0x19-2
vaulted clg

Dn

open to below

Second Floor
507 sq. ft.

28'-2"

34'-0"

Br 2
11-4x10-3

Br 1
11-3x11-5

F

R

Kit
9-1x7-9

Up

Living
25-4x13-8

First Floor
884 sq. ft.

Deck

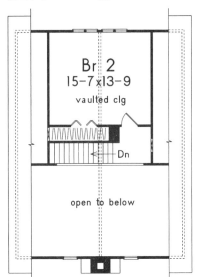

**Second Floor
327 sq. ft.**

Br 2
15-7x13-9
vaulted clg

open to below

Dn

PLAN DATA

Total Living Area: 1,211
Bedrooms: 2
Baths: 1
Foundation Types:
  Crawl space standard
  Basement
Features:
  Additional plan for
  second floor has an
  third bedroom with
  223 square feet

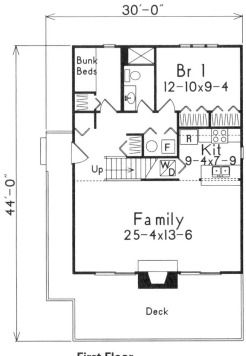

**First Floor
884 sq. ft.**

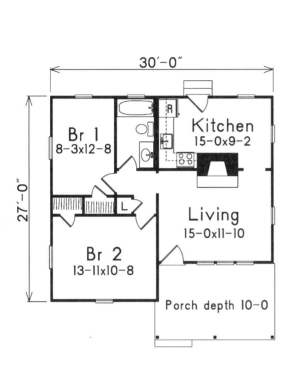

30'-0"

Br 1
8-3x12-8

Kitchen
15-0x9-2

27'-0"

Living
15-0x11-10

Br 2
13-11x10-8

Porch depth 10-0

PLAN DATA

Total Living Area:	733
Bedrooms:	2
Baths:	1
Foundation Type:	
Pier	

PLAN #563-0543

Price Code AA

PLAN DATA

Total Living Area:	1,160
Bedrooms:	3
Baths:	1 1/2
Foundation Types:	
Crawl space standard	
Basement	
Slab	

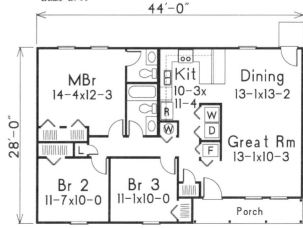

44'-0"

MBr
14-4x12-3

Kit
10-3x
11-4

Dining
13-1x13-2

28'-0"

Great Rm
13-1x10-3

Br 2
11-7x10-0

Br 3
11-1x10-0

Porch

PLAN #563-DBI-8013

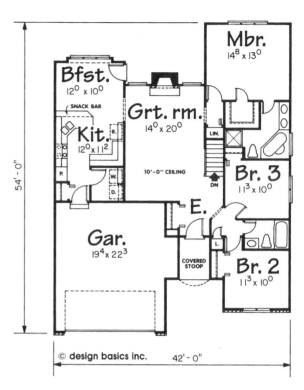

Mbr.
14⁸ x 13⁰

Bfst.
12⁰ x 10⁰

SNACK BAR

Grt. rm.
14⁰ x 20⁰

LIN.

Kit.
12⁰ x 11²

R.

10'-0" CEILING

DN

Br. 3
11³ x 10⁰

W.
D.

P.

Gar.
19⁴ x 22³

E.

L

Br. 2
11³ x 10⁰

COVERED STOOP

54' - 0"

© design basics inc.   42' - 0"

PLAN DATA

Total Living Area:	1,392
Bedrooms:	3
Baths:	2
Garage:	2-car
Foundation Type:	
Basement	

PLAN #563-0258

PLAN DATA

Total Living Area:	1,438
Bedrooms:	3
Baths:	2
Garage:	2-car
Foundation Types:	
Crawl space standard	
Slab	

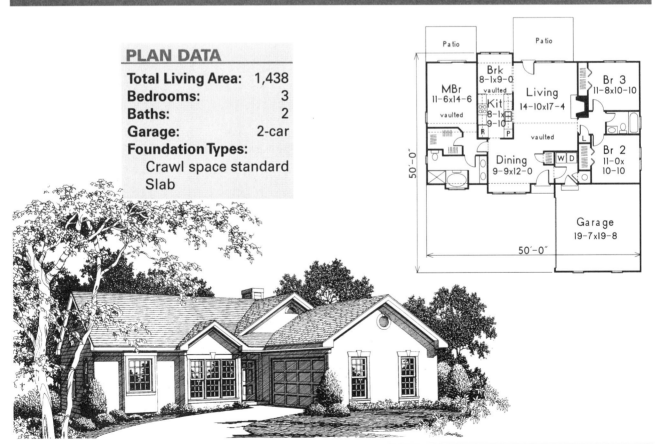

Patio

Patio

Brk
8-1x9-0
vaulted

Living
14-10x17-4

Br 3
11-8x10-10

MBr
11-6x14-6
vaulted

Kit
8-1x
9-10

R.   P.

vaulted

L

Br 2
11-0x
10-10

Dining
9-9x12-0

W D

Garage
19-7x19-8

50'-0"

50'-0"

PLAN DATA

Total Living Area: 1,426
Bedrooms: 1
Baths: 1
Foundation Type:
Crawl space

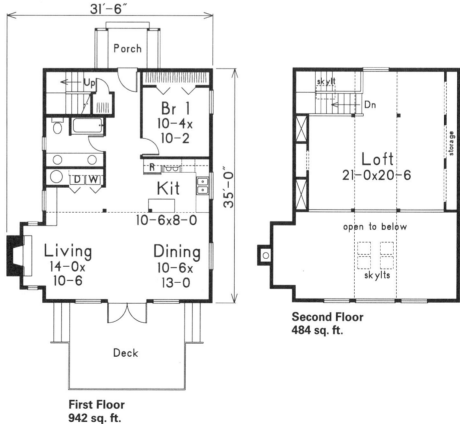

31'-6"

Porch

Up

Br 1
10-4x
10-2

35'-0"

Kit
10-6x8-0

D   W

Living
14-0x
10-6

Dining
10-6x
13-0

Deck

First Floor
942 sq. ft.

skylt

Dn

storage

Loft
21-0x20-6

open to below

skylts

Second Floor
484 sq. ft.

PLAN #563-0294

PLAN DATA

Total Living Area: 1,655
Bedrooms: 3
Baths: 2
Garage: 2-car
Foundation Type:
  Crawl space
Features:
- 9' ceiling in master bedroom
- 10' ceiling in family room

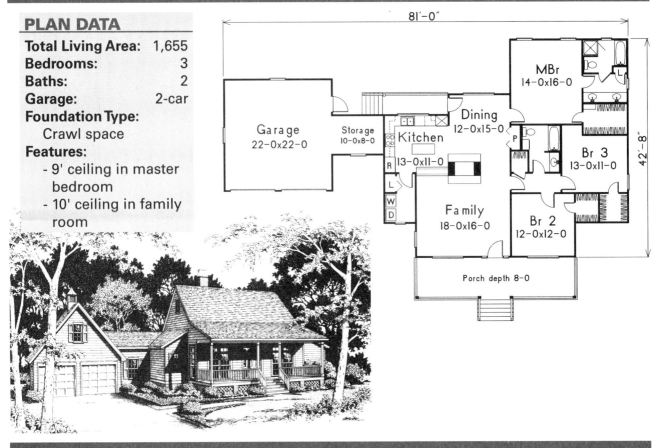

PLAN #563-0296

PLAN DATA

Total Living Area: 1,396
Bedrooms: 3
Baths: 2
Garage: 1-car carport
Foundation Types:
  Basement standard
  Crawl space

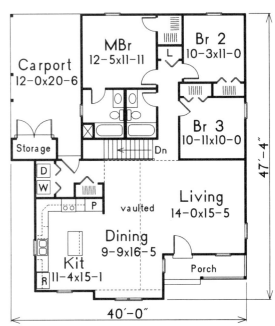

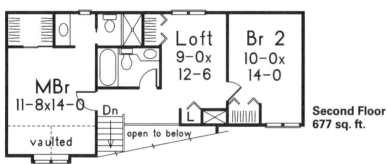

Loft
9-0x
12-6

Br 2
10-0x
14-0

MBr
11-8x14-0

Dn

L

open to below

vaulted

**Second Floor
677 sq. ft.**

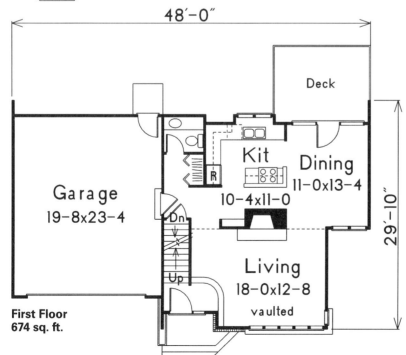

48'-0"

Deck

Garage
19-8x23-4

Kit
10-4x11-0

Dining
11-0x13-4

Dn

R

Up

Living
18-0x12-8
vaulted

29'-10"

**First Floor
674 sq. ft.**

PLAN DATA

Total Living Area:	1,351
Bedrooms:	3
Baths:	2 1/2
Garage:	2-car
Foundation Type:	
Basement	

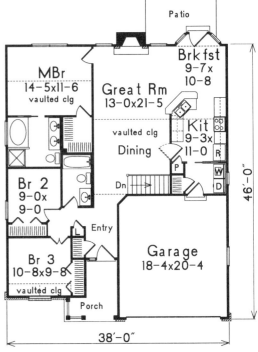

PLAN DATA

Total Living Area:	1,268
Bedrooms:	3
Baths:	2
Garage:	2-car
Foundation Type:	
Basement	

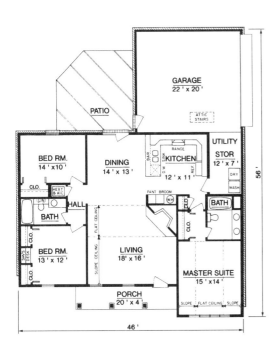

PLAN DATA

Total Living Area:	1,984
Bedrooms:	3
Baths:	2
Garage:	2-car
Foundation Types:	
Slab	
Crawl space	
Please specify when ordering	

**Second Floor
907 sq. ft.**

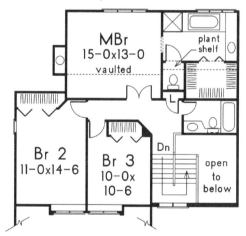

MBr
15-0x13-0
vaulted

plant
shelf

Br 2
11-0x14-6

Br 3
10-0x
10-6

Dn

open
to
below

PLAN DATA

Total Living Area:	1,835
Bedrooms:	3
Baths:	2 1/2
Garage:	2-car
Foundation Type:	
Basement	

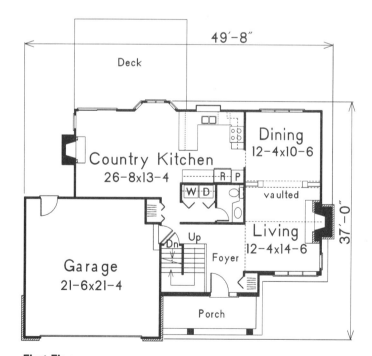

49'-8"

Deck

Dining
12-4x10-6

Country Kitchen
26-8x13-4

R P

W D

vaulted

37'-0"

Living
12-4x14-6

Up

Dn

Foyer

Garage
21-6x21-4

Porch

**First Floor
928 sq. ft.**

PLAN DATA

Total Living Area:	1,735
Bedrooms:	3
Baths:	2
Garage:	2-car
Foundation Type:	
Slab	

Width: 50'-0"
Depth: 55'-0"

PLAN #563-0542

Price Code C

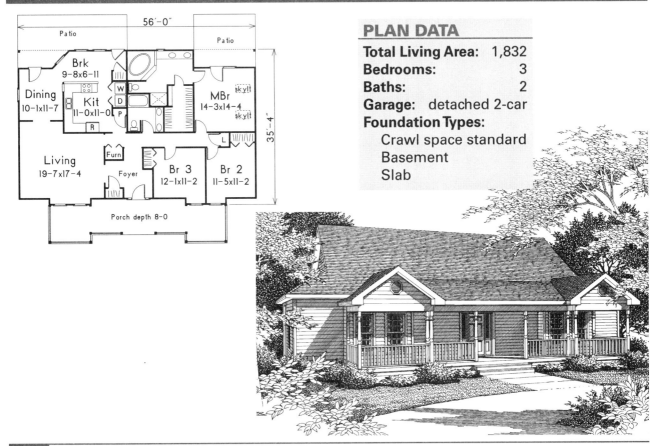

PLAN DATA

Total Living Area:	1,832
Bedrooms:	3
Baths:	2
Garage:	detached 2-car
Foundation Types:	
Crawl space standard	
Basement	
Slab	

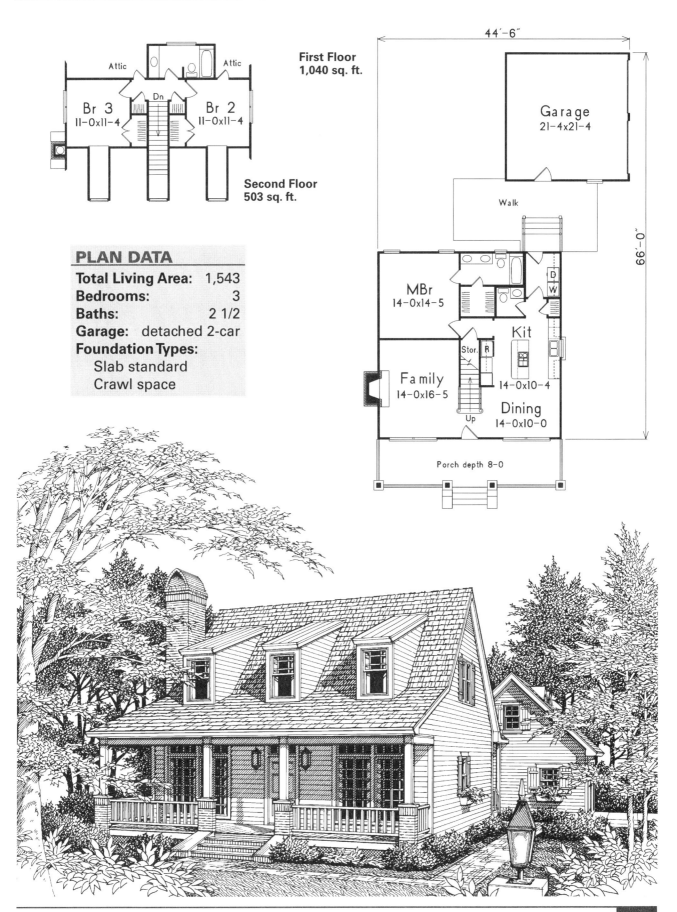

Attic

Br 3
11-0x11-4

Dn

Attic

Br 2
11-0x11-4

First Floor
1,040 sq. ft.

Second Floor
503 sq. ft.

44'-6"

Garage
21-4x21-4

66'-0"

Walk

PLAN DATA

Total Living Area: 1,543
Bedrooms: 3
Baths: 2 1/2
Garage: detached 2-car
Foundation Types:
  Slab standard
  Crawl space

MBr
14-0x14-5

D
W

Kit
14-0x10-4

Stor. R

Family
14-0x16-5

Up

Dining
14-0x10-0

Porch depth 8-0

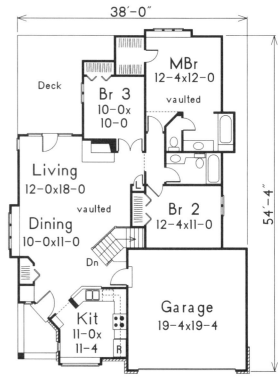

38'-0"

54'-4"

Deck

MBr
12-4x12-0
vaulted

Br 3
10-0x
10-0

Living
12-0x18-0
vaulted

Dining
10-0x11-0

Br 2
12-4x11-0

Dn

Kit
11-0x
11-4

Garage
19-4x19-4

PLAN DATA

Total Living Area: 1,270
Bedrooms: 3
Baths: 2
Garage: 2-car
Foundation Type:
  Basement

PLAN DATA

Total Living Area: 1,050
Bedrooms: 3
Baths: 2
Garage: 1-car
Foundation Types:
  Basement
  Slab
Please specify when ordering

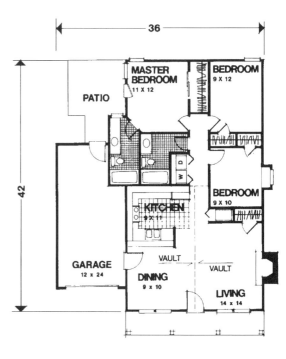

36

42

MASTER
BEDROOM
11 X 12

BEDROOM
9 X 12

PATIO

BEDROOM
9 X 10

KITCHEN
9 X 11

GARAGE
12 x 24

VAULT

VAULT

DINING
9 x 10

LIVING
14 x 14

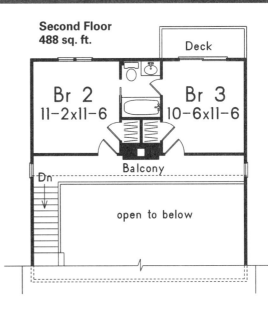

Second Floor
488 sq. ft.

Deck

Br 2
11-2x11-6

Br 3
10-6x11-6

Balcony

Dn

open to below

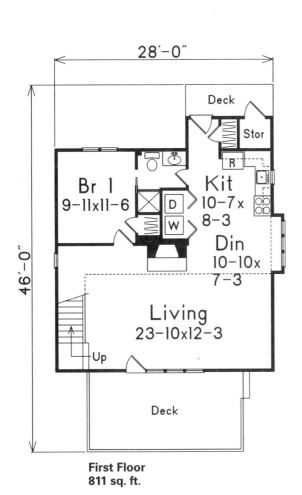

28'-0"

46'-0"

Deck

Stor

R

Br 1
9-11x11-6

Kit
10-7 x
8-3

D

W

Din
10-10x
7-3

Living
23-10x12-3

Up

Deck

First Floor
811 sq. ft.

PLAN DATA

Total Living Area:	1,299
Bedrooms:	3
Baths:	2
Foundation Types:	
Crawl space standard	
Slab	

PLAN DATA

Total Living Area:	1,954
Bedrooms:	3
Baths:	2 1/2
Garage:	2-car
Foundation Type:	
Basement	

Second Floor
902 sq. ft.

MBr
13-8x16-8

Br 3
10-6x10-3

L

Dn

Br 2
10-8x12-4

plant shelf

open to below

First Floor
1,052 sq. ft.

43'-0"

Family
13-5x16-4

Brk
8-8x
10-6

Kit
10-6x
12-6

W D

Dn

R

P

Dining
11-0x11-6

Garage
21-8x22-0

Up

Foyer

Living
13-8x14-0
Vaulted

Porch

47'-0"

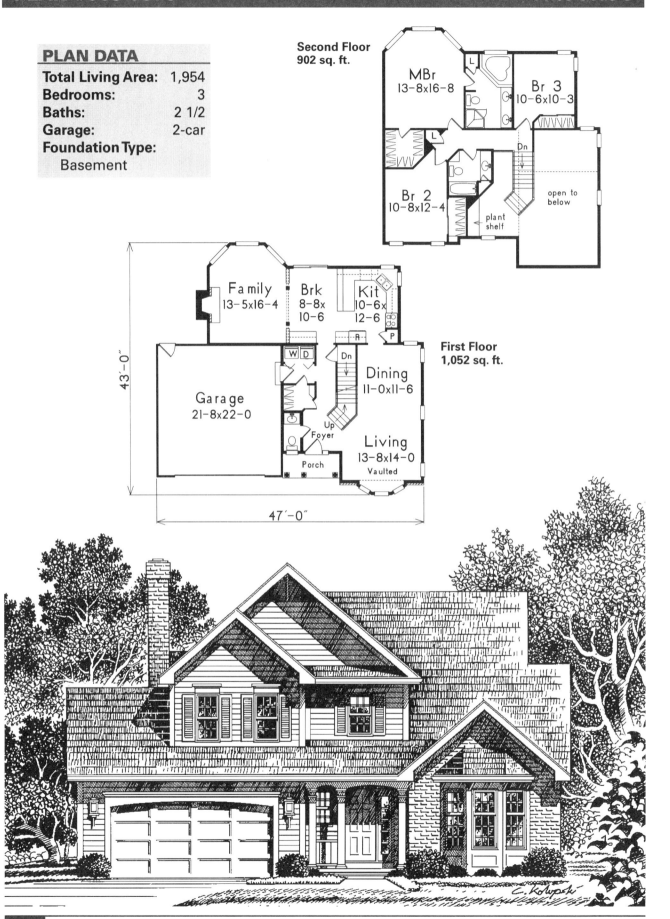

C. Kolupok

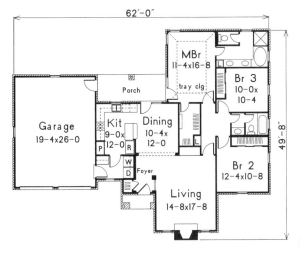

PLAN DATA

Total Living Area: 1,539
Bedrooms: 3
Baths: 2
Garage: 2-car
Foundation Type:
  Slab
Features:
  - 9' ceilings through-out
  - 10' ceiling in master bedroom

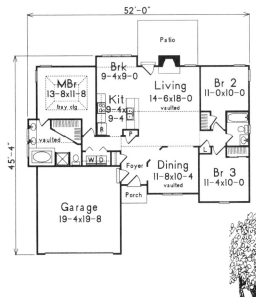

PLAN DATA

Total Living Area: 1,358
Bedrooms: 3
Baths: 2
Garage: 2-car
Foundation Type:
  Slab

PLAN DATA

Total Living Area: 1,472
Bedrooms: 4
Baths: 2
Foundation Types:
  Crawl space
  Slab
Please specify when ordering
Features:
  Optional bonus room on the second floor has an additional 199 square feet of living area

Second Floor
332 sq. ft.

First Floor
1,140 sq. ft.

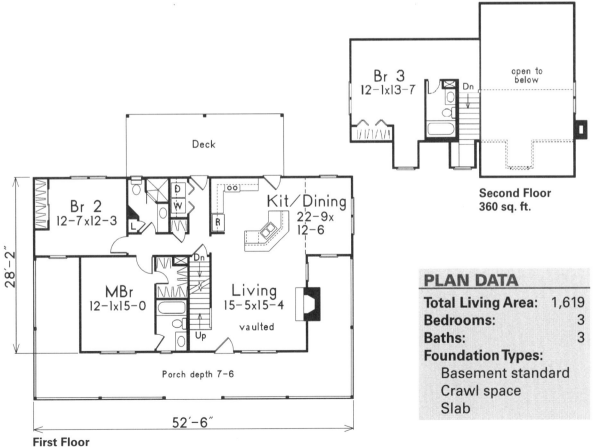

Second Floor
360 sq. ft.

Br 3
12-1x13-7

open to below

Dn

Deck

Br 2
12-7x12-3

Kit/Dining
22-9x
12-6

MBr
12-1x15-0

Living
15-5x15-4
vaulted

28'-2"

Dn

Up

Porch depth 7-6

52'-6"

First Floor
1,259 sq. ft.

PLAN DATA

Total Living Area: 1,619
Bedrooms: 3
Baths: 3
Foundation Types:
Basement standard
Crawl space
Slab

PLAN #563-0693

Price Code AA

PLAN DATA
Total Living Area: 1,013
Bedrooms: 2
Baths: 1
Foundation Type:
   Slab

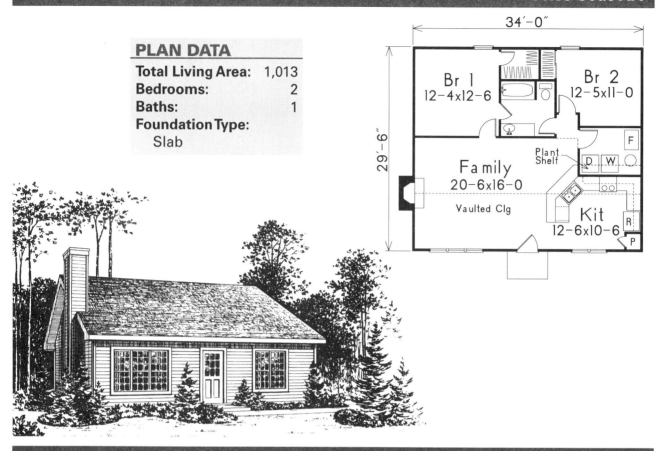

34'-0"

29'-6"

Br 1
12-4x12-6

Br 2
12-5x11-0

F

Plant
Shelf

D | W

Family
20-6x16-0

Vaulted Clg

Kit
12-6x10-6

R

P

PLAN #563-0272

Price Code A

51'-4"

40'-8"

Deck

Brk
vaulted

Br 3
9-0x11-4

MBr
14-6x14-6

Kit
10-6x
18-8

R

P

Dn

Dining

Great Rm
13-6x21-0

vaulted

Br 2
11-0x10-3

Garage
19-4x19-4

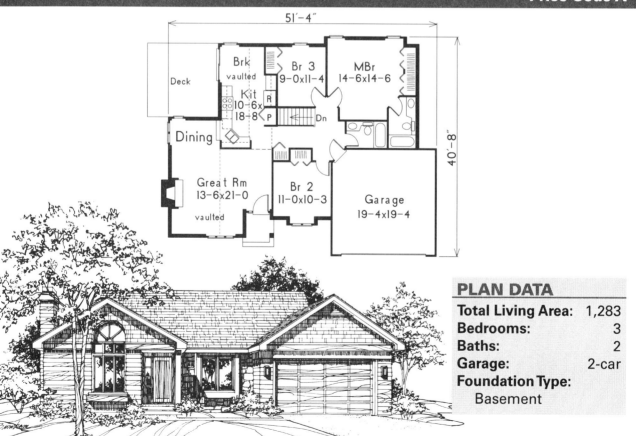

PLAN DATA
Total Living Area: 1,283
Bedrooms: 3
Baths: 2
Garage: 2-car
Foundation Type:
   Basement

Second Floor
415 sq. ft.

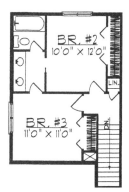

BR. #2
10'0" x 12'0"

LIN.

BR. #3
11'0" x 11'0"

DN.

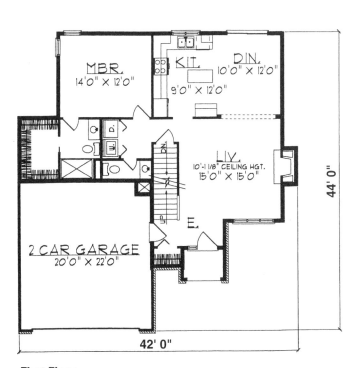

MBR.
14'0" x 12'0"

KIT.
9'0" x 12'0"

DIN.
10'0" x 12'0"

LIV.
10'-1 1/8" CEILING HGT.
15'0" x 15'0"

DN.

UP

2 CAR GARAGE
20'0" x 22'0"

44' 0"

42' 0"

First Floor
927 sq. ft.

PLAN DATA

Total Living Area:	1,342
Bedrooms:	3
Baths:	2 1/2
Garage:	2-car
Foundation Type:	
Basement	

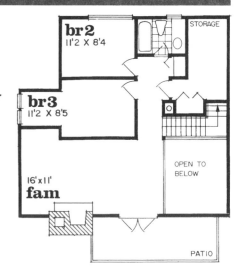

Second Floor
625 sq. ft.

PLAN DATA

Total Living Area:	1,735
Bedrooms:	3
Baths:	2
Foundation Type:	
Crawl space	

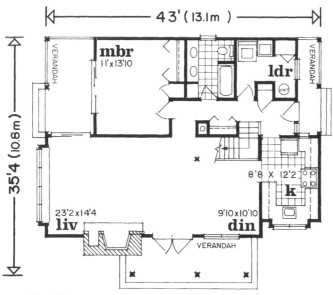

First Floor
1,110 sq. ft.

Second Floor
952 sq. ft.

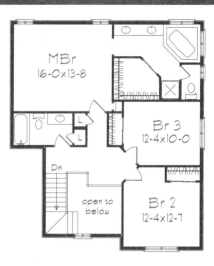

First Floor
1,228 sq. ft.

PLAN DATA

Total Living Area:	2,180
Bedrooms:	3
Baths:	2 1/2
Garage:	2-car
Foundation Type:	
Basement	

© COPYRIGHT 1990 RALPH JONES & ASSOC.

Optional Second Floor

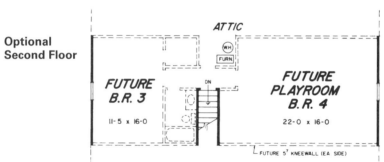

ATTIC

(WH) FURN

FUTURE B.R. 3
11-5 x 16-0

DN

FUTURE PLAYROOM B.R. 4
22-0 x 16-0

FUTURE 5' KNEEWALL (EA SIDE)

← 46' 0" →

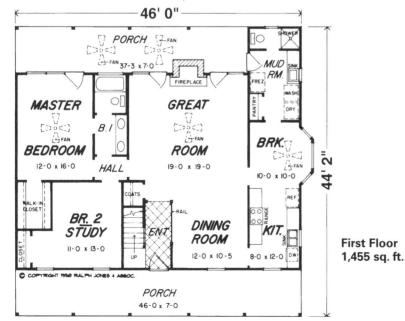

PORCH
FAN FAN
FAN 37-3 x 7-0
FIREPLACE

MUD RM.

SHOWER
SINK
FREZ
PANTRY
WASH
DRY

MASTER
B.1
BEDROOM
12-0 x 16-0
HALL

GREAT
ROOM
19-0 x 19-0
FAN

BRK.
10-0 x 10-0
FAN

WALK-IN CLOSET
CLOSET

BR. 2
STUDY
11-0 x 13-0

COATS
ENT
RAIL
UP

DINING ROOM
12-0 x 10-5

KIT.
8-0 x 12-0
REF
RANGE
SINK
DW

© COPYRIGHT 1990 RALPH JONES & ASSOC.

PORCH
46-0 x 7-0

44' 2"

First Floor 1,455 sq. ft.

PLAN DATA
Total Living Area: 1,455
Bedrooms: 2
Baths: 2
Foundation Types:
 Crawl space
 Slab
Please specify when ordering
Features:
 Optional second floor has an additional 744 square feet of living area

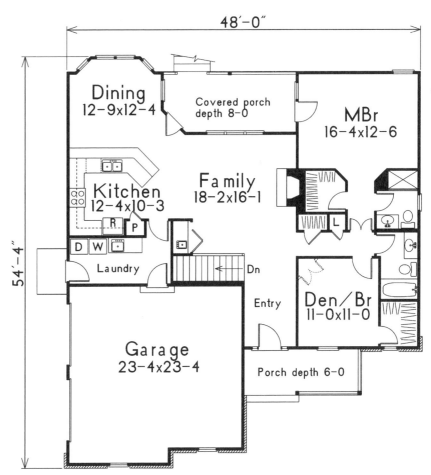

48'-0"

54'-4"

Dining
12-9x12-4

Covered porch
depth 8-0

MBr
16-4x12-6

Kitchen
12-4x10-3

Family
18-2x16-1

R P

D W

Laundry

Dn

Entry

Den/Br
11-0x11-0

Garage
23-4x23-4

Porch depth 6-0

PLAN DATA

Total Living Area:	1,440
Bedrooms:	2
Baths:	2
Foundation Type:	
Basement	

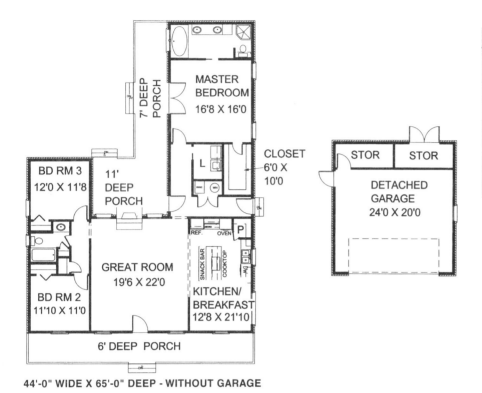

MASTER BEDROOM
16'8 X 16'0

7' DEEP PORCH

CLOSET
6'0 X 10'0

BD RM 3
12'0 X 11'8

11' DEEP PORCH

L

BD RM 2
11'10 X 11'0

GREAT ROOM
19'6 X 22'0

REF. OVEN P

SNACK BAR COOKTOP

KITCHEN/ BREAKFAST
12'8 X 21'10

6' DEEP PORCH

STOR STOR

DETACHED GARAGE
24'0 X 20'0

44'-0" WIDE X 65'-0" DEEP - WITHOUT GARAGE

PLAN DATA

Total Living Area: 1,716
Bedrooms: 3
Baths: 2
Garage: detached 2-car
Foundation Types:
  Crawl space
  Slab
Please specify when ordering

© Michael E. Nelson

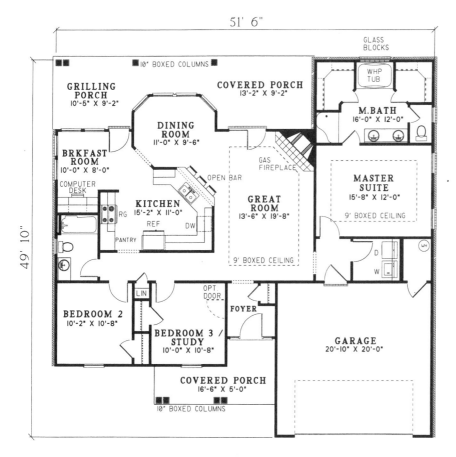

51' 6"

49' 10"

GLASS BLOCKS

10" BOXED COLUMNS

GRILLING PORCH
10'-5" X 9'-2"

COVERED PORCH
13'-2" X 9'-2"

WHP TUB

M.BATH
16'-0" X 12'-0"

BRKFAST ROOM
10'-0" X 8'-0"

DINING ROOM
11'-0" X 9'-6"

GAS FIREPLACE

OPEN BAR

COMPUTER DESK

MASTER SUITE
15'-8" X 12'-0"

9' BOXED CEILING

KITCHEN
15'-2" X 11'-0"

RG

REF

DW

GREAT ROOM
13'-6" X 19'-8"

PANTRY

9' BOXED CEILING

D

W

WH

LIN

OPT DOOR

FOYER

BEDROOM 2
10'-2" X 10'-8"

BEDROOM 3 / STUDY
10'-0" X 10'-8"

GARAGE
20'-10" X 20'-0"

COVERED PORCH
16'-6" X 5'-0"

10" BOXED COLUMNS

PLAN DATA

Total Living Area:	1,525
Bedrooms:	3
Baths:	2
Garage:	2-car

Foundation Types:
  Basement
  Walk-out basement
  Crawl space
  Slab
Please specify when ordering

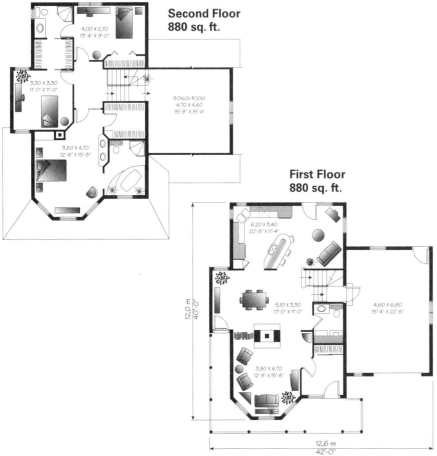

Second Floor
880 sq. ft.

4,00 X 2,70
13'-4" X 9'-0"

3,30 X 3,30
11'-0" X 11'-0"

BONUS ROOM
4,70 X 4,60
15'-8" X 15'-4"

3,80 X 4,70
12'-8" X 15'-8"

First Floor
880 sq. ft.

6,20 X 3,40
20'-8" X 11'-4"

5,10 X 3,30
17'-0" X 11'-0"

4,60 X 6,80
15'-4" X 22'-8"

3,80 X 4,70
12'-8" X 15'-8"

12,0 m
40'-0"

12,6 m
42'-0"

PLAN DATA

Total Living Area: 1,760
Bedrooms: 3
Baths: 2 1/2
Garage: 1-car
Foundation Type:
   Basement
Features:
   - 9' ceilings on first floor
   - 2" x 6" exterior walls
   - Bonus room on the second floor has an additional 256 square feet of living area

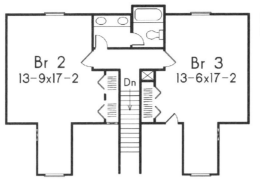

Second Floor
820 sq. ft.

Br 2
13-9x17-2

Dn

Br 3
13-6x17-2

PLAN DATA

Total Living Area: 1,875
Bedrooms: 3
Baths: 2
Garage: 2-car
Foundation Types:
  Crawl space standard
  Basement
  Slab

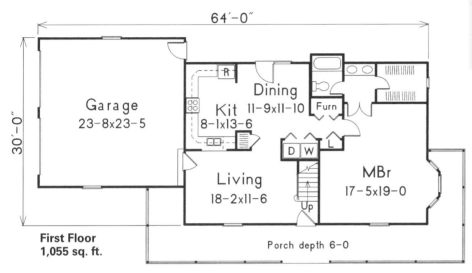

64'-0"

30'-0"

Garage
23-8x23-5

R

Dining
11-9x11-10

Kit
8-1x13-6

Furn

D W L

Living
18-2x11-6

Up

MBr
17-5x19-0

First Floor
1,055 sq. ft.

Porch depth 6-0

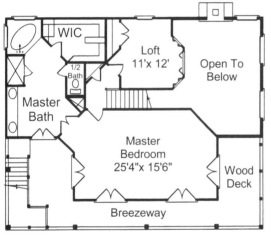

WIC

Loft
11'x 12'

Open To
Below

1/2
Bath

Master
Bath

Master
Bedroom
25'4"x 15'6"

Wood
Deck

Breezeway

**Second Floor
920 sq. ft.**

PLAN DATA

Total Living Area:	2,172
Bedrooms:	3
Baths:	2
Garage:	2-car

Foundation Types:
  Crawl space
  Slab
  Pier
Please specify when ordering

Features:
  -10' ceilings through-
   out first floor
  - 9' ceilings through-
   out second floor

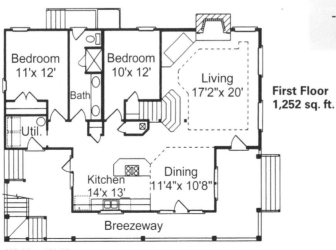

Bedroom
11'x 12'

Bedroom
10'x 12'

Living
17'2"x 20'

Bath

Util.

Kitchen
14'x 13'

Dining
11'4"x 10'8"

Breezeway

**First Floor
1,252 sq. ft.**

Width: 46'-0"
Depth: 40'-6"

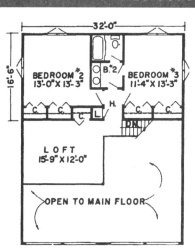

Second Floor
735 sq. ft.

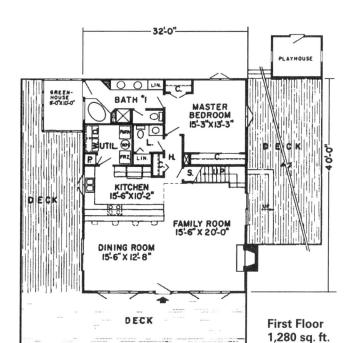

First Floor
1,280 sq. ft.

PLAN DATA

Total Living Area:	2,015
Bedrooms:	3
Baths:	2 1/2
Foundation Type:	
Crawl space	

PLAN DATA

Total Living Area: 1,803
Bedrooms: 3
Baths: 2
Garage: 3-car
Foundation Type:
   Basement
Features:
   Drive-under garage

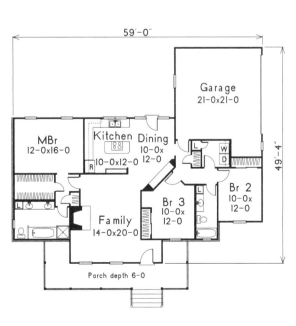

PLAN DATA

Total Living Area: 1,595
Bedrooms: 3
Baths: 2
Garage: 2-car
Foundation Types:
   Slab standard
   Crawl space

PLAN DATA

Total Living Area: 1,275
Bedrooms: 4
Baths: 2
Foundation Types:
   Basement standard
   Crawl space
   Slab

Second Floor
443 sq. ft.

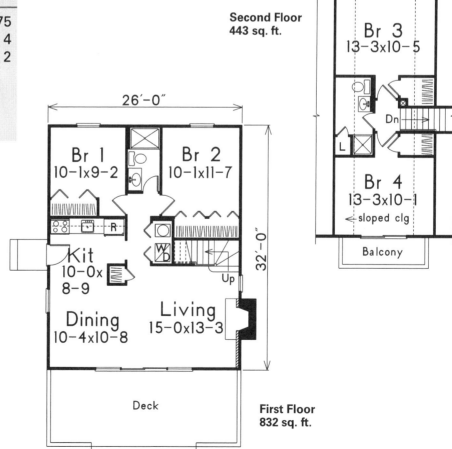

Br 3
13-3x10-5

Dn

L

Br 4
13-3x10-1

← sloped clg

Balcony

26'-0"

Br 1
10-1x9-2

Br 2
10-1x11-7

R

Kit
10-0x
8-9

W
D

Up

32'-0"

Dining
10-4x10-8

Living
15-0x13-3

Deck

First Floor
832 sq. ft.

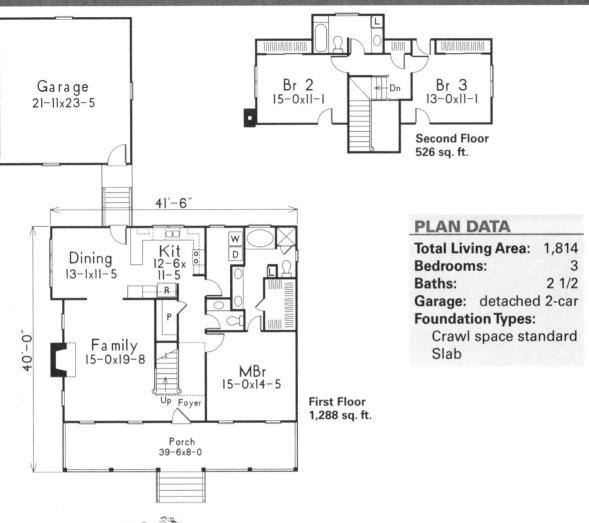

Garage
21-11x23-5

Br 2
15-0x11-1

Dn

Br 3
13-0x11-1

Second Floor
526 sq. ft.

41'-6"

W
D

L

Dining
13-1x11-5

Kit
12-6x
11-5

R

40'-0"

P

Family
15-0x19-8

MBr
15-0x14-5

Up Foyer

First Floor
1,288 sq. ft.

Porch
39-6x8-0

PLAN DATA

Total Living Area: 1,814
Bedrooms: 3
Baths: 2 1/2
Garage: detached 2-car
Foundation Types:
  Crawl space standard
  Slab

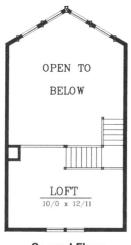

OPEN TO

BELOW

LOFT
10/0 x 12/11

**Second Floor
240 sq. ft.**

PLAN DATA

Total Living Area: 1,888
Bedrooms: 2
Baths: 2
Foundation Type:
Basement

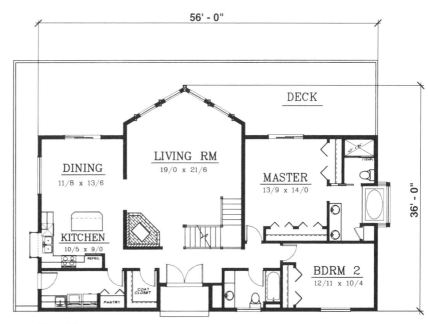

56' - 0"

DECK

DINING
11/8 x 13/6

LIVING RM
19/0 x 21/6

MASTER
13/9 x 14/0

KITCHEN
10/5 x 9/0

REFRIG.

36' - 0"

COAT
CLOSET

PANTRY

BDRM 2
12/11 x 10/4

**First Floor
1,648 sq. ft.**

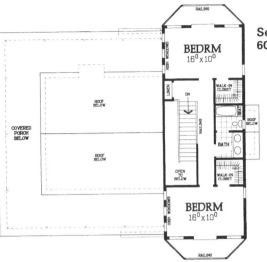

Second Floor
600 sq. ft.

BEDRM
16⁰ x 10⁰

BEDRM
16⁰ x 10⁰

First Floor
1,374 sq. ft.

51'8"

50'8"

NOOK
16⁰ x 10⁰

KIT
16⁰ x 10⁴

GREAT RM
17¹⁰ x 21⁰
VOL. CLG

POWDER RM

MASTER BATH

FOYER
VOL. CLG

WALK-IN CLOSET

MASTER BEDRM
16⁰ x 13⁸

PLAN DATA

Total Living Area: 1,974
Bedrooms: 3
Baths: 2 1/2
Foundation Types:
　Basement
　Crawl space
Please specify when ordering

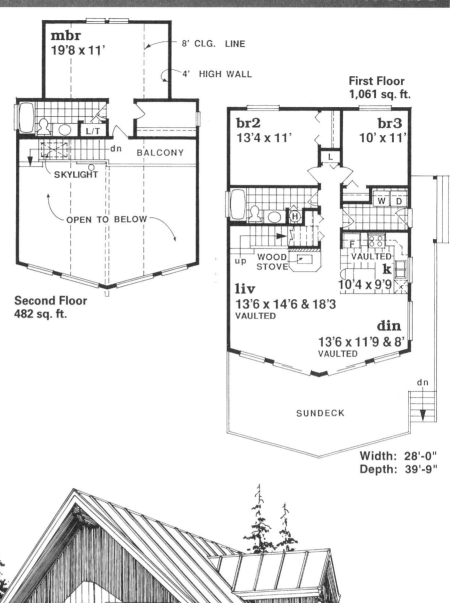

mbr
19'8 x 11'

8' CLG. LINE

4' HIGH WALL

dn

BALCONY

L/T

SKYLIGHT

OPEN TO BELOW

Second Floor
482 sq. ft.

First Floor
1,061 sq. ft.

br2
13'4 x 11'

br3
10' x 11'

L

W D

H

F

VAULTED

up

WOOD
STOVE

k
10'4 x 9'9

liv
13'6 x 14'6 & 18'3
VAULTED

din
13'6 x 11'9 & 8'
VAULTED

SUNDECK

dn

Width: 28'-0"
Depth: 39'-9"

PLAN DATA

Total Living Area: 1,543
Bedrooms: 3
Baths: 2
Foundation Type:
  Crawl space

**Second Floor
511 sq. ft.**

BR3
11' x 11'7

BATH 2

Foyer Below

BR2
11'4 x 11'11

**First Floor
1,281 sq. ft.**

DIN RM
11'8 x 11'11

KIT
9'8 x 11'7

DIN
8'8 x 11'5

MBR
15'8 x 13'5

MBATH

DW

PANTRY

REF

Dress'g

LIV RM
15' x 13'8

Lav

WI Closet

Mud Rm/Entry

Two-Story
FOYER

Laun

COUNTER

W

D

Covered Entry

GARAGE
21'4 x 21'8

**Width: 58'-0"
Depth: 44'-0"**

PLAN DATA

Total Living Area:	1,792
Bedrooms:	3
Baths:	2 1/2
Garage:	2-car
Foundation Type:	
Basement	

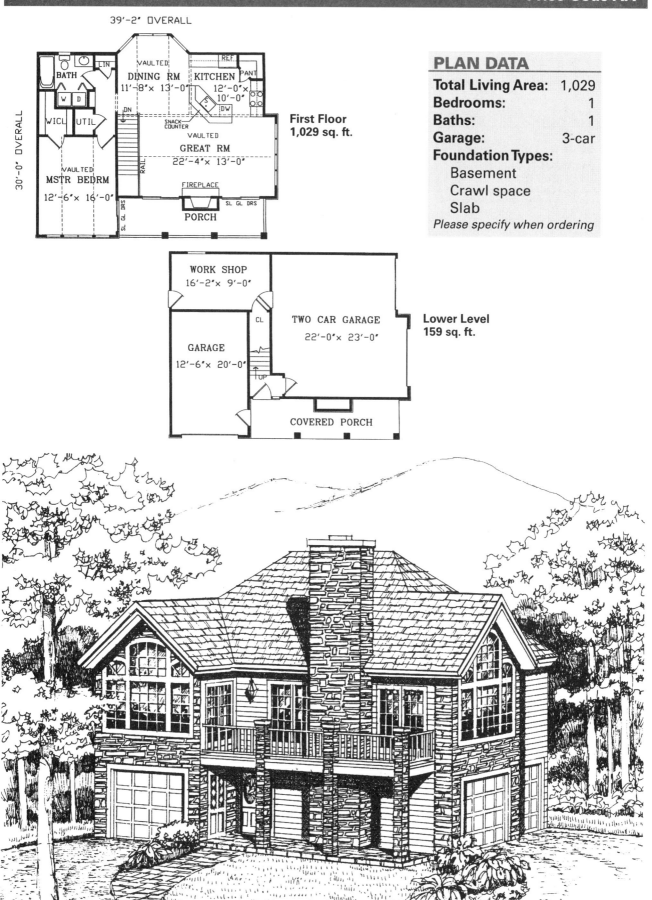

39'-2" OVERALL

30'-0" OVERALL

BATH
LIN
VAULTED
DINING RM
11'-8" x 13'-0"
REF.
KITCHEN
12'-0" x
10'-0"
PANT

W D
WICL
UTIL
DN
SNACK COUNTER

VAULTED
MSTR BEDRM
12'-6" x 16'-0"

RAIL

VAULTED
GREAT RM
22'-4" x 13'-0"

FIREPLACE
SL GL DRS
SL GL DRS
PORCH

First Floor
1,029 sq. ft.

WORK SHOP
16'-2" x 9'-0"

CL
TWO CAR GARAGE
22'-0" x 23'-0"

GARAGE
12'-6" x 20'-0"
UP

COVERED PORCH

Lower Level
159 sq. ft.

PLAN DATA

Total Living Area: 1,029
Bedrooms: 1
Baths: 1
Garage: 3-car
Foundation Types:
  Basement
  Crawl space
  Slab
Please specify when ordering

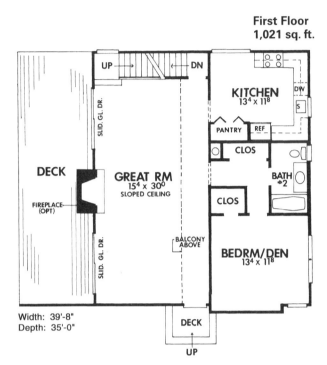

First Floor
1,021 sq. ft.

UP →   ← DN

KITCHEN
13⁴ x 11⁸

DW

S

PANTRY   REF

DECK

SLID. GL. DR.

GREAT RM
15⁴ x 30⁰
SLOPED CEILING

FIREPLACE (OPT)

CLOS

BATH #2

CLOS

SLID. GL. DR.

BALCONY ABOVE

BEDRM/DEN
13⁴ x 11⁸

Width: 39'-8"
Depth: 35'-0"

DECK

UP

DN

BEDRM #2
13⁴ x 11⁴

RAIL

BALCONY

UPPER
GREAT RM

CL

WALK
IN
CLOS

BATH #1

MASTER BEDRM
17² x 14⁰

Second Floor
616 sq. ft.

PLAN DATA

Total Living Area:	1,637
Bedrooms:	3
Baths:	2
Foundation Types:	
Basement	
Crawl space	
Slab	

Please specify when ordering

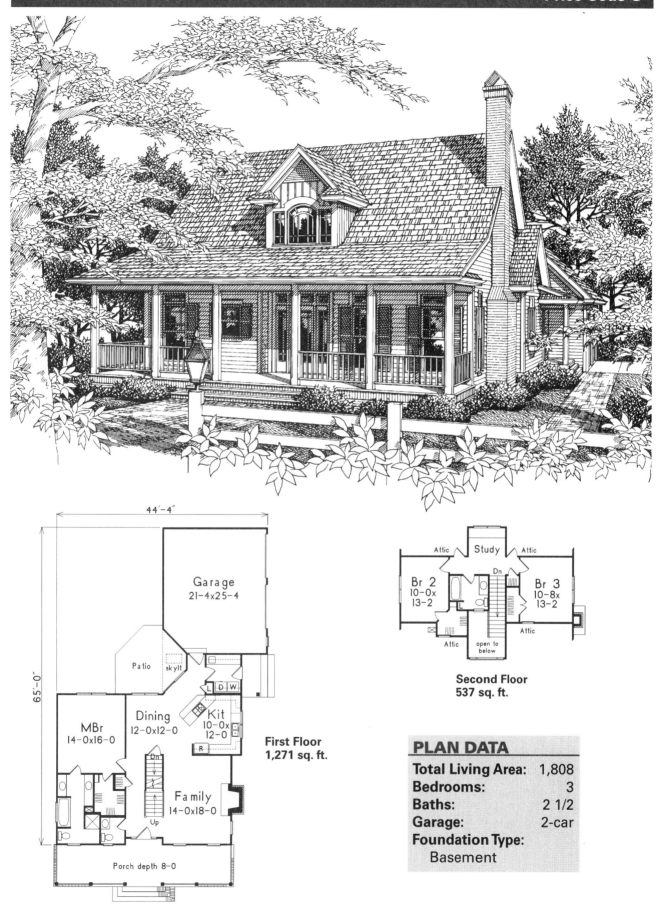

First Floor
1,271 sq. ft.

44'-4"

65'-0"

Garage
21-4x25-4

Patio

skylt

L D W

MBr
14-0x16-0

Dining
12-0x12-0

Kit
10-0x
12-0

R

Dn

Family
14-0x18-0

Up

Porch depth 8-0

Second Floor
537 sq. ft.

Attic   Study   Attic

Br 2
10-0x
13-2

Dn

Br 3
10-8x
13-2

Attic   open to   Attic
         below

PLAN DATA

Total Living Area:	1,808
Bedrooms:	3
Baths:	2 1/2
Garage:	2-car
Foundation Type:	
Basement	

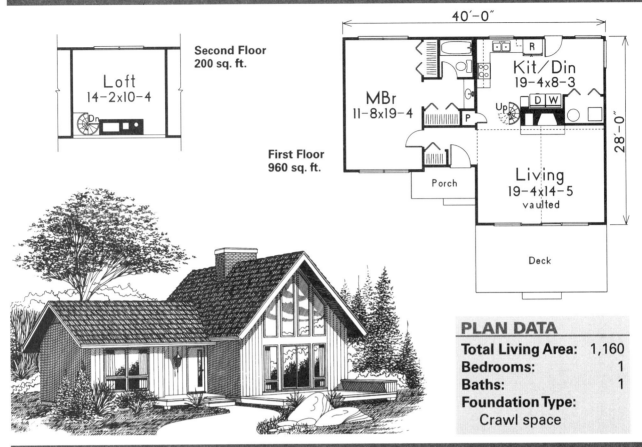

Second Floor
200 sq. ft.

Loft
14-2x10-4

Dn

40'-0"

Kit/Din
19-4x8-3

D W

R

MBr
11-8x19-4

Up

P

First Floor
960 sq. ft.

28'-0"

Living
19-4x14-5
vaulted

Porch

Deck

PLAN DATA

Total Living Area:	1,160
Bedrooms:	1
Baths:	1
Foundation Type:	
Crawl space	

PLAN DATA

Total Living Area:	1,462
Bedrooms:	3
Baths:	2
Garage:	2-car
Foundation Type:	
Basement	

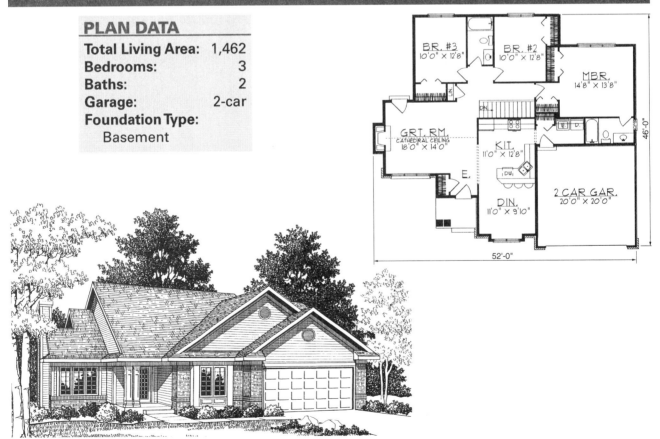

BR. #3
10'0" x 12'8"

BR. #2
10'0" x 12'8"

MBR
14'8" x 13'8"

46'-0"

GRT. RM.
CATHEDRAL CEILING
18'0" x 14'0"

KIT.
11'0" x 12'8"

2 CAR GAR.
20'0" x 20'0"

DIN.
11'0" x 9'10"

52'-0"

Second Floor
507 sq. ft.

31'-8"

38'-4"

First Floor
980 sq. ft.

PLAN DATA

Total Living Area: 1,397
Bedrooms: 3
Baths: 2
Foundation Types:
   Crawl space
   Slab
Please specify when ordering

PLAN DATA

Total Living Area: 1,779
Bedrooms: 3
Baths: 3
Foundation Type:
  Pier

Second Floor
872 sq. ft.

Width: 34'-0"
Depth: 30'-0"

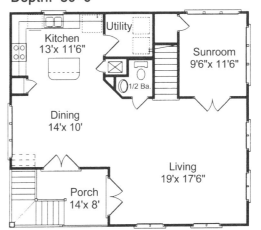

First Floor
907 sq. ft.

PLAN #563-0340

Price Code C

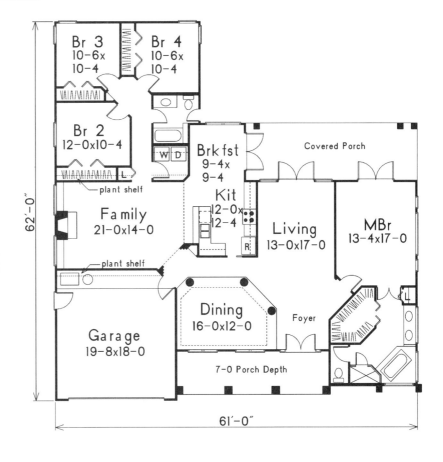

PLAN DATA

Total Living Area:	2,153
Bedrooms:	4
Baths:	2
Garage:	2-car
Foundation Type:	
Slab	

PLAN DATA

Total Living Area:	1,882
Bedrooms:	4
Baths:	2
Garage:	2-car
Foundation Type:	
Basement	

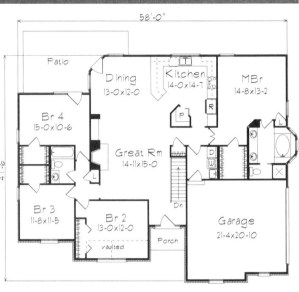

PLAN DATA

Total Living Area:	1,611
Bedrooms:	3
Baths:	2
Garage:	2-car
Foundation Type:	
Basement	

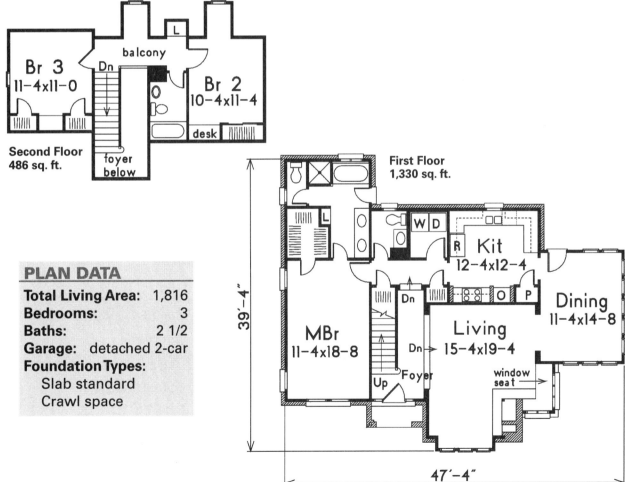

Br 3
11-4x11-0

balcony

Dn

L

Br 2
10-4x11-4

desk

Second Floor
486 sq. ft.

foyer
below

First Floor
1,330 sq. ft.

L

W D

R

Kit
12-4x12-4

39'-4"

Dn

O P

Dining
11-4x14-8

MBr
11-4x18-8

Living
15-4x19-4

Dn

Up

Foyer

window
seat

47'-4"

PLAN DATA

Total Living Area: 1,816
Bedrooms: 3
Baths: 2 1/2
Garage: detached 2-car
Foundation Types:
   Slab standard
   Crawl space

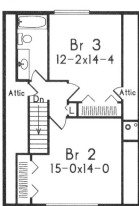

Second Floor
560 sq. ft.

Br 3
12-2x14-4

Attic   Attic

Dn

Br 2
15-0x14-0

First Floor
1,245 sq. ft.

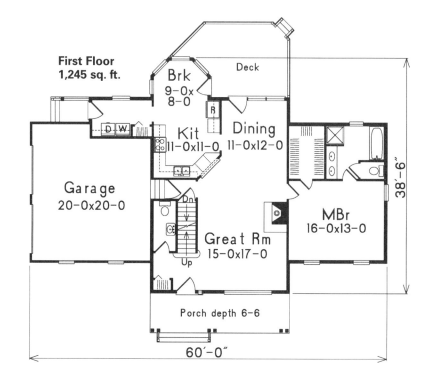

PLAN DATA

Total Living Area:	1,805
Bedrooms:	3
Baths:	2 1/2
Garage:	2-car

Foundation Types:
   Basement standard
   Slab

Features:
   2" x 6" exterior walls

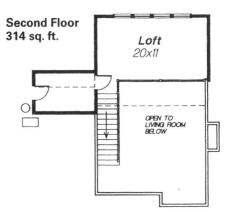

**Second Floor
314 sq. ft.**

Loft
20x11

OPEN TO
LIVING ROOM
BELOW

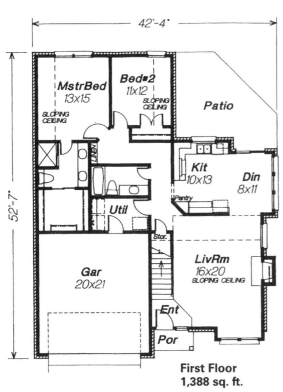

42'-4"

52'-7"

MstrBed
13x15
SLOPING CEILING

Bed#2
11x12
SLOPING CEILING

Patio

Kit
10x13

Din
8x11

Pantry

Util

Stor.

Gar
20x21

LivRm
16x20
SLOPING CEILING

Ent

Por

**First Floor
1,388 sq. ft.**

PLAN DATA	
Total Living Area:	1,702
Bedrooms:	2
Baths:	2
Garage:	2-car
Foundation Type:	
Slab	

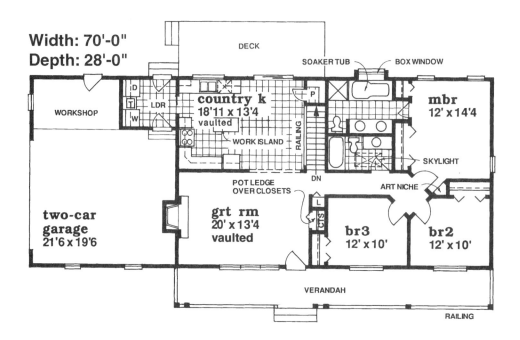

Width: 70'-0"
Depth: 28'-0"

DECK

SOAKER TUB   BOX WINDOW

WORKSHOP

D
T
W
LDR

country k
18'11 x 13'4
vaulted

WORK ISLAND

RAILING

P

mbr
12' x 14'4

SKYLIGHT

ART NICHE

POT LEDGE
OVER CLOSETS

DN

two-car garage
21'6 x 19'6

grt rm
20' x 13'4
vaulted

L
CTS

br3
12' x 10'

br2
12' x 10'

VERANDAH

RAILING

PLAN DATA

Total Living Area:	1,408
Bedrooms:	3
Baths:	2
Garage:	2-car
Foundation Types:	
Basement	
Crawl space	

Please specify when ordering

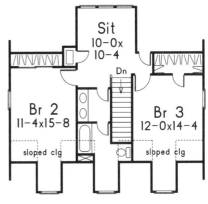

**Second Floor
751 sq. ft.**

**First Floor
1,308 sq. ft.**

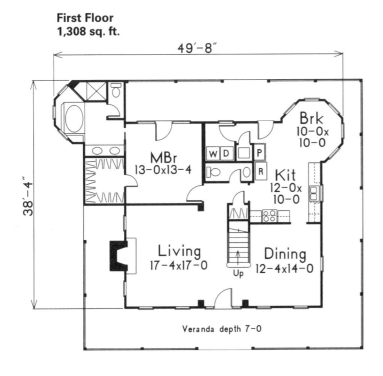

PLAN DATA

Total Living Area: 2,059
Bedrooms: 3
Baths: 2 1/2
Garage: detached 2-car
Foundation Types:
  Slab standard
  Basement
  Crawl space
Features:
  9' ceilings throughout

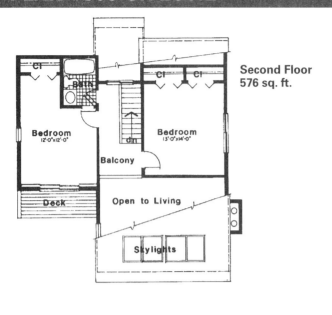

Second Floor
576 sq. ft.

First Floor
911 sq. ft.

PLAN DATA

Total Living Area: 1,487
Bedrooms: 3
Baths: 1 1/2
Foundation Type:
   Basement

**Second Floor
1,209 sq. ft.**

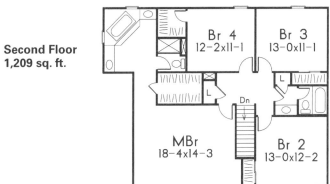

Br 4
12-2x11-1

Br 3
13-0x11-1

Dn

MBr
18-4x14-3

Br 2
13-0x12-2

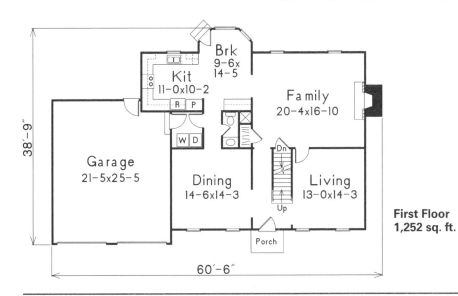

Brk
9-6x
14-5

Kit
11-0x10-2

Family
20-4x16-10

R P

W D

Garage
21-5x25-5

Dining
14-6x14-3

Dn

Living
13-0x14-3

Up

Porch

38'-9"

60'-6"

**First Floor
1,252 sq. ft.**

PLAN DATA
Total Living Area: 2,461
Bedrooms: 4
Baths: 2 1/2
Garage: 2-car
Foundation Types:
   Basement standard
   Crawl space
   Slab

PLAN DATA

Total Living Area: 2,334
Bedrooms: 3
Baths: 2
Garage: 2-car
Foundation Type:
Walk-out basement

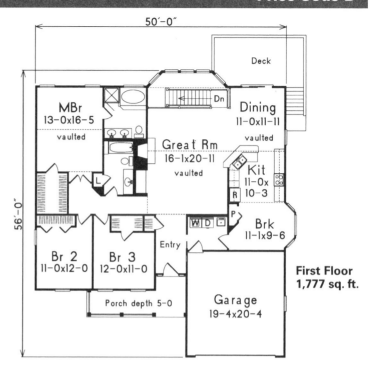

**First Floor
1,777 sq. ft.**

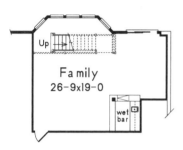

**Lower Level
557 sq. ft.**

Rear View

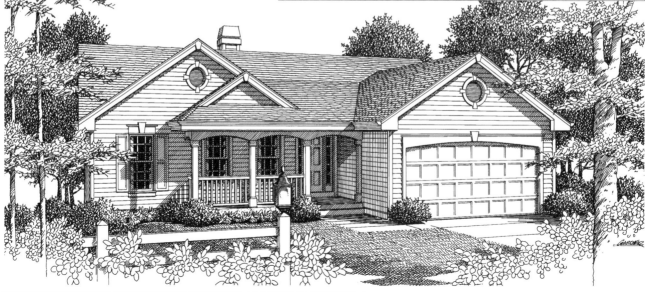

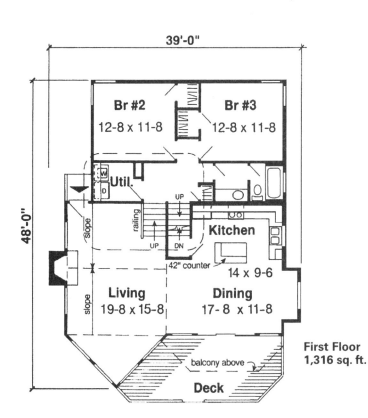

39'-0"

48'-0"

Br #2
12-8 x 11-8

Br #3
12-8 x 11-8

Util.

W
D

slope
railing

UP

UP   DN

Kitchen

42" counter

14 x 9-6

Living
19-8 x 15-8

slope

slope

Dining
17-8 x 11-8

First Floor
1,316 sq. ft.

balcony above

Deck

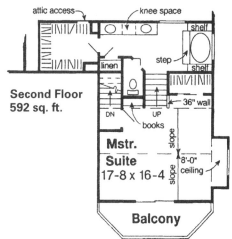

attic access   knee space

shelf

linen   step   shelf

Second Floor
592 sq. ft.

36" wall

DN   UP

books

**Mstr.
Suite**
17-8 x 16-4

slope

slope

8'-0"
ceiling

Balcony

PLAN DATA

Total Living Area: 1,908
Bedrooms: 3
Baths: 2
Foundation Types:
  Basement
  Crawl space
Please specify when ordering

PLAN DATA

Total Living Area: 1,593
Bedrooms: 3
Baths: 2
Garage: 2-car
Foundation Type:
  Basement

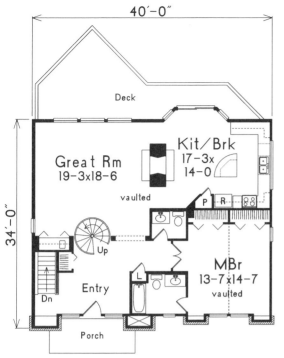

40'-0"

34'-0"

Deck

Great Rm
19-3x18-6
vaulted

Kit/Brk
17-3x
14-0

P   R

MBr
13-7x14-7
vaulted

Up

Dn

Entry

Porch

First Floor
1,314 sq. ft.

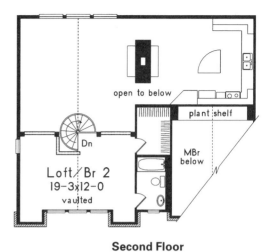

open to below

plant shelf

Dn

MBr below

Loft/Br 2
19-3x12-0
vaulted

Second Floor
397 sq. ft.

PLAN DATA

Total Living Area:	1,711
Bedrooms:	2
Baths:	2 1/2
Foundation Type:	
Basement	

Rear View

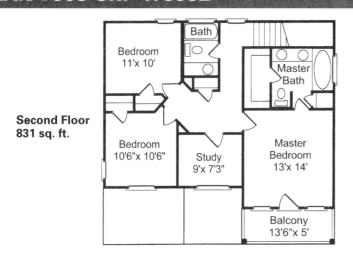

Second Floor
831 sq. ft.

Bath

Bedroom
11'x 10'

Master
Bath

Bedroom
10'6"x 10'6"

Study
9'x 7'3"

Master
Bedroom
13'x 14'

Balcony
13'6"x 5'

PLAN DATA

Total Living Area: 1,743
Bedrooms: 3
Baths: 3
Garage: 2-car carport
Foundation Type:
Pier
Features:
9' ceilings on first
floor

Utility
9'7"x 6'10"

1/2 Ba.

Kitchen
12'8"x 12'2"

Living
14'2"x 19'6"

First Floor
912 sq. ft.

Dining
11'4"x 12'

Porch
22'x8'

Width: 34'-0"
Depth: 32'-0"

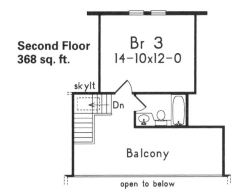

**Second Floor
368 sq. ft.**

Br 3
14-10x12-0

skylt

Dn

Balcony

open to below

PLAN DATA

Total Living Area: 1,660
Bedrooms: 3
Baths: 3
Foundation Types:
   Partial basement/
   crawl space standard
   Slab

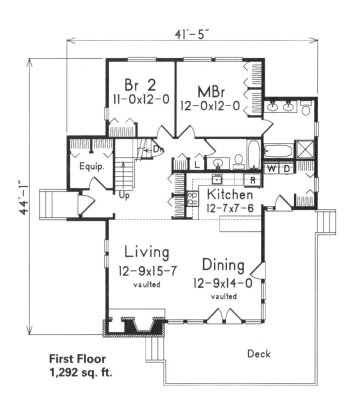

41'-5"

Br 2
11-0x12-0

MBr
12-0x12-0

Equip.

44'-1"

Dn

Up

L

W D

Kitchen
12-7x7-6

R

Living
12-9x15-7
vaulted

Dining
12-9x14-0
vaulted

**First Floor
1,292 sq. ft.**

Deck

PLAN DATA

Total Living Area: 1,577
Bedrooms: 3
Baths: 2 1/2
Foundation Type:
  Crawl space

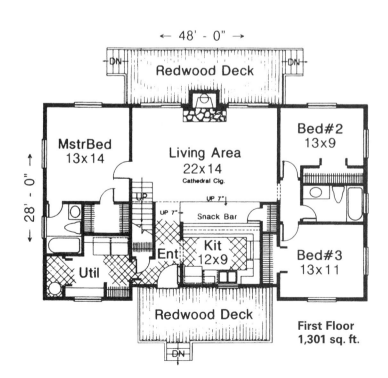

← 48' - 0" →

← 28' - 0" →

DN Redwood Deck DN

MstrBed
13 x 14

Living Area
22 x 14
Cathedral Clg.

Bed#2
13x9

UP

UP 7"

UP 7"

Snack Bar

Ent   Kit
       12x9

Util

Bed#3
13 x 11

Redwood Deck

DN

First Floor
1,301 sq. ft.

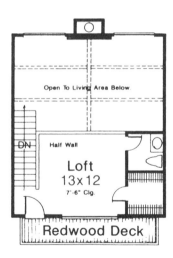

Open To Living Area Below

DN   Half Wall

Loft
13x12
7'-6" Clg.

Redwood Deck

Second Floor
276 sq. ft.

Second Floor
600 sq. ft.

BEDRM
$11^8 \times 10^0$
8'-0" CLG

OPEN OVER
FAMILY-GREAT RM
2-STORY CLG
SLOPING CEILING

BEDRM
$11^8 \times 15^2$
8'-0" CLG

RAILING

BALCONY

BATH

OPEN OVER
ENTRY HALL
2-STORY CLG

PLANT
SHELF

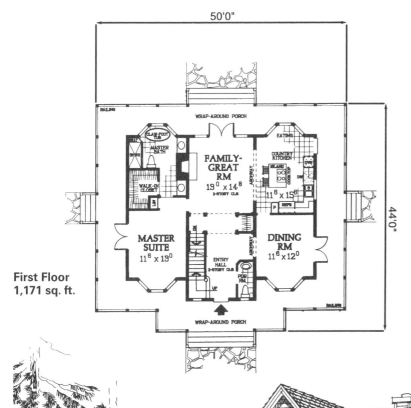

First Floor
1,171 sq. ft.

50'0"

44'0"

WRAP-AROUND PORCH

RAILING

CLAW-FOOT TUB

MASTER BATH

WALK-IN CLOSET

FAMILY-GREAT RM
$13^0 \times 14^8$
2-STORY CLG

ARCHWAY

EATING

COUNTRY KITCHEN
ISLAND
COOKTOP
$11^8 \times 15^8$

OVEN

DW

P REFG

MASTER SUITE
$11^8 \times 13^0$

ARCHWAY

DINING RM
$11^8 \times 12^0$

ENTRY HALL
2-STORY CLG

UP

PDR RM

RAILING

WRAP-AROUND PORCH

PLAN DATA

Total Living Area:	1,771
Bedrooms:	3
Baths:	2 1/2
Garage:	2-car
	optional detached
Foundation Type:	
Basement	

KOIZUMI

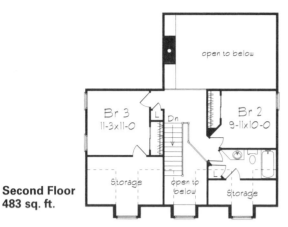

**Second Floor
483 sq. ft.**

Br 3
11-3x11-0

Dn

Br 2
9-11x10-0

open to below

Storage

open to below

Storage

PLAN DATA

Total Living Area:	1,711
Bedrooms:	3
Baths:	2 1/2
Garage:	2-car
Foundation Type:	
Basement	

**First Floor
1,228 sq. ft.**

63'-0"

43'-0"

Covered Porch

Family
20-4x13-0
vaulted

Deck

MBr
13-8x13-8

Dn

Kit
8-3x11-3

Brk
10-6x10-0

Up

Dining
12-4x12-8

Garage
21-4x21-4

Porch

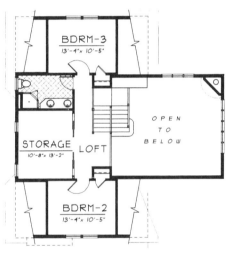

Second Floor
669 sq. ft.

BDRM-3
13'-4" x 10'-5"

STORAGE
10'-8" x 13'-2"

LOFT

OPEN TO BELOW

BDRM-2
13'-4" x 10'-5"

PLAN DATA

Total Living Area:	2,104
Bedrooms:	3
Baths:	2
Garage:	2-car
Foundation Type:	
Crawl space	
Features:	
9' ceilings on first floor	

65'-4"

43'-2"

GARAGE
23'-6" x 24'-0"

WALK-IN

MASTER
15'-0" x 12'-11"

BATH

UTILITY & MUD ROOM

LIVING RM
18'-2" x 19'-0"

DECK
160 SQ. FT.

DINING
12'-5" x 13'-0"

KITCHEN
12'-7" x 10'-0"

PORCH
COVERED

First Floor
1,435 sq. ft.

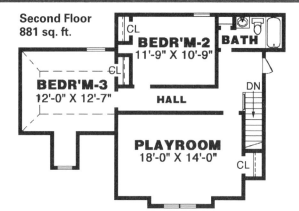

Second Floor
881 sq. ft.

CL

BEDR'M-2
11'-9" X 10'-9"

BATH

CL

BEDR'M-3
12'-0" X 12'-7"

HALL

DN

PLAYROOM
18'-0" X 14'-0"

CL

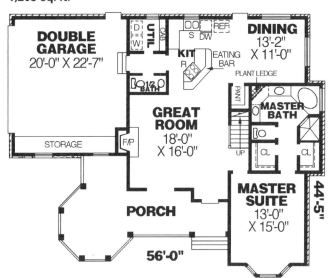

First Floor
1,203 sq. ft.

DOUBLE GARAGE
20'-0" X 22'-7"

D/W

UTIL

CAB

S

DW

REF

DINING
13'-2" X 11'-0"

KIT

R

EATING BAR

PLANT LEDGE

BATH

PANT

MASTER BATH

GREAT ROOM
18'-0" X 16'-0"

STORAGE

F/P

UP

CL

CL

PORCH

MASTER SUITE
13'-0" X 15'-0"

44'-5"

56'-0"

PLAN DATA

Total Living Area: 2,084
Bedrooms: 3
Baths: 2 1/2
Garage: 2-car
Foundation Types:
  Basement
  Crawl space
  Slab
Please specify when ordering

56'-8"

54'-0"

Garage
21-4x21-4

MBr
13-6x16-0

Dining
11-0x11-8

Kitchen
12-6x11-8

W D

Dn   Up

Brk
10-8x12-6

R

Family
14-2x19-4

Porch depth 6-0

First Floor
1,339 sq. ft.

Br 3
10-0x
14-6

Optional
Br 4
10-0x13-4

Dn

Br 2
12-8x11-0

Second Floor
490 sq. ft.

PLAN DATA

Total Living Area:	1,829
Bedrooms:	3
Baths:	2 1/2
Garage:	2-car
Foundation Type:	
Partial basement/ crawl space	

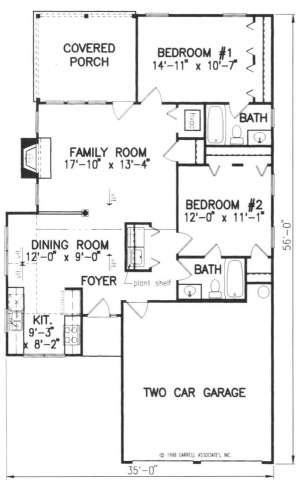

COVERED PORCH

BEDROOM #1
14'-11" x 10'-7"

BATH

hvac

FAMILY ROOM
17'-10" x 13'-4"

BEDROOM #2
12'-0" x 11'-1"

56'-0"

DINING ROOM
12'-0" x 9'-0"

FOYER

BATH

plant shelf

KIT.
9'-3" x 8'-2"

TWO CAR GARAGE

© 1998 GARRELL ASSOCIATES, INC.

35'-0"

PLAN DATA

Total Living Area: 1,093
Bedrooms: 2
Baths: 2
Garage: 2-car
Foundation Type:
Slab

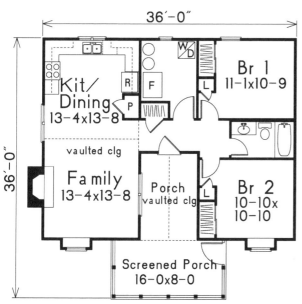

36'-0"

36'-0"

Kit/
Dining
13-4x13-8

Br 1
11-1x10-9

vaulted clg

Family
13-4x13-8

Porch
vaulted clg

Br 2
10-10x
10-10

Screened Porch
16-0x8-0

PLAN DATA
Total Living Area:	924
Bedrooms:	2
Baths:	1
Foundation Type:	
Slab	

PLAN DATA
Total Living Area:	1,340
Bedrooms:	3
Baths:	2
Garage:	2-car
Foundation Type:	
Basement	
Features:	

- Drive-under garage
- Lower level has
  space for additional
  bedroom

38'-0"

Patio

MBr
14-9x11-6

vaulted clg

plant shelf

Brkfst

Kit
13-6x15-6

shelves

Dining

38'-4"

Br 2
8-11x9-0

Living
18-2x18-8
vaulted clg

Dn   Up

Br 3
12-4x10-0

Porch

vaulted clg

PLAN DATA

Total Living Area: 1,442
Bedrooms: 3
Baths: 2
Foundation Type:
  Basement
Features:
  2" x 6" exterior walls

First Floor
922 sq. ft.

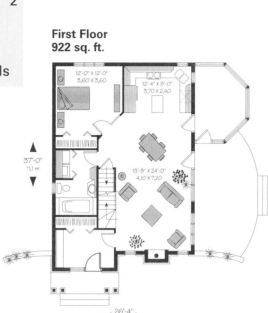

Second Floor
520 sq. ft.

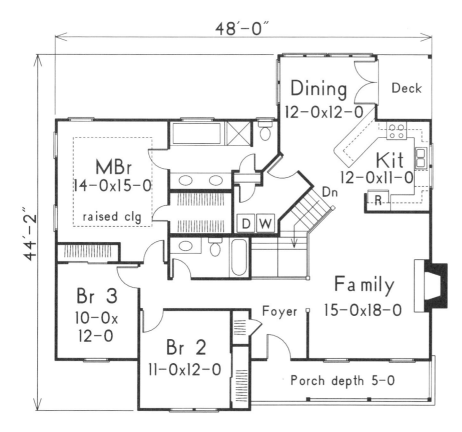

48'-0"

44'-2"

Dining
12-0x12-0

Deck

MBr
14-0x15-0

raised clg

Kit
12-0x11-0

Dn

D W

R

Family
15-0x18-0

Br 3
10-0x
12-0

Foyer

Br 2
11-0x12-0

Porch depth 5-0

PLAN DATA

Total Living Area:	1,631
Bedrooms:	3
Baths:	2
Garage:	2-car
Foundation Type:	
Basement	
Features:	

- 9' ceilings through-
  out
- Drive-under garage

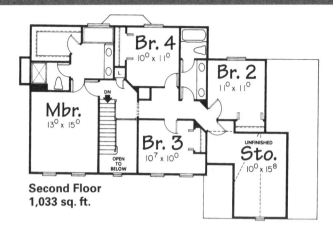

**Second Floor
1,033 sq. ft.**

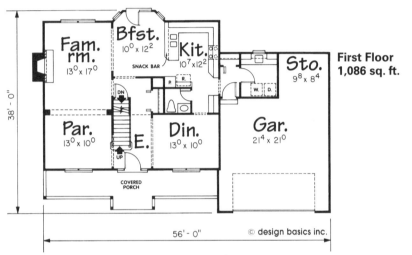

**First Floor
1,086 sq. ft.**

PLAN DATA

Total Living Area:	2,119
Bedrooms:	4
Baths:	2 1/2
Garage:	2-car
Foundation Type:	
Basement	

© design basics inc.

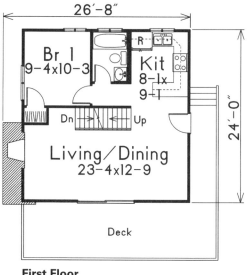

26'-8"

Br 1
9-4x10-3

Kit
8-1x
9-1

Dn ← → Up

Living/Dining
23-4x12-9

24'-0"

Deck

First Floor
576 sq. ft.

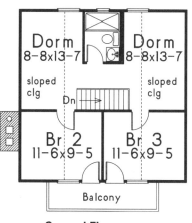

Dorm
8-8x13-7

Dorm
8-8x13-7

sloped clg

sloped clg

Dn

Br 2
11-6x9-5

Br 3
11-6x9-5

Balcony

Second Floor
528 sq. ft.

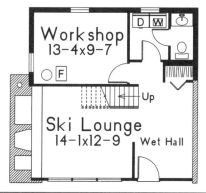

Workshop
13-4x9-7

D W

F

Up

Ski Lounge
14-1x12-9   Wet Hall

Lower Level
576 sq. ft.

PLAN DATA

Total Living Area: 1,680
Bedrooms: 5
Baths: 2 1/2
Foundation Type:
  Basement

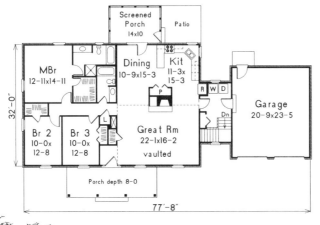

PLAN DATA

Total Living Area: 1,674
Bedrooms: 3
Baths: 2
Garage: 2-car
Foundation Types:
   Basement standard
   Crawl space
   Slab

PLAN DATA

Total Living Area: 1,442
Bedrooms: 3
Baths: 2
Garage: 2-car
Foundation Types:
   Slab standard
   Crawl space
Features:
   Living room with
   recessed fireplace
   and 10' ceiling

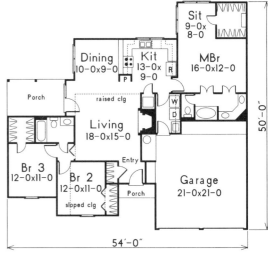

PLAN DATA

Total Living Area: 2,076
Bedrooms: 3
Baths: 2
Garage: 2-car
Foundation Type:
  Basement

**Second Floor
633 sq. ft.**

Br 2
11-0x10-7

Br 3
11-4x11-0

Br 4
11-4x11-0

Dn

open to
foyer

plant
shelf

L

73'-4"

38'-6"

Garage
21-4x23-4

Dining
13-4x10-0

Kitchen
13-4x10-0

Family
13-4x18-2

MBr
13-4x15-0

Foyer

plant
shelf

**First Floor
1,241 sq. ft.**

Porch
41-4x8-0

PLAN DATA

Total Living Area: 1,874
Bedrooms: 4
Baths: 2 1/2
Garage: 2-car
Foundation Types:
    Basement standard
    Slab
Features:
    9' ceilings on first
    floor

PLAN DATA

Total Living Area: 1,827
Bedrooms: 4
Baths: 2
Garage: 2-car
Foundation Types:
   Crawl space standard
   Basement
   Slab

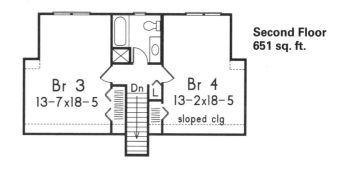

**Second Floor
651 sq. ft.**

Br 3
13-7x18-5

Dn

Br 4
13-2x18-5

sloped clg

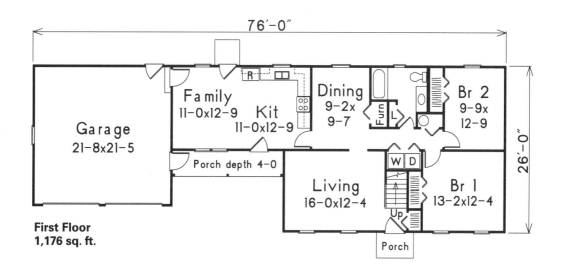

76'-0"

Garage
21-8x21-5

Family
11-0x12-9

Kit
11-0x12-9

Dining
9-2x
9-7

Br 2
9-9x
12-9

Furn

Porch depth 4-0

Living
16-0x12-4

W D

Br 1
13-2x12-4

Up

Porch

26'-0"

**First Floor
1,176 sq. ft.**

First Floor
952 sq. ft.

Second Floor
400 sq. ft.

PLAN DATA

Total Living Area: 1,352
Bedrooms: 3
Baths: 2
Foundation Types:
   Basement
   Crawl space
   Slab
Please specify when ordering

Rear View

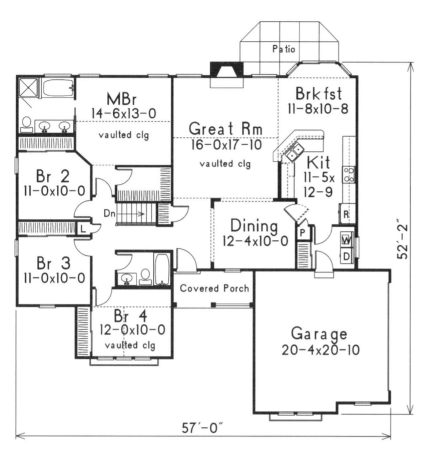

MBr
14-6x13-0
vaulted clg

Brk fst
11-8x10-8

Great Rm
16-0x17-10
vaulted clg

Kit
11-5x
12-9

Br 2
11-0x10-0

Dn

Dining
12-4x10-0

Br 3
11-0x10-0

Covered Porch

Br 4
12-0x10-0
vaulted clg

Garage
20-4x20-10

Patio

52'-2"

57'-0"

R

P

W
D

L

PLAN DATA

Total Living Area:	1,761
Bedrooms:	4
Baths:	2
Garage:	2-car
Foundation Type:	
Basement	

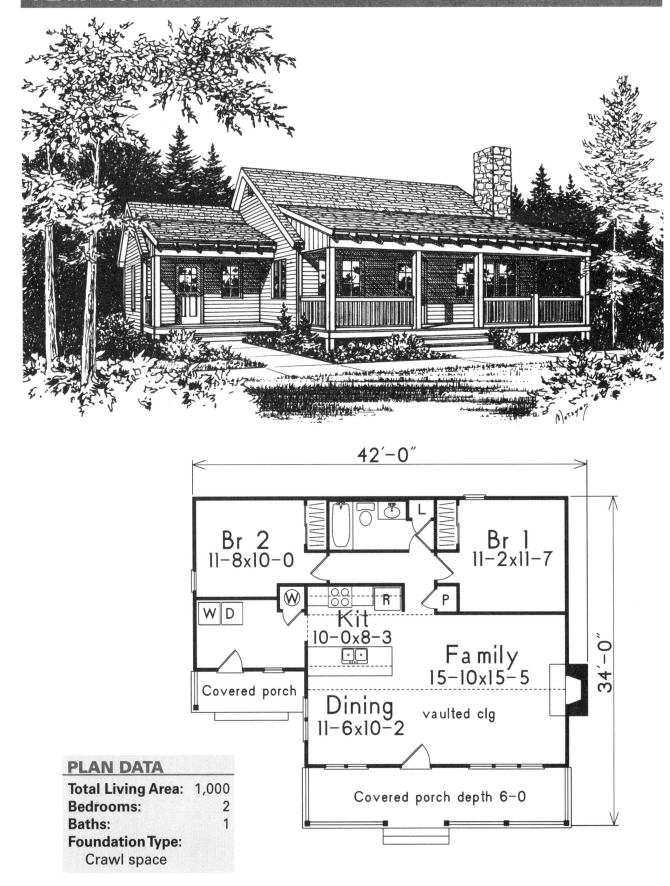

42'-0"

34'-0"

Br 2
11-8x10-0

Br 1
11-2x11-7

L

W D

W

R

P

Kit
10-0x8-3

Family
15-10x15-5

Covered porch

Dining
11-6x10-2

vaulted clg

Covered porch depth 6-0

PLAN DATA

Total Living Area:	1,000
Bedrooms:	2
Baths:	1
Foundation Type:	
Crawl space	

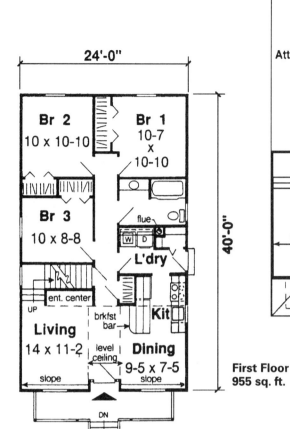

24'-0"

Br 2
10 x 10-10

Br 1
10-7 x 10-10

Br 3
10 x 8-8

flue

L'dry

ent. center

UP

brkfst bar

Kit

Living
14 x 11-2

level ceiling

slope

Dining
9-5 x 7-5

slope

40'-0"

W D

First Floor
955 sq. ft.

DN

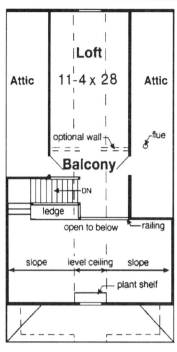

Loft
11-4 x 28

Attic

Attic

flue

optional wall

Balcony

DN

ledge

open to below

railing

slope

level ceiling

slope

plant shelf

Second Floor
336 sq. ft.

PLAN DATA

Total Living Area: 1,291
Bedrooms: 3
Baths: 1
Foundation Types:
  Basement
  Crawl space
  Slab
Please specify when ordering

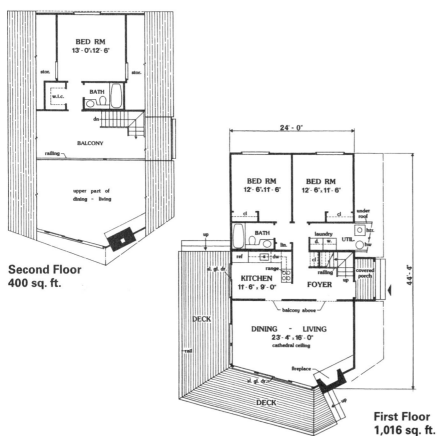

Second Floor
400 sq. ft.

First Floor
1,016 sq. ft.

BED RM
13'-0"x12'-6"

stor.

stor.

w.i.c.

BATH

dn

BALCONY

railing

upper part of
dining - living

24'-0"

BED RM
12'-6"x11'-6"

BED RM
12'-6"x11'-6"

cl

cl

under
roof

BATH

lin.

ref

dw

range

KITCHEN
11'-6" x 9'-0"

laundry

d. w.

UTIL

htr.

hw

cl

railing

up

FOYER

covered
porch

up

DECK

rail

balcony above

44'-4"

DINING - LIVING
23'-4" x 16'-0"
cathedral ceiling

sl. gl. dr.

fireplace

sl. gl. dr.

DECK

up

PLAN DATA

Total Living Area: 1,416
Bedrooms: 3
Baths: 2
Foundation Types:
  Basement
  Crawl space
  Slab
Please specify when ordering

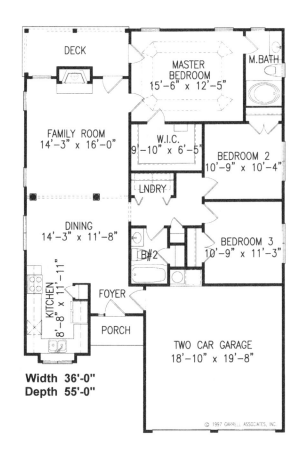

DECK

MASTER BEDROOM
15'-6" x 12'-5"

M.BATH

FAMILY ROOM
14'-3" x 16'-0"

W.I.C.
9'-10" x 6'-5"

BEDROOM 2
10'-9" x 10'-4"

LNDRY

DINING
14'-3" x 11'-8"

B#2

BEDROOM 3
10'-9" x 11'-3"

KITCHEN
8'-8" x 11'-11"

FOYER

PORCH

TWO CAR GARAGE
18'-10" x 19'-8"

Width 36'-0"
Depth 55'-0"

© 1997 GARRELL ASSOCIATES, INC

PLAN DATA

Total Living Area:	1,277
Bedrooms:	3
Baths:	2
Garage:	2-car
Foundation Type:	
Slab	

© 2003, Garrell Associates, Inc.

Christine Canova 2/02

PLAN DATA
Total Living Area: 1,950
Bedrooms: 4
Baths: 2
Garage: 3-car
Foundation Type:
  Crawl space

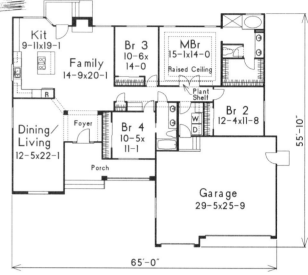

Kit
9-11x19-1

Family
14-9x20-1

Br 3
10-6x
14-0

MBr
15-1x14-0
Raised Ceiling

Plant Shelf

Dining/
Living
12-5x22-1

Foyer

Br 4
10-5x
11-1

W.D.

Br 2
12-4x11-8

Porch

Garage
29-5x25-9

55'-10"

65'-0"

PLAN DATA
Total Living Area: 1,422
Bedrooms: 3
Baths: 2
Garage: 2-car
Foundation Type:
  Basement

WHIRLPOOL

LIN.

Mbr.
14⁰ x 12²
9'-0" CEILING

Grt. rm.
14⁰ x 20⁰

Din.
12³ x 10⁰

COVERED
PORCH

BOOKS

12'-0" CEILING

Kit.
12⁰ x 10⁰

P.

Sto.
8⁴ x 10⁴

Br. 2
10⁰ x 11⁰

Br. 3
10⁰ x 11²
10'-0" CLG.
OPT. DEN

L

E
DN

W.D.

R

WORK
BENCH

Gar.
20⁴ x 21⁸

CVRD.
STOOP

58'-0"

50'-0"

© design basics inc.

PLAN DATA

Total Living Area:	1,760
Bedrooms:	3
Baths:	2
Garage:	2-car
Foundation Type:	
Slab	

@50 = 88,000
@60 = 105,600

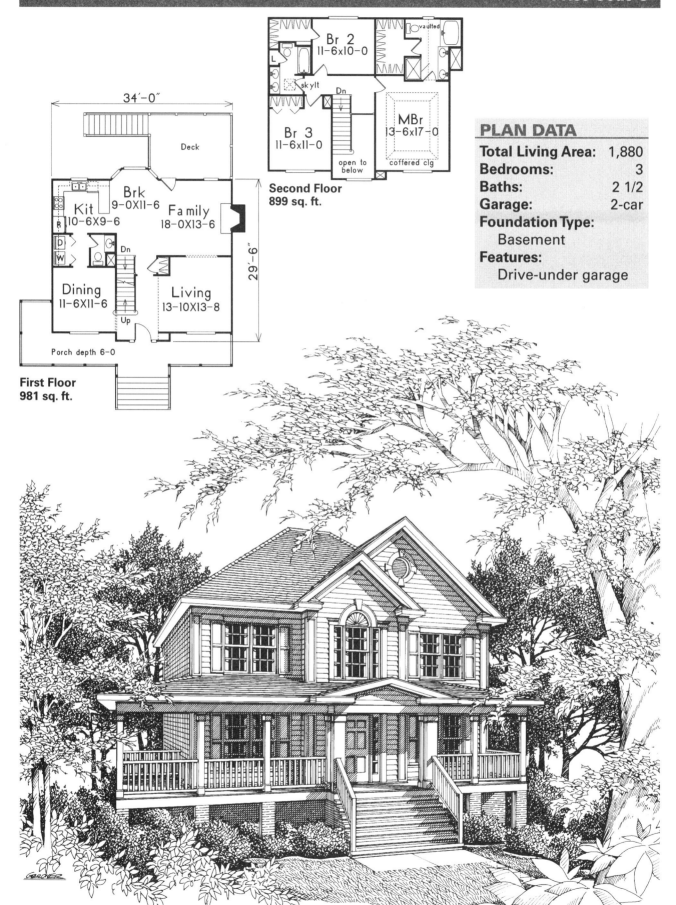

34'-0"

Deck

Br 2
11-6x10-0

vaulted

L

skylt

Dn

Br 3
11-6x11-0

MBr
13-6x17-0

open to
below

coffered clg

Second Floor
899 sq. ft.

Brk
9-0X11-6

Kit
10-6X9-6

Family
18-0X13-6

R

29'-6"

D

W

Dn

Dining
11-6X11-6

Living
13-10X13-8

Up

Porch depth 6-0

First Floor
981 sq. ft.

PLAN DATA

Total Living Area:	1,880
Bedrooms:	3
Baths:	2 1/2
Garage:	2-car
Foundation Type:	
Basement	
Features:	
Drive-under garage	

PLAN DATA

Total Living Area:	1,400
Bedrooms:	3
Baths:	2
Garage:	2-car
Foundation Types:	
Basement standard	
Crawl space	

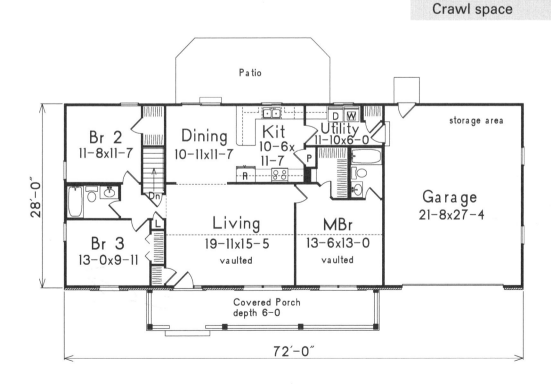

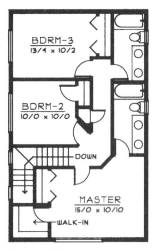

Second Floor
792 sq. ft.

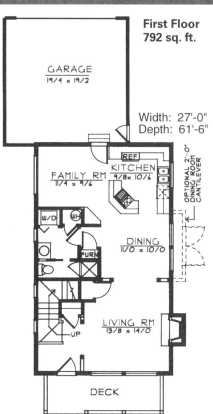

First Floor
792 sq. ft.

Width: 27'-0"
Depth: 61'-6"

PLAN DATA

Total Living Area:	1,584
Bedrooms:	3
Baths:	2 1/2
Garage:	2-car
Foundation Type:	
Crawl space	

36´-0˝

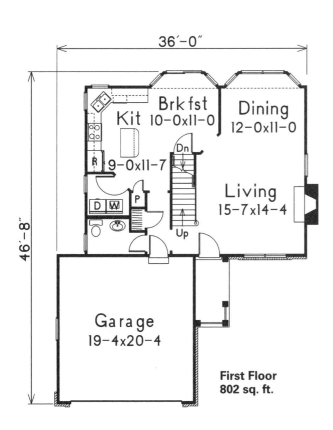

Kit
9-0x11-7

Brkfst
10-0x11-0

Dining
12-0x11-0

Dn

Living
15-7x14-4

Up

P

D W

46´-8˝

Garage
19-4x20-4

First Floor
802 sq. ft.

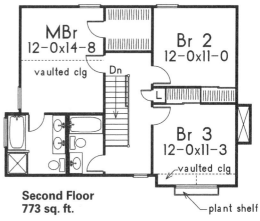

MBr
12-0x14-8

vaulted clg

Dn

Br 2
12-0x11-0

L

Br 3
12-0x11-3

vaulted clg

Second Floor
773 sq. ft.

plant shelf

PLAN DATA

Total Living Area:	1,575
Bedrooms:	3
Baths:	2 1/2
Garage:	2-car
Foundation Type:	
Basement	

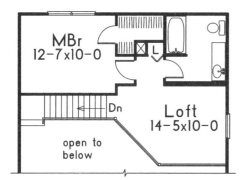

Second Floor
416 sq. ft.

MBr
12-7x10-0

Loft
14-5x10-0

open to
below

Dn

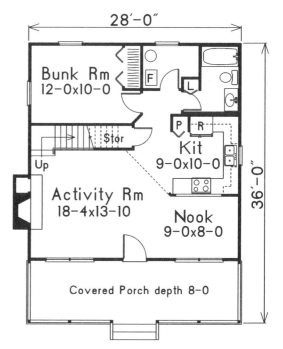

28'-0"

Bunk Rm
12-0x10-0

F

L

Stor

Up

Kit
9-0x10-0

P   R

Activity Rm
18-4x13-10

Nook
9-0x8-0

36'-0"

First Floor
784 sq. ft.

Covered Porch depth 8-0

PLAN DATA

Total Living Area: 1,200
Bedrooms: 2
Baths: 2
Foundation Type:
  Crawl space

PLAN DATA

Total Living Area: 2,847
Bedrooms: 4
Baths: 3 1/2
Garage: 2-car
Foundation Type:
Basement

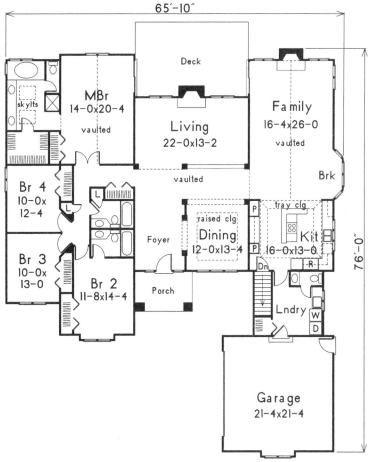

65'-10"

76'-0"

Deck

MBr
14-0x20-4
vaulted

skylts

Living
22-0x13-2
vaulted

Family
16-4x26-0
vaulted

Br 4
10-0x
12-4

Brk

vaulted

raised clg

tray clg

Br 3
10-0x
13-0

Foyer

Dining
12-0x13-4

Kit
16-0x13-0

Br 2
11-8x14-4

Porch

Dn

Lndry

W D

Garage
21-4x21-4

PLAN #563-0191

PLAN DATA

Total Living Area:	1,868
Bedrooms:	3
Baths:	2
Garage:	2-car

Foundation Types:
 Slab standard
 Crawl space

Features:
- 2" x 6" exterior walls
- 12' ceiling in living room

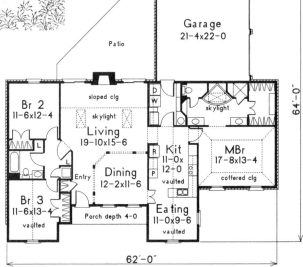

PLAN #563-0659

PLAN DATA

Total Living Area:	1,516
Bedrooms:	3
Baths:	2
Garage:	2-car

Foundation Type:
 Basement

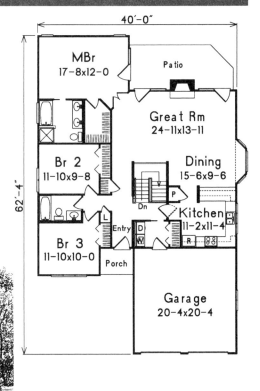

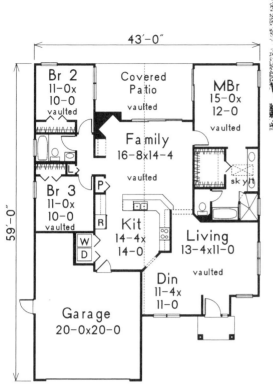

PLAN DATA

Total Living Area: 1,550
Bedrooms: 3
Baths: 2
Garage: 2-car
Foundation Type:
 Slab

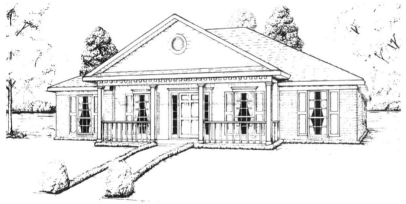

PLAN DATA

Total Living Area: 1,556
Bedrooms: 3
Baths: 2
Garage: 2-car carport
Foundation Type:
 Slab

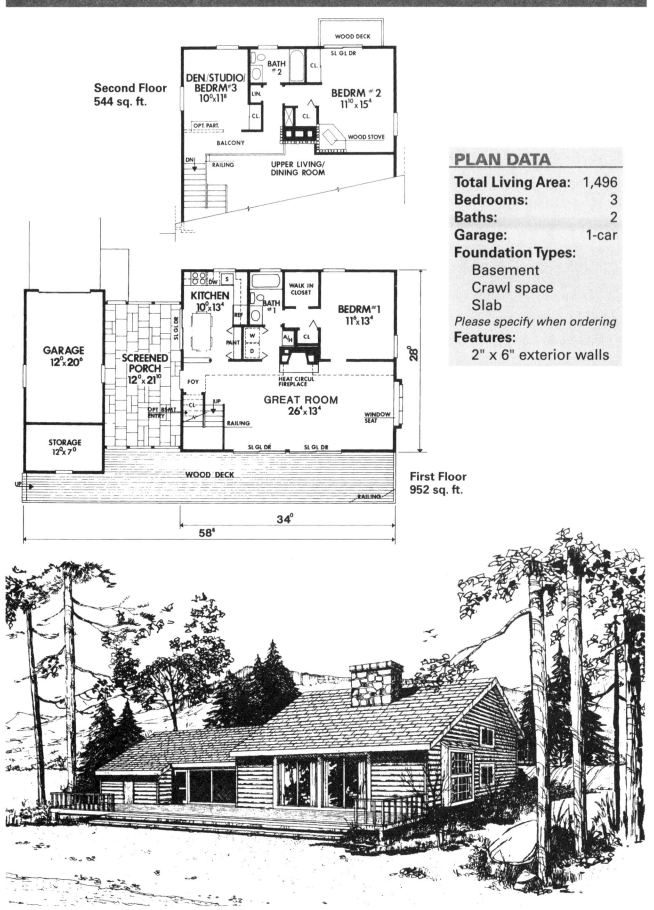

Second Floor
544 sq. ft.

WOOD DECK

SL GL DR

BATH #2

CL.

DEN./STUDIO/ BEDRM#3
10⁰x11⁸

LIN.

BEDRM # 2
11¹⁰ x 15⁴

CL.

CL.

OPT. PART.

CL.

WOOD STOVE

BALCONY

DN

RAILING

UPPER LIVING/ DINING ROOM

DW | S

KITCHEN
10⁰x13⁴

WALK IN CLOSET

REF

BATH #1

BEDRM #1
11⁶x13⁴

SL GL DR

GARAGE
12⁰x20⁶

SCREENED PORCH
12⁰x21¹⁰

PANT

W

D

A/H

CL

28⁰

FOY

OPT BSMT ENTRY

CL

UP

HEAT CIRCUL FIREPLACE

STORAGE
12⁰x7⁰

RAILING

GREAT ROOM
26⁴x13⁴

WINDOW SEAT

SL GL DR

SL GL DR

UP

WOOD DECK

RAILING

First Floor
952 sq. ft.

34⁰

58⁸

PLAN DATA

Total Living Area:	1,496
Bedrooms:	3
Baths:	2
Garage:	1-car

Foundation Types:
  Basement
  Crawl space
  Slab
Please specify when ordering
Features:
  2" x 6" exterior walls

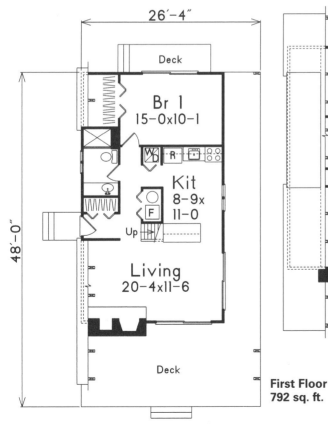

26′-4″

Deck

Br 1
15-0x10-1

W D R

Kit
8-9x
11-0

F

Up

Living
20-4x11-6

48′-0″

Deck

First Floor
792 sq. ft.

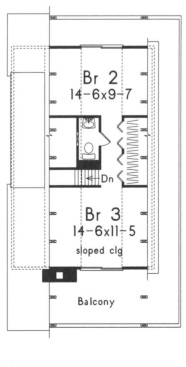

Br 2
14-6x9-7

Dn

Br 3
14-6x11-5
sloped clg

Balcony

Second Floor
480 sq. ft.

PLAN DATA

Total Living Area: 1,272
Bedrooms: 3
Baths: 1 1/2
Foundation Type:
Crawl space

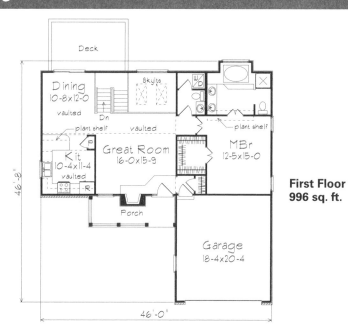

Deck

Dining
10-8x12-0
vaulted

Dn

Skylts

W/D

plant shelf   vaulted   plant shelf

Kit
10-4x11-4
vaulted

P

Great Room
16-0x15-9

MBr
12-5x15-0

R

Porch

**First Floor
996 sq. ft.**

Garage
18-4x20-4

46'-8"

46'-0"

46'-0"

Br 3
9-9x10-4

Atrium
9-6x7-1

Br 2
12-3x11-6

Up

Br 4
9-9x10-1

Family
16-0x15-5

Bar

Storage
18-0x9-3

D W

24'-4"

**Lower Level
945 sq. ft.**

PLAN DATA

Total Living Area:	1,941
Bedrooms:	4
Baths:	2 1/2
Garage:	2-car
Foundation Type:	
Walk-out basement	

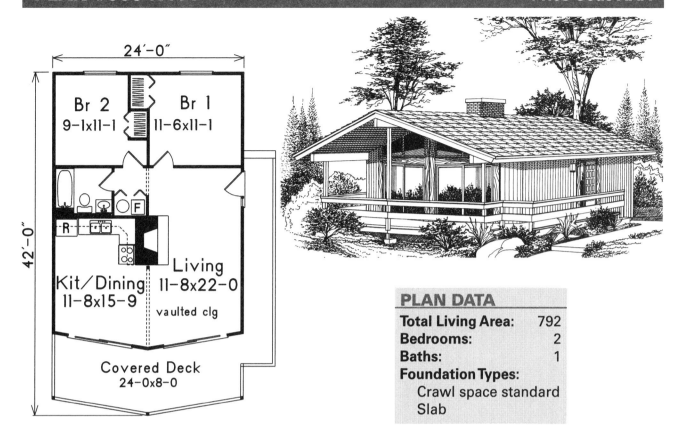

24'-0"

Br 2
9-1x11-1

Br 1
11-6x11-1

42'-0"

R

F

Kit/Dining
11-8x15-9

Living
11-8x22-0
vaulted clg

Covered Deck
24-0x8-0

PLAN DATA

Total Living Area:	792
Bedrooms:	2
Baths:	1
Foundation Types:	
Crawl space standard	
Slab	

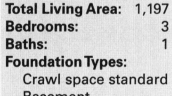

PLAN DATA

Total Living Area:	1,197
Bedrooms:	3
Baths:	1
Foundation Types:	
Crawl space standard	
Basement	
Slab	

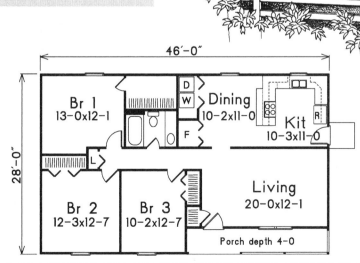

46'-0"

28'-0"

Br 1
13-0x12-1

D
W

Dining
10-2x11-0

Kit
10-3x11-0

R

F

L

Br 2
12-3x12-7

Br 3
10-2x12-7

Living
20-0x12-1

Porch depth 4-0

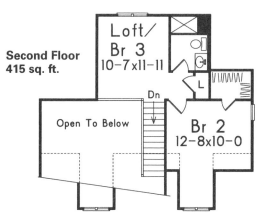

Second Floor
415 sq. ft.

Loft/
Br 3
10-7x11-11

Open To Below

Dn

L

Br 2
12-8x10-0

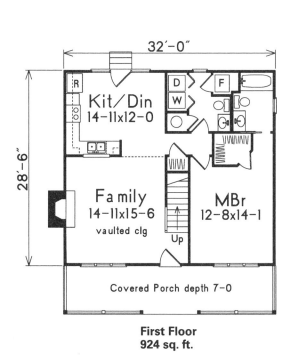

32'-0"

28'-6"

R

Kit/Din
14-11x12-0

D
W
F

Family
14-11x15-6
vaulted clg

Up

MBr
12-8x14-1

Covered Porch depth 7-0

First Floor
924 sq. ft.

PLAN DATA

Total Living Area: 1,339
Bedrooms: 3
Baths: 2 1/2
Foundation Type:
Crawl space

br2
12'4x12'8

br3
10'x10'
OR OPTIONAL LOFT

DN

3'6 RAILING

OPEN TO BELOW

Second Floor
556 sq. ft.

PORCH

mbr
12'4x12'8

W D

CABINETS

din
12'x10'

k
8'4x10'

DN

UP

BREAKFAST BAR

great rm
17'x13'6

First Floor
1,012 sq. ft.

PORCH

Width: 34'-0"
Depth: 38'-0"

PLAN DATA

Total Living Area: 1,568
Bedrooms: 3
Baths: 2 1/2
Foundation Types:
  Basement
  Crawl space
Please specify when ordering

Second Floor
520 sq. ft.

BR3
13' x 10'7

BATH 2

WI Closet

BR2
13' x 12'10

Dining Room Below

FIRST LEVEL PLANT SHELF

SECOND LEVEL PLANT SHELF

Balcony

Great Room Below

Foyer Below

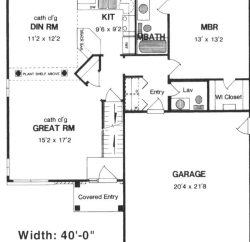

First Floor
973 sq. ft.

DW

KIT
9'6 x 9'2

cath cl'g
DIN RM
11'2 x 12'2

MBATH

MBR
13' x 13'2

REF

PLANT SHELF ABOVE

cath cl'g
GREAT RM
15'2 x 17'2

Entry

Lav

WI Closet

GARAGE
20'4 x 21'8

Covered Entry

PLAN DATA

Total Living Area:	1,493
Bedrooms:	3
Baths:	2 1/2
Garage:	2-car
Foundation Type:	
Basement	

Width: 40'-0"
Depth: 41'-0"

MARIBEL MAXON

PLAN DATA

Total Living Area: 914
Bedrooms: 2
Baths: 1
Garage: 2-car
Foundation Type:
  Basement
Features:
 - Basement includes
   storage area,
   finished laundry and
   mechanical room
 - Drive-under garage

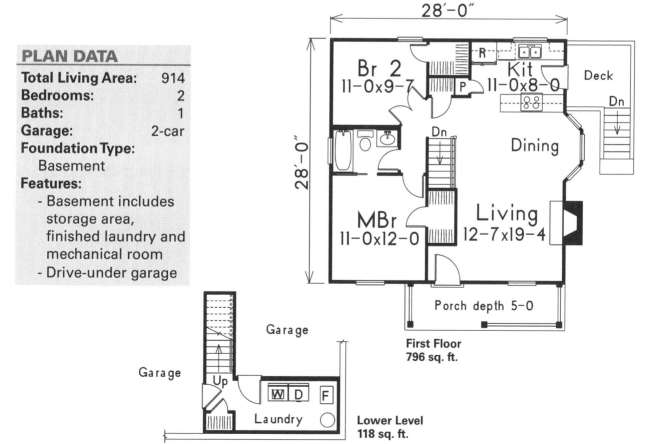

28'-0"

28'-0"

Br 2
11-0x9-7

Kit
11-0x8-0

R

P

Deck

Dn

Dn

Dining

MBr
11-0x12-0

Living
12-7x19-4

Porch depth 5-0

First Floor
796 sq. ft.

Garage

Garage

Up

W D F

Laundry

Lower Level
118 sq. ft.

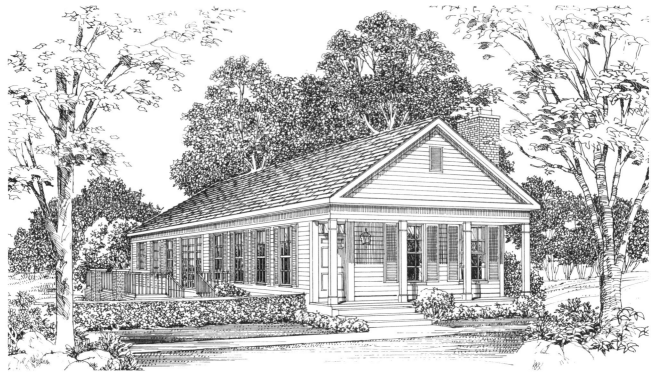

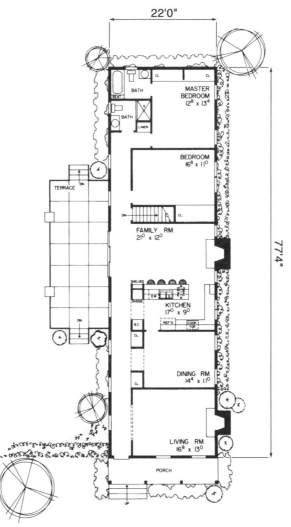

22'0"

77'4"

MASTER BEDROOM 12⁸ x 13⁴

BATH

SEAT

BATH

LINEN

CL

CL

BEDROOM 16⁸ x 11⁰

TERRACE

DN

DN

CL

FAMILY RM. 21⁰ x 12⁰

DN

SHELVES

DW

OVENS

B.C.

REF'G

KITCHEN 17⁰ x 9⁰

COOK TOP

CL

CL

DINING RM. 14⁴ x 11⁰

LIVING RM. 16⁸ x 13⁰

PORCH

PLAN DATA

Total Living Area: 1,700
Bedrooms: 2
Baths: 2
Foundation Type:
  Basement
Features:
  9' ceilings on first
  floor

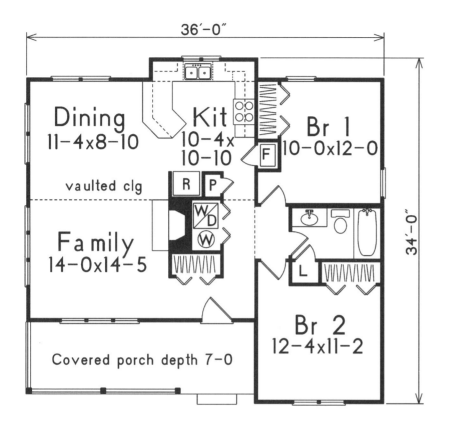

36'-0"

Dining
11-4x8-10

Kit
10-4x
10-10

Br 1
10-0x12-0

vaulted clg

F

R P

Family
14-0x14-5

W/D

W

L

34'-0"

Covered porch depth 7-0

Br 2
12-4x11-2

PLAN DATA
Total Living Area:	990
Bedrooms:	2
Baths:	1
Foundation Type:	
Crawl space	

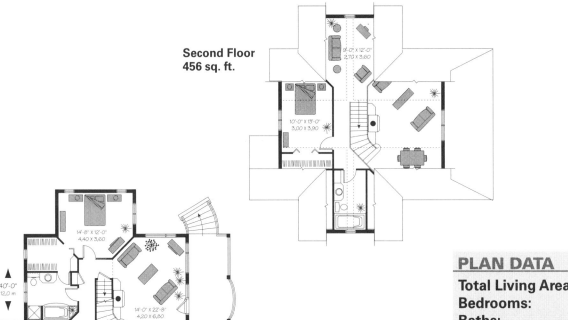

Second Floor
456 sq. ft.

9'-0" X 12'-0"
2,70 X 3,60

10'-0" X 13'-0"
3,00 X 3,90

14'-8" X 12'-0"
4,40 X 3,60

40'-0"
12,0 m

14'-0" X 22'-8"
4,20 X 6,80

First Floor
1,024 sq. ft.

14'-8" X 12'-0"
4,40 X 3,60

32'-0"
9,6 m

PLAN DATA

Total Living Area: 1,480
Bedrooms: 2
Baths: 2
Foundation Type:
  Basement
Features:
  2" x 6" exterior walls

PLAN DATA

Total Living Area:	1,508
Bedrooms:	3
Baths:	2
Garage:	2-car

Foundation Types:
  Basement
  Crawl space
Please specify when ordering

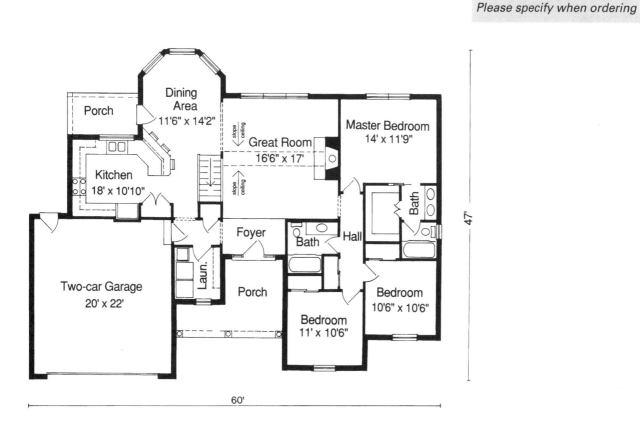

Porch

Dining Area
11'6" x 14'2"

slope ceiling

Great Room
16'6" x 17'

slope ceiling

Master Bedroom
14' x 11'9"

Kitchen
18' x 10'10"

Bath

Two-car Garage
20' x 22'

Laun.

Foyer

Bath

Hall

Porch

Bedroom
10'6" x 10'6"

Bedroom
11' x 10'6"

47'

60'

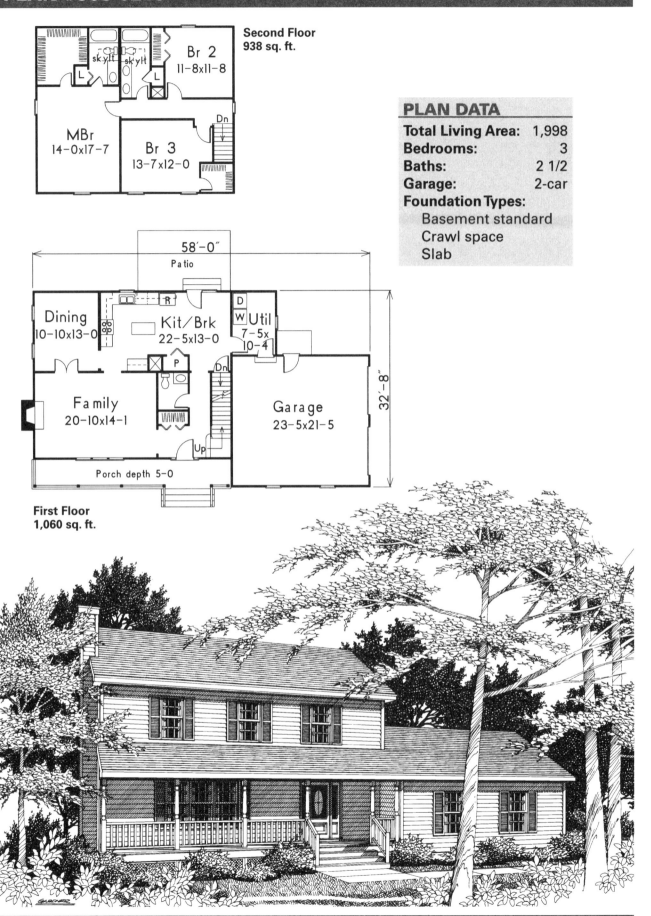

Second Floor
938 sq. ft.

Br 2
11-8x11-8

sk ylt sk ylt

L

L

MBr
14-0x17-7

Br 3
13-7x12-0

Dn

PLAN DATA

Total Living Area:	1,998
Bedrooms:	3
Baths:	2 1/2
Garage:	2-car
Foundation Types:	

Basement standard
Crawl space
Slab

58'-0"

Patio

Dining
10-10x13-0

Kit/Brk
22-5x13-0

R

D
W Util
7-5x
10-4

P

Dn

Family
20-10x14-1

Garage
23-5x21-5

Up

32'-8"

Porch depth 5-0

First Floor
1,060 sq. ft.

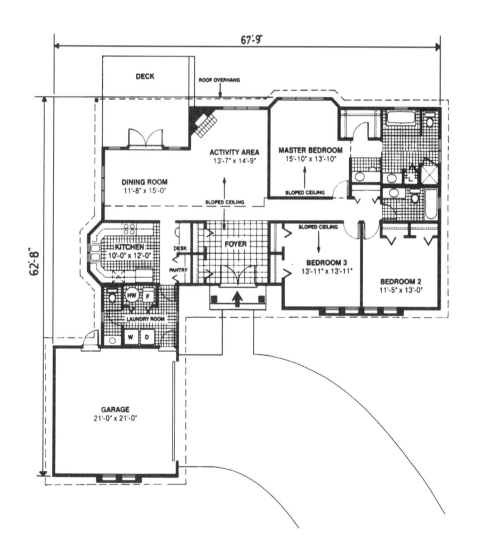

DECK

ROOF OVERHANG

ACTIVITY AREA
13'-7" x 14'-9"

MASTER BEDROOM
15'-10" x 13'-10"

DINING ROOM
11'-8" x 15'-0"

SLOPED CEILING

SLOPED CEILING

KITCHEN
10'-0" x 12'-0"

DESK

FOYER

SLOPED CEILING

PANTRY

BEDROOM 3
13'-11" x 13'-11"

BEDROOM 2
11'-5" x 13'-0"

HW F

LAUNDRY ROOM

W   D

GARAGE
21'-0" x 21'-0"

67'-9"

62'-8"

PLAN DATA

Total Living Area:	1,800
Bedrooms:	3
Baths:	2 1/2
Garage:	2-car
Foundation Type:	Slab

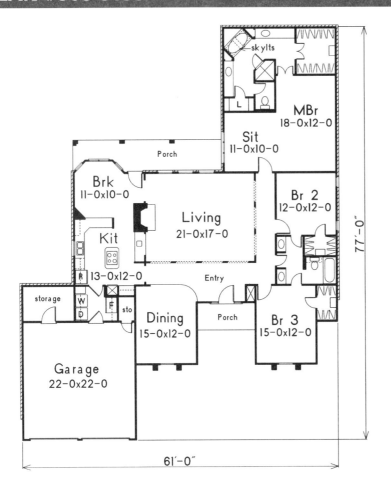

Brk 11-0x10-0

MBr 18-0x12-0

Sit 11-0x10-0

Br 2 12-0x12-0

Living 21-0x17-0

Kit 13-0x12-0

Porch

Entry

Dining 15-0x12-0

Porch

Br 3 15-0x12-0

storage

sto

Garage 22-0x22-0

77'-0"

61'-0"

sk ylts

PLAN DATA

Total Living Area:	2,177
Bedrooms:	3
Baths:	2
Garage:	2-car
Foundation Types:	
Slab standard	
Basement	
Crawl space	

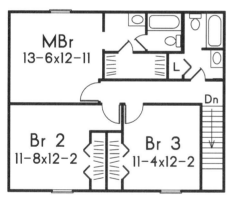

Second Floor
832 sq. ft.

MBr
13-6x12-11

L

Dn

Br 2
11-8x12-2

Br 3
11-4x12-2

PLAN DATA

Total Living Area:	1,664
Bedrooms:	3
Baths:	2 1/2
Foundation Types:	
Crawl space standard	
Slab	
Basement	

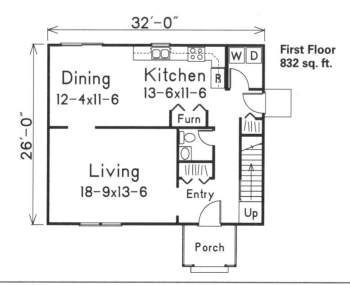

32'-0"

26'-0"

First Floor
832 sq. ft.

W D

Dining
12-4x11-6

Kitchen
13-6x11-6

R

Furn

Living
18-9x13-6

Entry

Up

Porch

PLAN DATA

Total Living Area: 1,477
Bedrooms: 3
Baths: 2
Garage: 2-car
Foundation Type:
  Basement

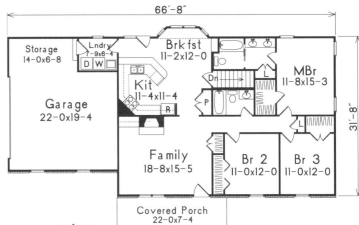

66'-8"

Storage
14-0x6-8

Lndry
7-9x6-4

D W

Brkfst
11-2x12-0

MBr
11-8x15-3

Garage
22-0x19-4

Kit
11-4x11-4

Dn

P

R

31'-8"

Family
18-8x15-5

Br 2
11-0x12-0

Br 3
11-0x12-0

Covered Porch
22-0x7-4

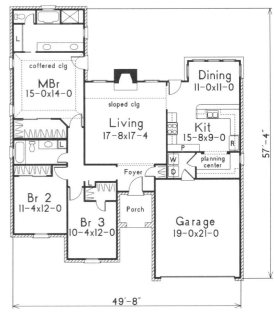

coffered clg

MBr
15-0x14-0

sloped clg

Dining
11-0x11-0

Living
17-8x17-4

Kit
15-8x9-0

P

R

W
D

planning
center

Foyer

Br 2
11-4x12-0

L

Br 3
10-4x12-0

Porch

Garage
19-0x21-0

57'-4"

49'-8"

PLAN DATA

Total Living Area: 1,770
Bedrooms: 3
Baths: 2
Garage: 2-car
Foundation Type:
  Slab

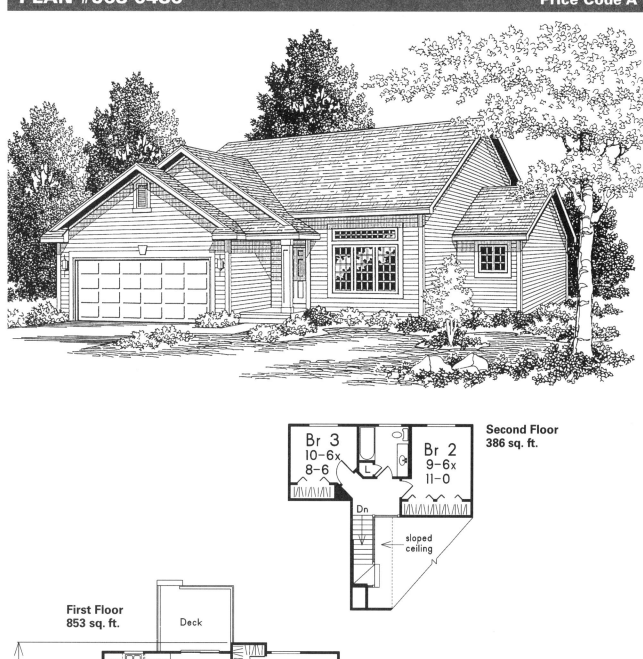

Second Floor
386 sq. ft.

Br 3
10-6x
8-6

L

Br 2
9-6x
11-0

Dn

sloped ceiling

First Floor
853 sq. ft.

Deck

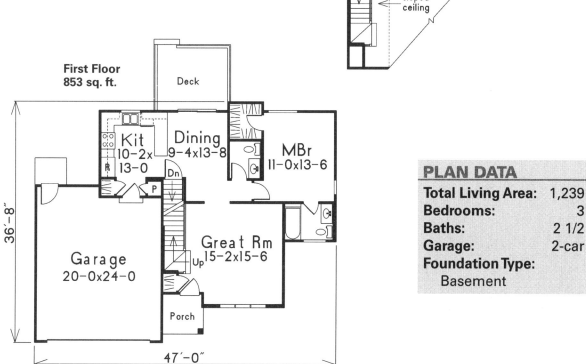

Kit
10-2x
13-0

Dining
9-4x13-8

MBr
11-0x13-6

Dn

P

36'-8"

Garage
20-0x24-0

Great Rm
15-2x15-6

Up

Porch

47'-0"

PLAN DATA

Total Living Area:	1,239
Bedrooms:	3
Baths:	2 1/2
Garage:	2-car
Foundation Type:	
Basement	

PLAN DATA

Total Living Area: 1,416
Bedrooms: 3
Baths: 2
Garage: 2-car
Foundation Types:
  Crawl space standard
  Basement

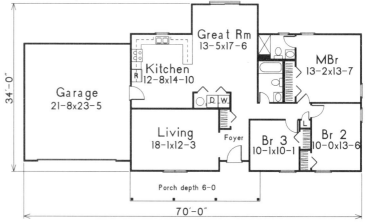

Great Rm
13-5x17-6

Kitchen
12-8x14-10

MBr
13-2x13-7

Garage
21-8x23-5

Living
18-1x12-3

Foyer

Br 3
10-1x10-1

Br 2
10-0x13-6

34'-0"

Porch depth 6-0

70'-0"

PLAN #563-0811

Price Code AA

PLAN DATA

Total Living Area: 1,161
Bedrooms: 3
Baths: 2
Foundation Type:
  Basement

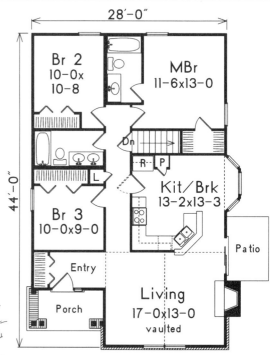

28'-0"

Br 2
10-0x
10-8

MBr
11-6x13-0

Dn

R   P

Br 3
10-0x9-0

Kit/Brk
13-2x13-3

Patio

Entry

44'-0"

Porch

Living
17-0x13-0
vaulted

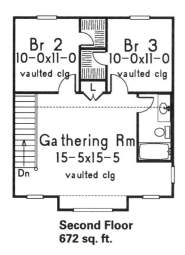

Br 2
10-0x11-0
vaulted clg

Br 3
10-0x11-0
vaulted clg

L

Gathering Rm
15-5x15-5
vaulted clg

Dn

Second Floor
672 sq. ft.

51'-0"

First Floor
1,112 sq. ft.

vaulted clg

Covered Porch
depth 9-0

D
W

Dining
10-3x10-5

Kit
10x10

R

MBr
12-0x17-6
vaulted clg

50'-7"

Stor

Up

P

Garage
13-5x22-0

Dn

Living
20-9x15-6

Covered Porch
depth 8-0

PLAN DATA

Total Living Area: 1,784
Bedrooms: 3
Baths: 2 1/2
Garage: 1-car
Foundation Types:
   Basement standard
   Crawl space

PLAN DATA

Total Living Area:	1,524
Bedrooms:	3
Baths:	2 1/2
Garage:	2-car
Foundation Type:	
Basement	

First Floor
951 sq. ft.

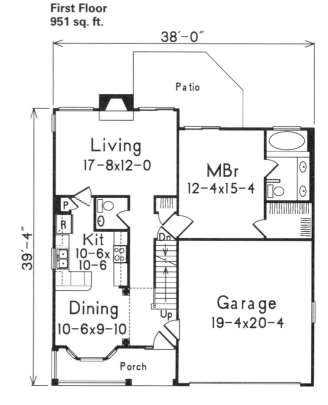

38'-0"

Patio

Living
17-8x12-0

MBr
12-4x15-4

39'-4"

P
R

Kit
10-6x
10-6

Dn

Dining
10-6x9-10

Up

Garage
19-4x20-4

Porch

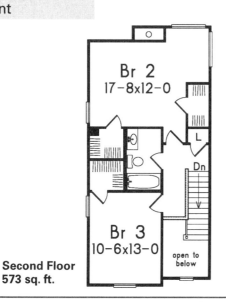

Br 2
17-8x12-0

L

Dn

Br 3
10-6x13-0

open to below

Second Floor
573 sq. ft.

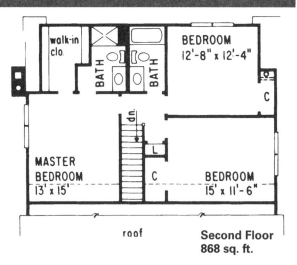

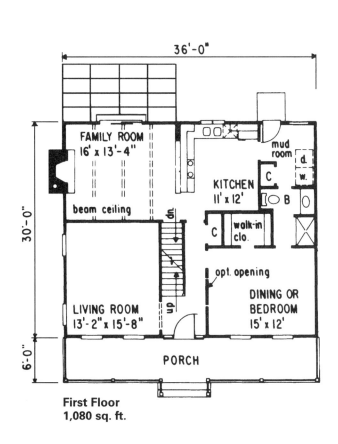

First Floor
1,080 sq. ft.

Second Floor
868 sq. ft.

PLAN DATA

Total Living Area:	1,948
Bedrooms:	3
Baths:	2 1/2
Foundation Types:	
Basement standard	
Crawl space	
Slab	

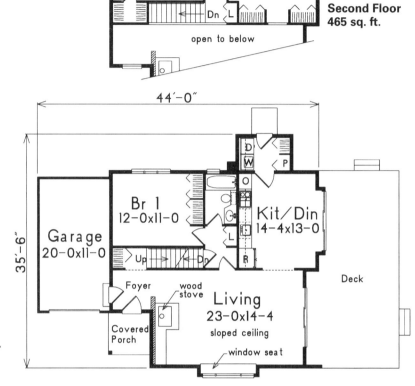

Second Floor
465 sq. ft.

Br 2
14-0x11-0

Br 3
12-4x12-0

Dn L

open to below

PLAN DATA

Total Living Area:	1,432
Bedrooms:	3
Baths:	2
Garage:	1-car

Foundation Types:
  Basement standard
  Slab

44'-0"

35'-6"

Garage
20-0x11-0

Br 1
12-0x11-0

Kit/Din
14-4x13-0

D
W
P
O
L
R

Deck

Foyer

wood
stove

Living
23-0x14-4
sloped ceiling

window seat

Covered
Porch

First Floor
967 sq. ft.

Second Floor
882 sq. ft.

Second Floor labels:
- VAULTED MASTER 14/4 X 12/8
- BR. 2 11/4 X 10/0 +/-
- LINEN
- W
- D
- DN.
- PLANT SHELF
- VAULTED BR. 3 10/0 X 11/0

PLAN DATA

Total Living Area:	1,994
Bedrooms:	3
Baths:	2 1/2
Garage:	2-car
Foundation Type:	Crawl space

First Floor labels:
- NOOK 11/0 X 9/0 +/- (9' CLG.)
- FAMILY 15/8 X 12/8 (9' CLG.)
- DEN 9/8 X 10/4 (9' CLG.)
- 11/0 X 10/6 +/-
- REF. P
- DINING 11/0 X 10/0 (9' CLG.)
- GARAGE 19/0 X 19/6
- UP
- VAULTED LIVING 13/0 X 12/0
- ©Alan Mascord Design Associates, Inc.
- 43'
- 40'

First Floor
1,112 sq. ft.

MASTER SUITE
11'-0" X 13'-0"

BEDROOM-2
11'-0" X 9'-8"

F/P

MASTER BATH

CL.
FURN.

WASH. DRY.
CL.

GREAT ROOM
14'-6" X 15'-1"

HALL

UTILITY

BATH-2

LIN.

37'-6"

FOYER

EATING BAR

REF.

D. W.

BEDROOM-3
11'-0" X 9'-0"

CTS.

DINING
10'-0" X 10'-0"

S.

R.

CL.

PORCH

KIT.

38'-0"

PLAN DATA

Total Living Area:	1,123
Bedrooms:	3
Baths:	2
Foundation Types:	
Crawl space	
Slab	

Please specify when ordering

PLAN DATA

Total Living Area:	1,458
Bedrooms:	3
Baths:	2
Garage:	2-car
Foundation Types:	
Crawl space standard	
Slab	

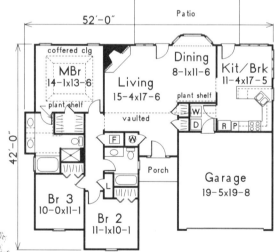

52'-0"

Patio

coffered clg

MBr
14-1x13-6

Dining
8-1x11-6

Kit/Brk
11-4x17-5

Living
15-4x17-6

plant shelf

W
D

R P

plant shelf

vaulted

42'-0"

F

W

Porch

Garage
19-5x19-8

Br 3
10-0x11-1

L

Br 2
11-1x10-1

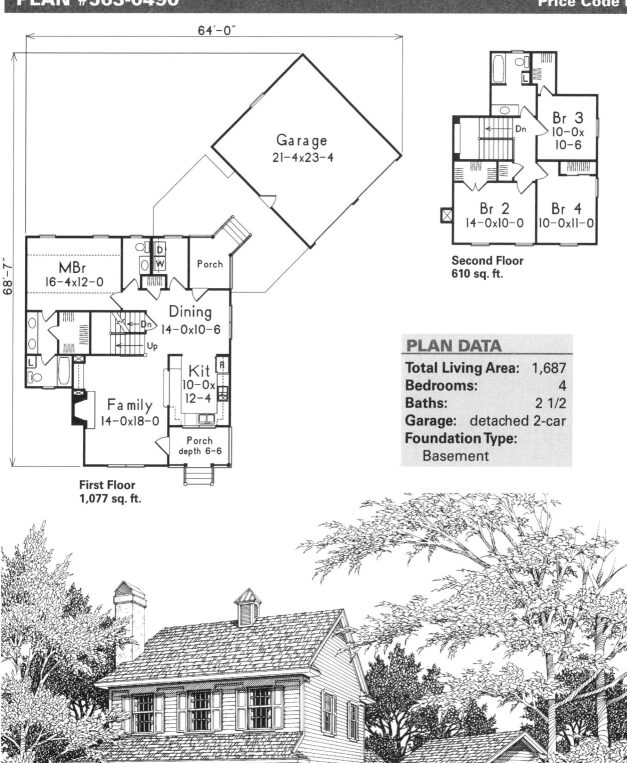

64'-0"

68'-7"

Garage
21-4x23-4

Porch

MBr
16-4x12-0

Dining
14-0x10-6

Dn
Up

Kit
10-0x
12-4

R

Family
14-0x18-0

Porch
depth 6-6

First Floor
1,077 sq. ft.

L

Br 3
10-0x
10-6

Dn

Br 2
14-0x10-0

Br 4
10-0x11-0

Second Floor
610 sq. ft.

PLAN DATA

Total Living Area: 1,687
Bedrooms: 4
Baths: 2 1/2
Garage: detached 2-car
Foundation Type:
  Basement

PLAN DATA

Total Living Area: 1,591
Bedrooms: 3
Baths: 2
Garage: 3-car
Foundation Type:
  Basement

PLAN DATA

Total Living Area: 1,316
Bedrooms: 3
Baths: 1
Foundation Type:
  Crawl space

First Floor
988 sq. ft.

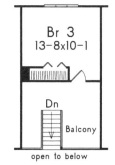

Br 3
13-8x10-1

Dn

Balcony

open to below

Second Floor
328 sq. ft.

Width: 42'-6"
Depth: 55'-0"

PLAN DATA

Total Living Area: 1,750
Bedrooms: 3
Baths: 2
Garage: 2-car
Foundation Type:
  Slab

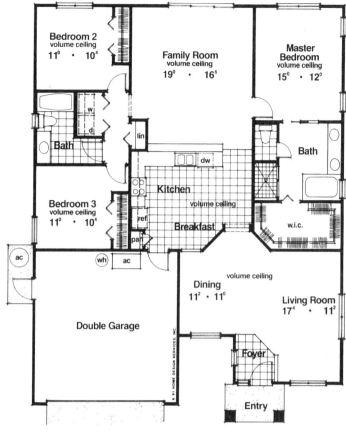

Bedroom 2
volume ceiling
11^0 · 10^4

Family Room
volume ceiling
19^0 · 16^6

Master
Bedroom
volume ceiling
15^0 · 12^0

Bath

Kitchen
volume ceiling

Bath

Bedroom 3
volume ceiling
11^0 · 10^4

Breakfast

w.i.c.

Double Garage

Dining
11^2 · 11^0

volume ceiling

Living Room
17^4 · 11^2

Foyer

Entry

© 91 HOME DESIGN SERVICES, INC.

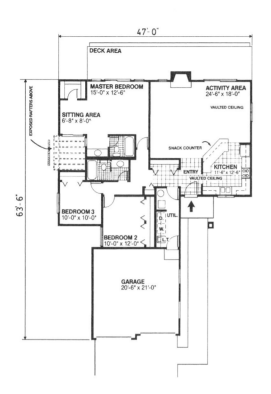

PLAN DATA

Total Living Area:	1,533
Bedrooms:	3
Baths:	2
Garage:	2-car
Foundation Types:	
Partial basement - standard	
Crawl space	

PLAN DATA

Total Living Area:	1,643
Bedrooms:	3
Baths:	2
Garage:	2-car
Foundation Types:	
Basement standard	
Crawl space	
Slab	

Width: 24'-0"
Depth: 36'-0"

Second Floor
401 sq. ft.

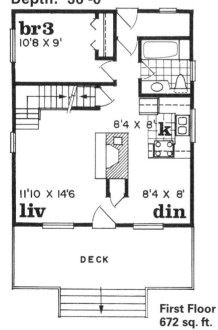

br3
10'8 X 9'

8'4 X 8' **k**

11'10 X 14'6

liv   8'4 X 8' **din**

DECK

First Floor
672 sq. ft.

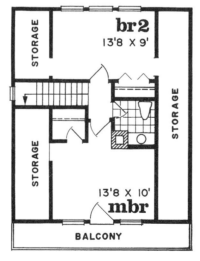

STORAGE

br2
13'8 X 9'

STORAGE

STORAGE

STORAGE

13'8 X 10'
mbr

BALCONY

PLAN DATA

Total Living Area: 1,073
Bedrooms: 3
Baths: 1 1/2
Foundation Types:
  Basement
  Crawl space
Please specify when ordering

PLAN #563-GM-1253

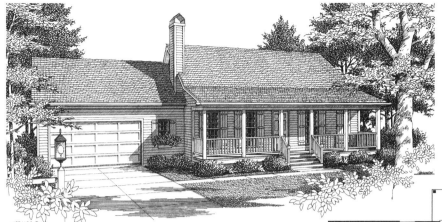

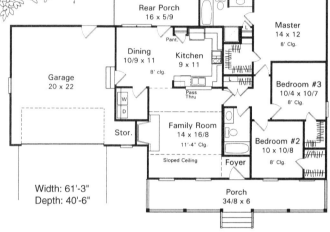

PLAN DATA

Total Living Area: 1,253
Bedrooms: 3
Baths: 2
Garage: 2-car
Foundation Types:
  Crawl space
  Slab
Please specify when ordering

Rear Porch
16 x 5/9

Garage
20 x 22

Dining
10/9 x 11
8' clg.

Kitchen
9 x 11

Pass Thru

Master
14 x 12
8' Clg.

Bedroom #3
10/4 x 10/7
8' Clg.

Family Room
14 x 16/8
11'-4" Clg.

Bedroom #2
10 x 10/8
8' Clg.

Stor.

W
D

Foyer

Sloped Ceiling

Width: 61'-3"
Depth: 40'-6"

Porch
34/8 x 6

PLAN #563-AP-1612

**Second Floor
579 sq. ft.**

STORAGE

BEDROOM 3
15X12

DN

OPEN TO BELOW

BEDROOM 2
15X12

PLAN DATA

Total Living Area: 1,643
Bedrooms: 3
Baths: 2 1/2
Garage: 2-car
Foundation Types:
  Basement
  Crawl space
Please specify when ordering
Features:
  Drive-under garage

DECK

SKYLIGHT

DINING
12x12

KITCHEN
10x12

VAULT

D
W

DN

VAULT

34

MASTER BEDRM
15x13

UP

FAMILY ROOM
18x15

**First Floor
1,064 sq. ft.**

◄38►

KOIZUMI/BUTLER

PLAN DATA

Total Living Area:	1,673
Bedrooms:	3
Baths:	2
Foundation Type:	
Crawl space	

Second Floor
580 sq. ft.

First Floor
1,093 sq. ft.

First Floor
1,031 sq. ft.

Second Floor
513 sq. ft.

PLAN DATA

Total Living Area: 1,544
Bedrooms: 3
Baths: 2
Foundation Types:
  Crawl space
  Slab
Please specify when ordering

First Floor
1,111 sq. ft.

32'8"

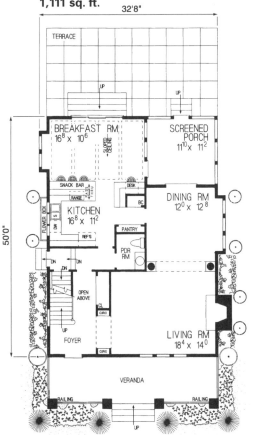

TERRACE

UP   UP

BREAKFAST RM
16⁸ x 10⁶

SCREENED
PORCH
11¹⁰ x 11²

SNACK BAR   DESK

RANGE

KITCHEN
16⁸ x 11²

DINING RM
12⁰ x 12⁸

BC

PANTRY

REF'S

FLOWER BOX

DW

PDR
RM

50'0"

DN   DN

OPEN
ABOVE

CL
CURIO

UP

FOYER

CURIO

LIVING RM
18⁴ x 14⁰

VERANDA

RAILING   RAILING

UP

PLAN DATA

Total Living Area:	1,997
Bedrooms:	3
Baths:	2 1/2
Foundation Type:	
Basement	

ROOF   ROOF

WALL BELOW

RECESSED ROOF

UPPER BREAKFAST RM

BEDROOM
11¹⁰ x 11⁴

BEDROOM
11⁴ x 11⁴

WALK-IN
CLOSET

LINEN   CL

DN
RAILING

BATH

WHIRLPOOL

S

BATH

OPEN
BELOW

DRESS. RM

Second Floor
886 sq. ft.

WALK-IN
CLOSET

UPPER
FOYER

MASTER
BEDROOM
12⁴ x 16⁰

RECESSED ROOF

ROOF   ROOF

PLAN DATA

Total Living Area: 2,089
Bedrooms: 4
Baths: 3
Garage: 2-car
Foundation Type:
  Slab

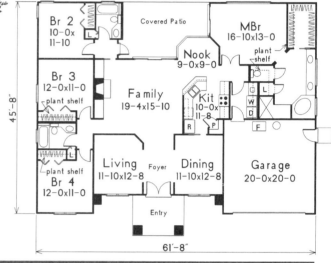

PLAN DATA

Total Living Area: 1,407
Bedrooms: 3
Baths: 2
Garage: 2-car
Foundation Type:
  Basement
Features:
  Drive-under garage

Second Floor
504 sq. ft.

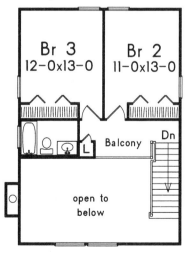

Br 3
12-0x13-0

Br 2
11-0x13-0

Balcony

Dn

L

open to below

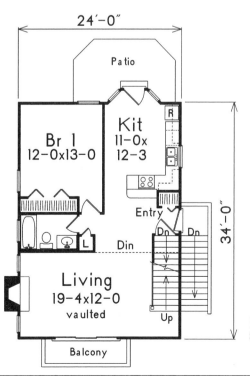

24'-0"

Patio

Br 1
12-0x13-0

Kit
11-0x
12-3

R

Entry

Din

Dn Dn

Living
19-4x12-0
vaulted

Up

L

34'-0"

Balcony

First Floor
828 sq. ft.

PLAN DATA	
Total Living Area:	1,332
Bedrooms:	3
Baths:	2
Garage:	4-car
	tandem basement
Foundation Type:	
Walk-out basement	

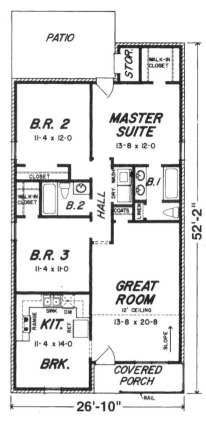

PATIO

STOR.

WALK-IN CLOSET

B.R. 2
11-4 x 12-0

MASTER SUITE
13-8 x 12-0

CLOSET

WALK-IN CLOSET

B.2

DRY. WASH.

B.1

HALL

COATS LINEN

B.R. 3
11-4 x 11-0

GREAT ROOM
12' CEILING
13-8 x 20-8

SLOPE

RANGE SINK D.W.

KIT.
11-4 x 14-0

REF.

BRK.

COVERED PORCH

RAIL

52'-2"

26'-10"

PLAN DATA

Total Living Area: 1,253
Bedrooms: 3
Baths: 2
Foundation Type:
  Slab

COPYRIGHT 1990 RALPH JONES 4 AS

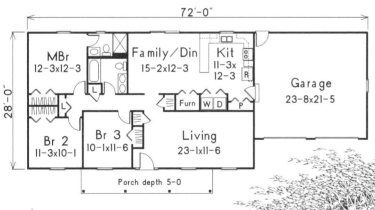

72'-0"

28'-0"

MBr
12-3x12-3

Family/Din
15-2x12-3

Kit
11-3x
12-3

Garage
23-8x21-5

Br 2
11-3x10-1

Br 3
10-1x11-6

Living
23-1x11-6

Furn W D P

Porch depth 5-0

PLAN DATA

Total Living Area: 1,344
Bedrooms: 3
Baths: 2
Garage: 2-car
Foundation Types:
  Crawl space standard
  Basement
  Slab

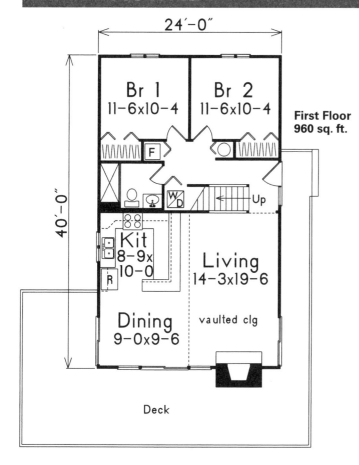

24'-0"

40'-0"

Br 1
11-6x10-4

Br 2
11-6x10-4

**First Floor
960 sq. ft.**

F

W/D

Up

Kit
8-9x
10-0

R

Living
14-3x19-6

Dining
9-0x9-6

vaulted clg

Deck

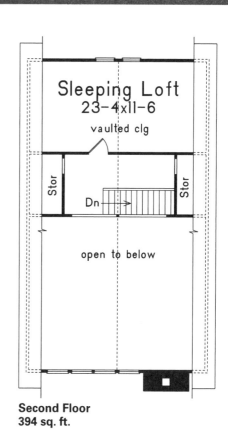

Sleeping Loft
23-4x11-6

vaulted clg

Stor

Dn

Stor

open to below

**Second Floor
394 sq. ft.**

PLAN DATA

Total Living Area:	1,354
Bedrooms:	3
Baths:	1
Foundation Type:	
Crawl space	

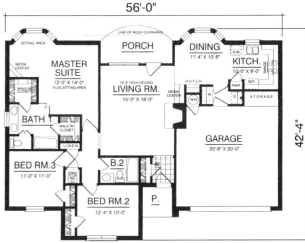

56'-0"

42'-4"

LINE OF ROOF OVERHANG

SITTING AREA

PORCH

DINING
11'-4" X 10'-6"

KITCH.
10'-0" X 9'-0"

MEDIA CENTER

MASTER SUITE
12'-0" X 14'-0"
PLUS SITTING AREA

D.W.

RANGE

HUTCH

WALK IN CLOSET

LIVING RM.
15'-0" X 18'-0"
10'-0" HIGH CEILING

MEDIA CENTER

REF.

PANT

W

D

STORAGE

WH

BATH

WALK IN CLOSET

LINEN

BED RM.3
11'-0" X 11'-0"

B.2

GARAGE
20'-8" X 20'-0"

BED RM.2
12'-4" X 10'-0"

P.

PLAN DATA

Total Living Area:	1,429
Bedrooms:	3
Baths:	2
Garage:	2-car
Foundation Types:	
Crawl space	
Slab	

Please specify when ordering

PLAN DATA

Total Living Area:	864
Bedrooms:	2
Baths:	1
Foundation Types:	
Crawl space	
Slab	

Please specify when ordering

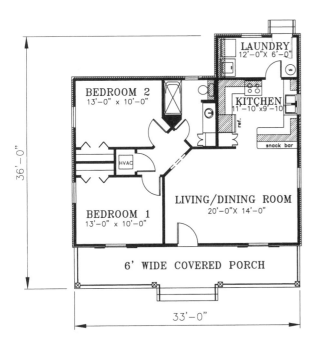

36'-0"

LAUNDRY
12'-0" X 6'-0"

BEDROOM 2
13'-0" x 10'-0"

KITCHEN
11'-10" x 9'-10"

ref.

snack bar

HVAC

BEDROOM 1
13'-0" x 10'-0"

LIVING/DINING ROOM
20'-0" X 14'-0"

6' WIDE COVERED PORCH

33'-0"

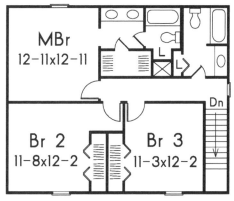

MBr
12-11x12-11

Br 2
11-8x12-2

Br 3
11-3x12-2

Dn

Second Floor
832 sq. ft.

PLAN DATA

Total Living Area: 1,664
Bedrooms: 3
Baths: 2 1/2
Garage: 2-car
Foundation Types:
  Crawl space standard
  Slab
  Basement

56'-0"

26'-0"

Dining
10-5x11-6

Kitchen
14-11x11-6

P

W D

R

Furn

Living
18-9x13-7

Foyer

Up

Garage
23-8x23-5

Porch depth 6-0

First Floor
832 sq. ft.

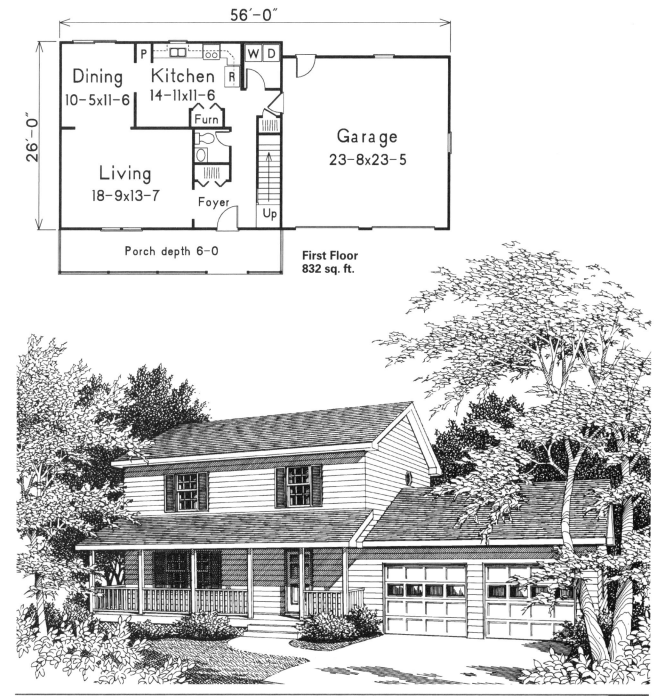

58'-4"

49'-6"

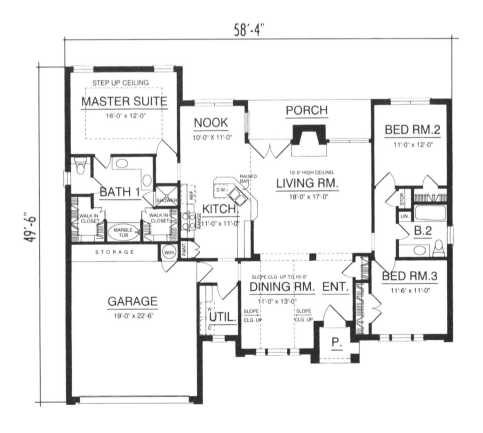

STEP UP CEILING

MASTER SUITE
16'-0" x 12'-0"

NOOK
10'-0" X 11'-0"

PORCH

BED RM.2
11'-0" x 12'-0"

BATH 1

SHOWER

RAISED BAR

D.W.

REF.

RANGE

10'-0" HIGH CEILING
LIVING RM.
18'-0" x 17'-0"

STOR.

LIN.

WALK IN CLOSET

WALK IN CLOSET

MARBLE TUB

KITCH.
11'-0" x 11'-0"

B.2

STORAGE

W/H

PANT.

GARAGE
19'-0" x 22'-6"

UTIL.

W

D

SLOPE CLG. UP TO 10'-0"

DINING RM.
11'-0" x 13'-0"

ENT.

BED RM.3
11'-6" x 11'-0"

SLOPE CLG. UP

SLOPE CLG. UP

P.

PLAN DATA

Total Living Area:	1,791
Bedrooms:	3
Baths:	2
Garage:	2-car

Foundation Types:
   Crawl space
   Slab
Please specify when ordering

Br 3
11-0x11-4

Br 4
8-6x11-0

L

Dn

Br 2
10-10x11-2

open to below

MBr
13-0x16-10

Second Floor
988 sq. ft.

56'-0"

30'-0"

Garage
19-4x21-4

Kit
9-4x11-6

Dinette
10-4x11-4

Family
13-0x15-4

R

D
P

W

Dn

Dining
11-2x11-4

Foyer

up

Living
11-4x13-0

Porch

First Floor
1,025 sq. ft.

PLAN DATA

Total Living Area:	2,013
Bedrooms:	4
Baths:	2 1/2
Garage:	2-car
Foundation Type:	
Basement	

PLAN DATA

Total Living Area:	1,251
Bedrooms:	3
Baths:	2
Garage:	2-car
Foundation Type:	
Crawl space	

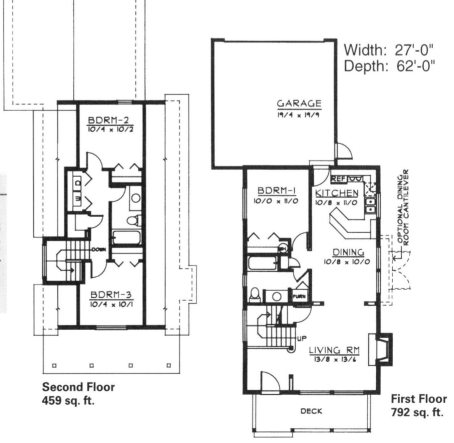

Width: 27'-0"
Depth: 62'-0"

GARAGE
19/4 x 19/9

BDRM-1
10/0 x 11/0

KITCHEN
10/8 x 11/0

REF

OPTIONAL DINING
ROOM CANTILEVER

DINING
10/8 x 10/0

FURN.

LIVING RM
13/8 x 13/6

UP

DECK

**First Floor
792 sq. ft.**

BDRM-2
10/4 x 10/2

DOWN

BDRM-3
10/4 x 10/1

**Second Floor
459 sq. ft.**

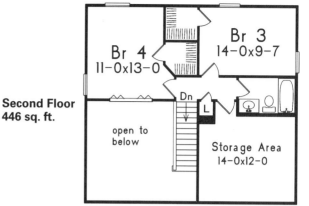

Second Floor 446 sq. ft.

Br 4
11-0x13-0

Br 3
14-0x9-7

Dn
L

open to below

Storage Area
14-0x12-0

PLAN DATA

Total Living Area:	1,330
Bedrooms:	4
Baths:	2
Garage:	1-car
Foundation Type:	
Basement	

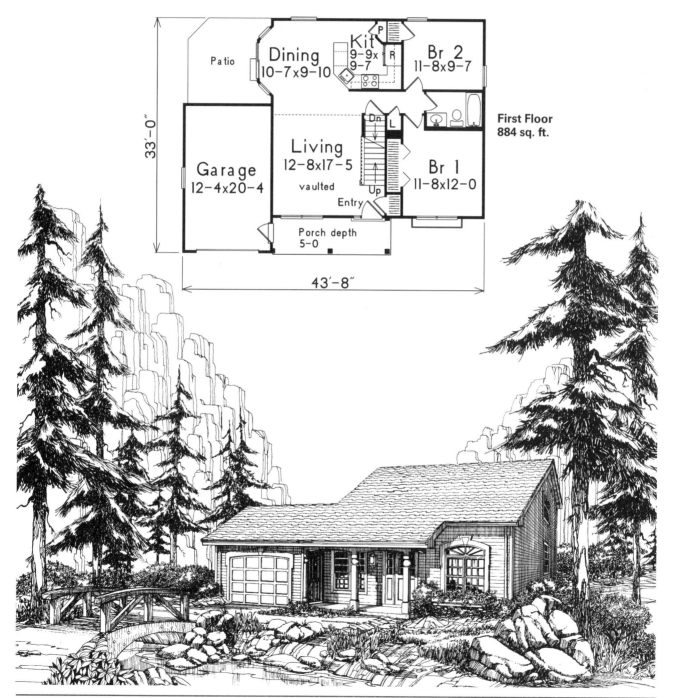

Patio

Dining
10-7x9-10

Kit
9-9x9-7
P
R

Br 2
11-8x9-7

First Floor 884 sq. ft.

Garage
12-4x20-4

Living
12-8x17-5
vaulted

Dn
L
Up

Br 1
11-8x12-0

Entry

Porch depth 5-0

33'-0"

43'-8"

PLAN DATA

Total Living Area: 1,408
Bedrooms: 3
Baths: 2
Garage: 2-car
Foundation Types:
  Crawl space standard
  Slab

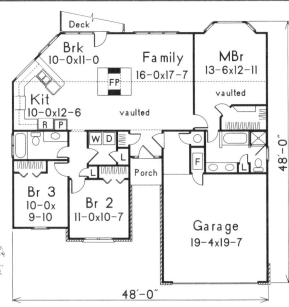

PLAN DATA

Total Living Area: 1,467
Bedrooms: 3
Baths: 2
Garage: 2-car
Foundation Type:
  Crawl space
Features:
  2" x 6" exterior walls

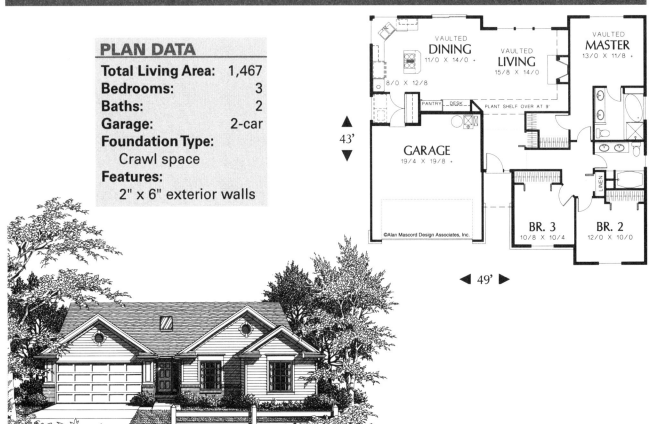

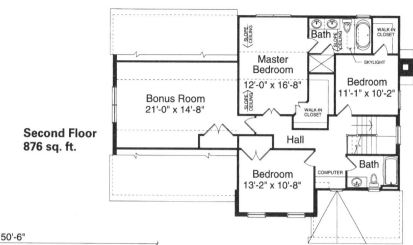

**Second Floor
876 sq. ft.**

Bath

Master
Bedroom
12'-0" x 16'-8"

WALK-IN
CLOSET

Bedroom
11'-1" x 10'-2"

SKYLIGHT

Bonus Room
21'-0" x 14'-8"

WALK-IN
CLOSET

Hall

Bedroom
13'-2" x 10'-8"

COMPUTER

Bath

50'-6"

Laun.

Breakfast
11'-6" x 10'-1"

Great Room
16'-0" x 16'-4"

Garage
21'-0" x 21'-4"

Kitchen
10'1"x11'9"

38'-0"

Dining Room
13'-2" x 11'-0"

Foyer

Bath

Porch

**First Floor
980 sq. ft.**

PLAN DATA

Total Living Area: 1,856
Bedrooms: 3
Baths: 2 1/2
Garage: 2-car
Foundation Types:
    Walk-out basement
    Basement
Please specify when ordering
Features:
    Bonus room on the
    second floor has an
    additional 325 square
    feet of living area

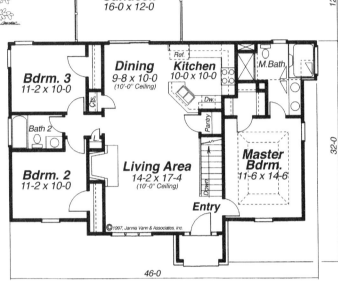

Sundeck
16-0 x 12-0

12-0

Bdrm. 3
11-2 x 10-0

Dining
9-8 x 10-0
(10'-0" Ceiling)

Kitchen
10-0 x 10-0

Ref.

M.Bath

Bath 2

Dw.

Pantry

Bdrm. 2
11-2 x 10-0

Living Area
14-2 x 17-4
(10'-0" Ceiling)

Down

Master
Bdrm.
11-6 x 14-6

Entry

©1997, Jannis Vann & Associates, inc.

32-0

46-0

PLAN DATA

Total Living Area:	1,273
Bedrooms:	3
Baths:	2
Garage:	2-car

Foundation Type:
Basement

Features:
- 10' ceilings in living and dining areas
- Drive-under garage

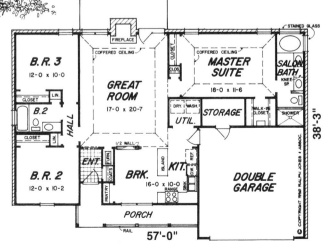

PATIO / DECK

FIREPLACE

STAINED GLASS

B.R. 3
12-0 x 10-0

COFFERED CEILING

COFFERED CEILING

CLOSET

MASTER
SUITE
18-0 x 11-6

SALON
BATH
KNEE-SP

CLOSET

LIN.

CLOSET

B.2

GREAT
ROOM
17-0 x 20-7

HALL

DRY. WASH.

STORAGE

WALK-IN
CLOSET

SHOWER

UTIL.

CLOSET

LIN.

38'-3"

1/2 WALL

ISLAND

REF.

ENT.

COATS

BRK.
16-0 x 10-0

KIT.

DOUBLE
GARAGE

B.R. 2
12-0 x 10-2

PANTRY

RANGE

SINK

© COPYRIGHT 1992 RALPH JONES & ASSOC.

PORCH

RAIL

57'-0"

PLAN DATA

Total Living Area:	1,482
Bedrooms:	3
Baths:	2
Garage:	2-car

Foundation Types:
Crawl space
Slab
Please specify when ordering

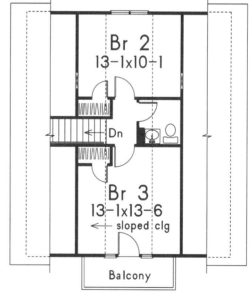

Second Floor
420 sq. ft.

Br 2
13-1x10-1

Dn

Br 3
13-1x13-6
← sloped clg

Balcony

26'-0"

30'-0"

Br 1
9-4x12-6

Kit
10-1x
9-5

R

Up

F   P

Living
25-4x13-2

Deck

First Floor
780 sq. ft.

PLAN DATA

Total Living Area: 1,200
Bedrooms: 3
Baths: 1 1/2
Foundation Types:
   Crawl space standard
   Slab

PLAN DATA

Total Living Area:	1,546
Bedrooms:	3
Baths:	2
Garage:	2-car
Foundation Type:	
Basement	

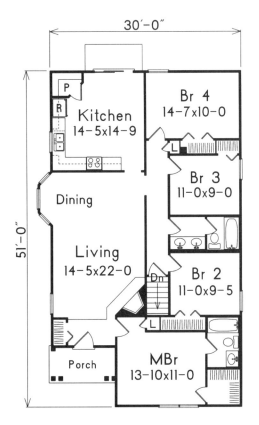

PLAN DATA

Total Living Area:	1,452
Bedrooms:	4
Baths:	2
Foundation Type:	
Basement	

PLAN DATA

Total Living Area:	1,496
Bedrooms:	3
Baths:	2
Garage:	2-car
Foundation Type:	
Slab	
Features:	
Drive-under garage	

PLAN DATA

Total Living Area:	1,747
Bedrooms:	4
Baths:	2
Garage:	2-car
Foundation Type:	
Slab	

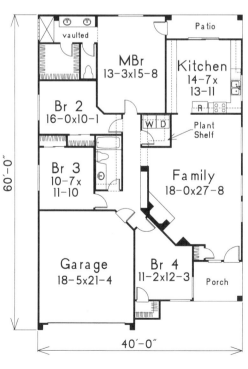

PLAN DATA

Total Living Area: 1,996
Bedrooms: 2
Baths: 2
Garage: 2-car carport
Foundation Type:
Slab

59'-0"

63'-0"

slope clg.

skylts

Patio

MBr
15-0x14-9

skylt

skylts

Activity Area
20-4x21-2

slope clg.

R

Kit
11-7x
12-0

F

Entry
vaulted

D W

Stor.

Br 2
15-8x14-2

Nook
9-7x
9-0

Porch

Carport

Stor.   Stor.

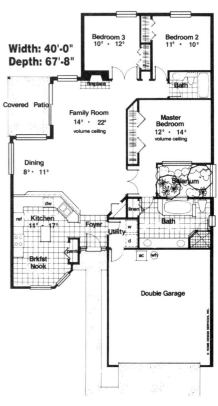

Width: 40'-0"
Depth: 67'-8"

Bedroom 3
10° · 12°

Bedroom 2
11° · 10°

Covered Patio

Family Room
14° · 22°
volume ceiling

fireplace

Bath

Master
Bedroom
12° · 14°
volume ceiling

Dining
8° · 11°

Solarium

linen

Bath

dw

ref   Kitchen
11° · 17°

Foyer

Utility

w
d

pantry

ac   wh

Brkfst
Nook

Double Garage

PLAN DATA

Total Living Area: 1,576
Bedrooms: 3
Baths: 2
Garage: 2-car
Foundation Type:
Slab

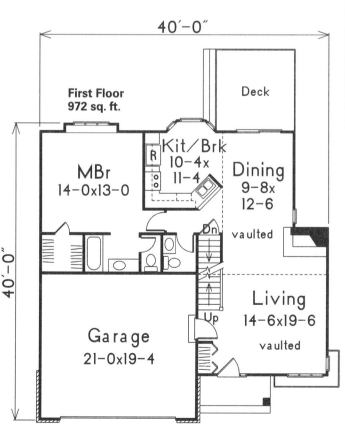

First Floor
972 sq. ft.

40'-0"

40'-0"

Deck

MBr
14-0x13-0

Kit/Brk
10-4x
11-4

R

Dining
9-8x
12-6

vaulted

Dn

Living
14-6x19-6

vaulted

Up

Garage
21-0x19-4

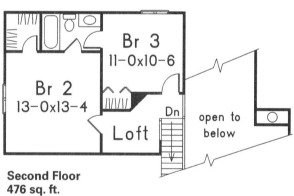

Second Floor
476 sq. ft.

Br 3
11-0x10-6

Br 2
13-0x13-4

Dn

Loft

open to below

PLAN DATA

Total Living Area:	1,448
Bedrooms:	3
Baths:	2 1/2
Garage:	2-car
Foundation Type:	
Basement	

PLAN DATA

Total Living Area:	1,565
Bedrooms:	3
Baths:	2 1/2
Garage:	2-car
Foundation Type:	
Basement	

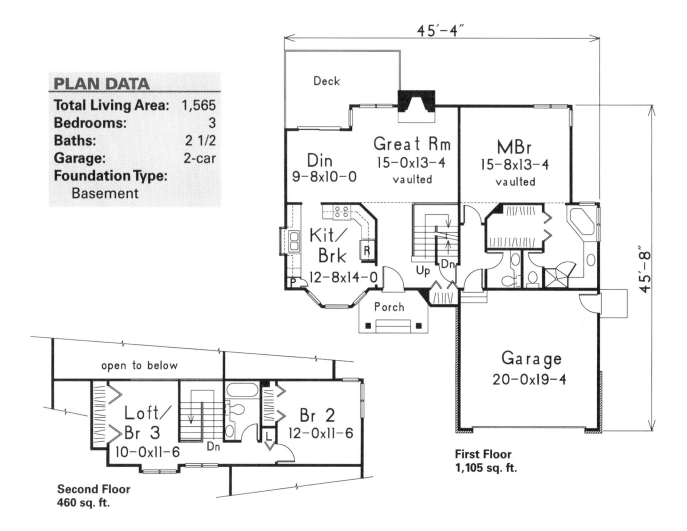

45'-4"

Deck

Great Rm
15-0x13-4
vaulted

MBr
15-8x13-4
vaulted

Din
9-8x10-0

Kit/
Brk
12-8x14-0

Up   Dn

Porch

Garage
20-0x19-4

45'-8"

First Floor
1,105 sq. ft.

open to below

Loft/
Br 3
10-0x11-6

Dn

Br 2
12-0x11-6

Second Floor
460 sq. ft.

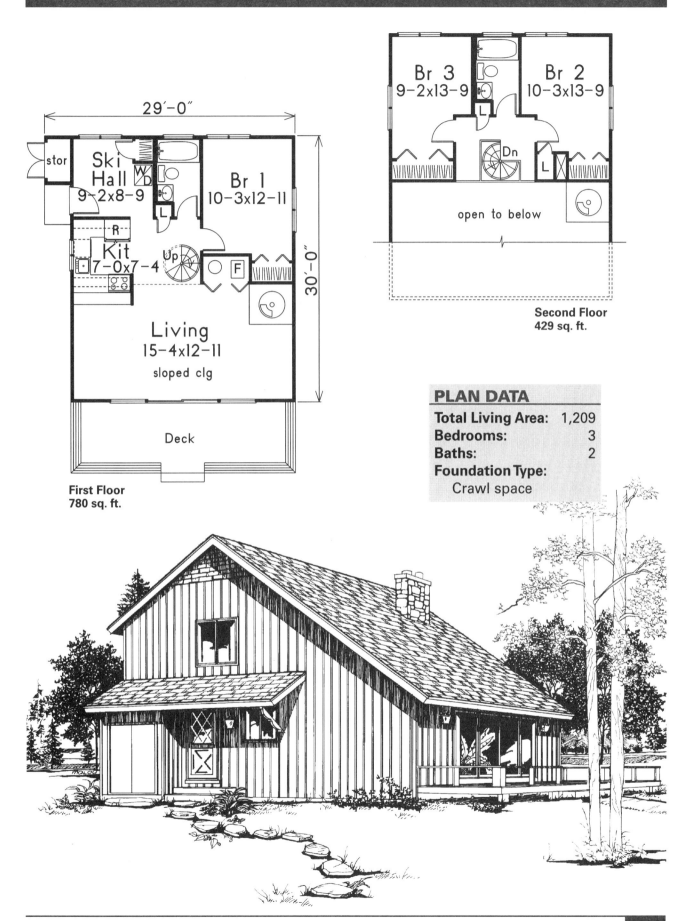

29'-0"

stor

Ski
Hall
9-2x8-9

W
D

L

Br 1
10-3x12-11

R

Kit
7-0x7-4

Up

F

30'-0"

Living
15-4x12-11

sloped clg

Deck

First Floor
780 sq. ft.

Br 3
9-2x13-9

L

Dn

Br 2
10-3x13-9

L

open to below

Second Floor
429 sq. ft.

PLAN DATA

Total Living Area:	1,209
Bedrooms:	3
Baths:	2
Foundation Type:	
Crawl space	

First Floor
792 sq. ft.

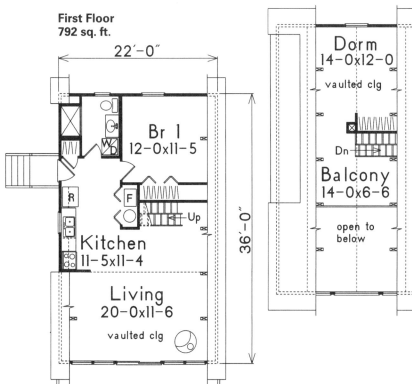

22'-0"

Br 1
12-0x11-5

36'-0"

Kitchen
11-5x11-4

Living
20-0x11-6

vaulted clg

Up

R

F

W
D

Deck

Second Floor
314 sq. ft.

Dorm
14-0x12-0

vaulted clg

Dn

Balcony
14-0x6-6

open to
below

PLAN DATA

Total Living Area:	1,106
Bedrooms:	2
Baths:	1
Foundation Type:	
Pier	

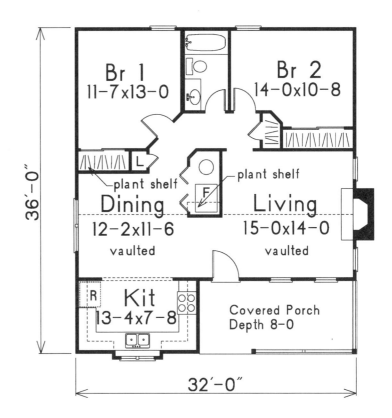

Br 1
11-7x13-0

Br 2
14-0x10-8

plant shelf

plant shelf

L

F

Dining
12-2x11-6
vaulted

Living
15-0x14-0
vaulted

R

Kit
13-4x7-8

Covered Porch
Depth 8-0

36'-0"

32'-0"

PLAN DATA

Total Living Area: 1,020
Bedrooms: 2
Baths: 1
Foundation Type:
Slab

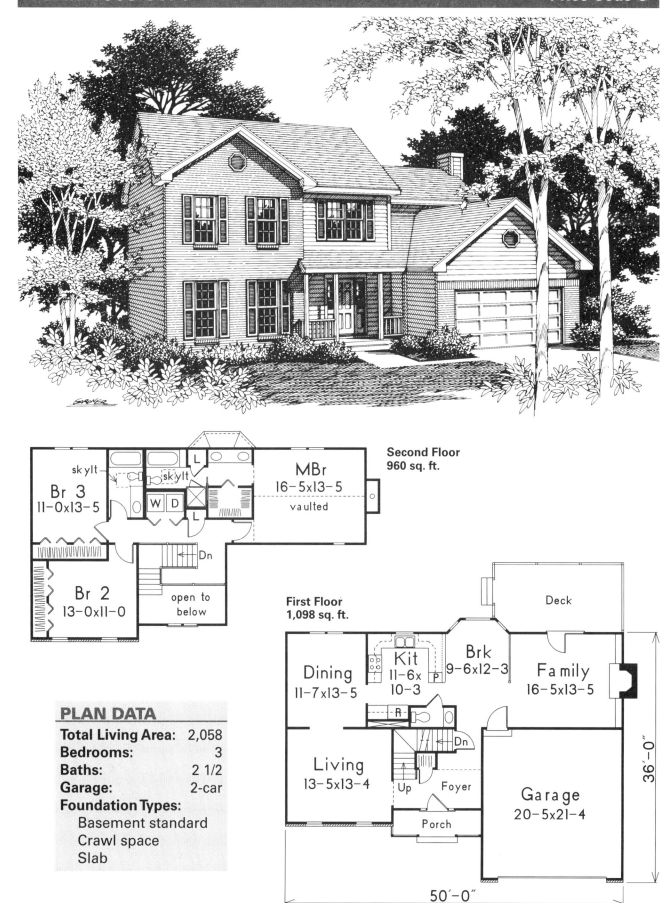

Second Floor
960 sq. ft.

skylt

Br 3
11-0x13-5

skylt

L

W | D

L

MBr
16-5x13-5
vaulted

o

Dn

Br 2
13-0x11-0

open to
below

First Floor
1,098 sq. ft.

Deck

Dining
11-7x13-5

Kit
11-6x
10-3

P

Brk
9-6x12-3

Family
16-5x13-5

R

36'-0"

Dn

Living
13-5x13-4

Up   Foyer

Garage
20-5x21-4

Porch

50'-0"

PLAN DATA

Total Living Area: 2,058
Bedrooms: 3
Baths: 2 1/2
Garage: 2-car
Foundation Types:
   Basement standard
   Crawl space
   Slab

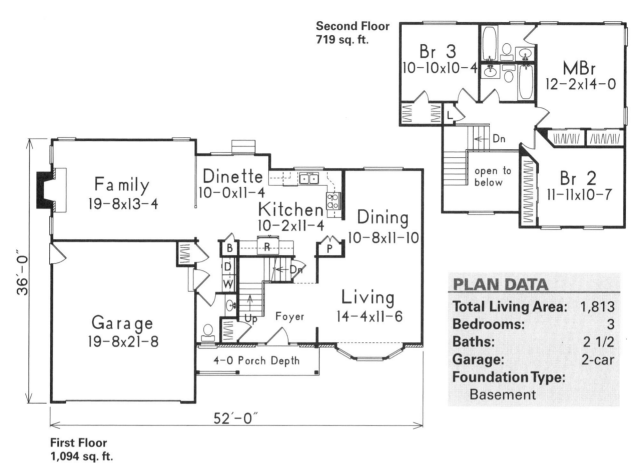

Second Floor
719 sq. ft.

Br 3
10-10x10-4

MBr
12-2x14-0

Br 2
11-11x10-7

open to below

Dn

L

Family
19-8x13-4

Dinette
10-0x11-4

Kitchen
10-2x11-4

Dining
10-8x11-10

Living
14-4x11-6

Foyer

Up

Dn

B
D
W
R
P

Garage
19-8x21-8

36'-0"

52'-0"

4-0 Porch Depth

First Floor
1,094 sq. ft.

PLAN DATA

Total Living Area:	1,813
Bedrooms:	3
Baths:	2 1/2
Garage:	2-car
Foundation Type:	
Basement	

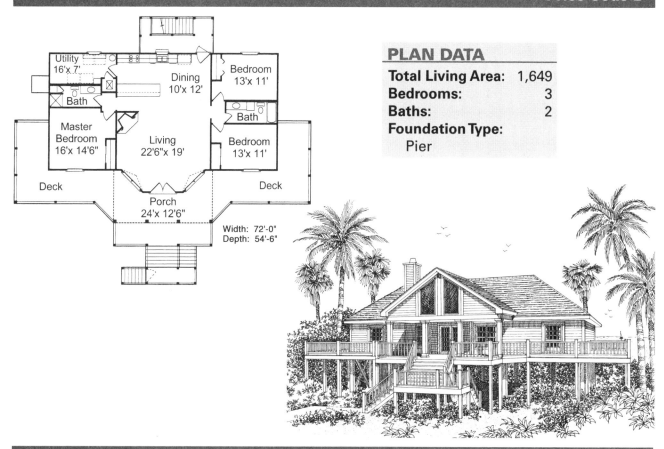

PLAN DATA

Total Living Area: 1,649
Bedrooms: 3
Baths: 2
Foundation Type:
  Pier

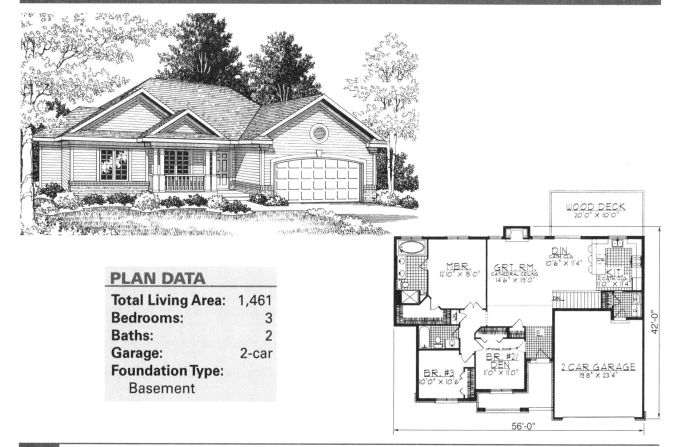

PLAN DATA

Total Living Area: 1,461
Bedrooms: 3
Baths: 2
Garage: 2-car
Foundation Type:
  Basement

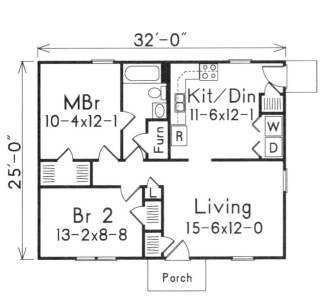

32'-0"

25'-0"

MBr
10-4x12-1

Kit/Din
11-6x12-1

Furn

R

W

D

Br 2
13-2x8-8

L

Living
15-6x12-0

Porch

PLAN DATA

Total Living Area:	800
Bedrooms:	2
Baths:	1
Foundation Types:	
Crawl space standard	
Basement	
Slab	

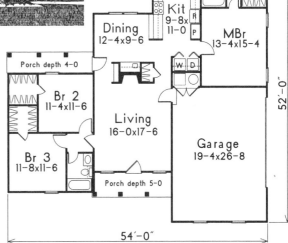

Porch depth 4-0

Kit
9-8x
11-0

R

P

Dining
12-4x9-6

MBr
13-4x15-4

Br 2
11-4x11-6

W D

52'-0"

Living
16-0x17-6

Garage
19-4x26-8

Br 3
11-8x11-6

Porch depth 5-0

54'-0"

PLAN DATA

Total Living Area:	1,444
Bedrooms:	3
Baths:	2
Garage:	2-car
Foundation Types:	
Slab standard	
Crawl space	
Features:	
11' ceilings in living and dining rooms	

PLAN DATA

Total Living Area: 1,882
Bedrooms: 3
Baths: 2
Garage: 2-car
Foundation Type:
   Basement

PLAN DATA

Total Living Area: 1,475
Bedrooms: 3
Baths: 2
Garage: 2-car
Foundation Types:
   Slab standard
   Crawl space

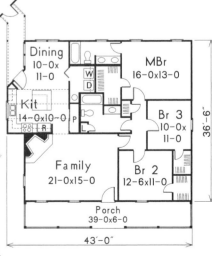

PLAN DATA

Total Living Area: 1,612
Bedrooms: 3
Baths: 2
Garage: 2-car
Foundation Type:
  Slab
Features:
  Side entry garage

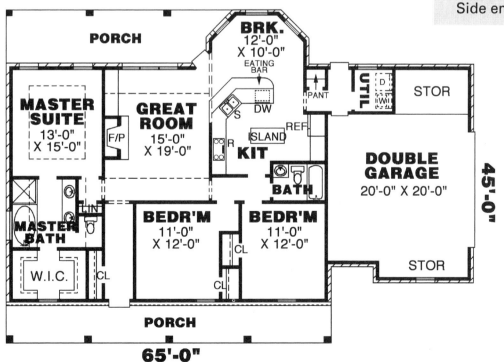

PORCH

BRK.
12'-0"
X 10'-0"

EATING BAR

UTIL

STOR

**MASTER
SUITE**
13'-0"
X 15'-0"

F/P

**GREAT
ROOM**
15'-0"
X 19'-0"

DW

PANT

D
W

ISLAND

S

REF

KIT

R

**DOUBLE
GARAGE**
20'-0" X 20'-0"

BATH

LIN

**MASTER
BATH**

BEDR'M
11'-0"
X 12'-0"

CL

BEDR'M
11'-0"
X 12'-0"

W.I.C.

CL

CL

STOR

45'-0"

PORCH

65'-0"

67'

40'

PLAN DATA

Total Living Area:	1,458
Bedrooms:	3
Baths:	2
Garage:	2-car

Foundation Types:
Slab
Crawl space
Please specify when ordering

PLAN DATA

Total Living Area:	947
Bedrooms:	2
Baths:	1

Foundation Types:
Slab
Crawl space
Please specify when ordering

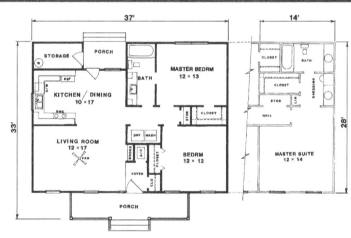

37'

14'

33'

28'

PLAN DATA

Total Living Area: 2,228
Bedrooms: 3
Baths: 2
Garage: 2-car
Foundation Type:
  Basement

Deck

Brk
12-11x9-4

Great Rm
18-0x17-6

MBr
15-8x12-0
coffered clg

vaulted

Kit
12-11x
12-4

Br 2
10-0x
10-9

Dn

D
W

Dining
11-6x14-0
tray clg

Foyer

Study
11-8x12-5

Br 3
13-5x10-0

Garage
19-4x20-4

Porch

51'-7"

64'-8"

PLAN #563-DB2638

Price Code C

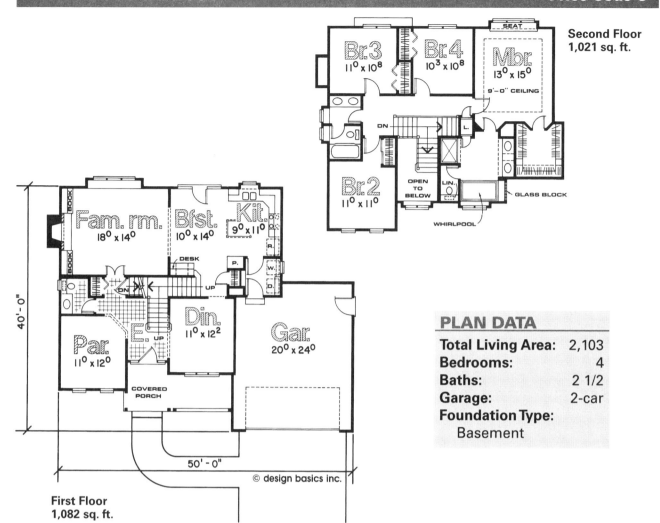

Second Floor
1,021 sq. ft.

Br.3 11⁰ x 10⁸
Br.4 10³ x 10⁸
Mbr. 13⁰ x 15⁰
9'-0" CEILING
Br.2 11⁰ x 11⁰
SEAT
DN
OPEN TO BELOW
LIN.
GLASS BLOCK
WHIRLPOOL

Fam. rm. 18⁰ x 14⁰
Bfst. 10⁰ x 14⁰
Kit. 9⁰ x 11⁰
DESK
Par. 11⁰ x 12⁰
Din. 11⁰ x 12²
Gar. 20⁰ x 24⁰
COVERED PORCH
UP

40'-0"
50'-0"

© design basics inc.

First Floor
1,082 sq. ft.

PLAN DATA

Total Living Area:	2,103
Bedrooms:	4
Baths:	2 1/2
Garage:	2-car
Foundation Type:	Basement

PLAN #563-DB2638

Price Code C

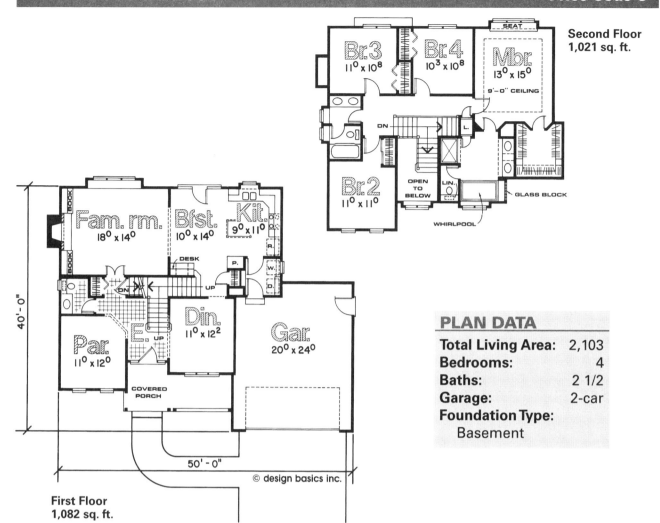

Second Floor
1,021 sq. ft.

First Floor
1,082 sq. ft.

PLAN DATA

Total Living Area:	2,103
Bedrooms:	4
Baths:	2 1/2
Garage:	2-car
Foundation Type:	Basement

Second Floor
745 sq. ft.

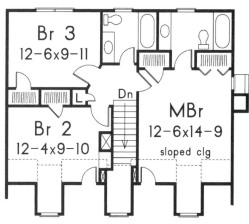

Br 3
12-6x9-11

Br 2
12-4x9-10

L

Dn

MBr
12-6x14-9
sloped clg

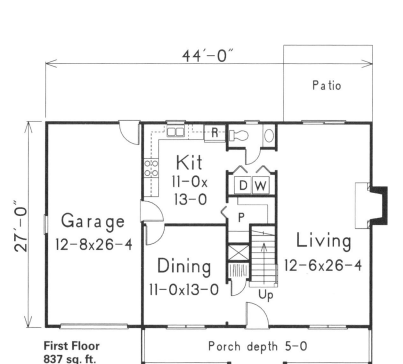

44'-0"

Patio

27'-0"

Garage
12-8x26-4

Kit
11-0x
13-0

D W

P

Dining
11-0x13-0

Up

Living
12-6x26-4

First Floor
837 sq. ft.

Porch depth 5-0

PLAN DATA

Total Living Area: 1,582
Bedrooms: 3
Baths: 2 1/2
Garage: 1-car
Foundation Types:
  Slab standard
  Crawl space

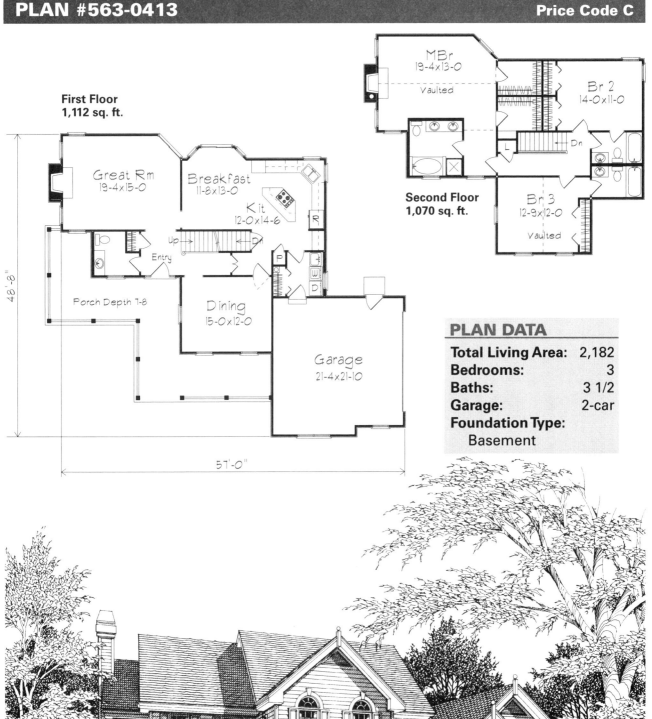

**First Floor
1,112 sq. ft.**

Great Rm
19-4x15-0

Breakfast
11-8x13-0

Kit
12-0x14-6

Up

Dn

Entry

Porch Depth 7-8

Dining
15-0x12-0

W D

Garage
21-4x21-10

48'-8"

57'-0"

MBr
19-4x13-0
Vaulted

Br 2
14-0x11-0

Dn

**Second Floor
1,070 sq. ft.**

Br 3
12-9x12-0
Vaulted

PLAN DATA

Total Living Area:	2,182
Bedrooms:	3
Baths:	3 1/2
Garage:	2-car
Foundation Type:	
Basement	

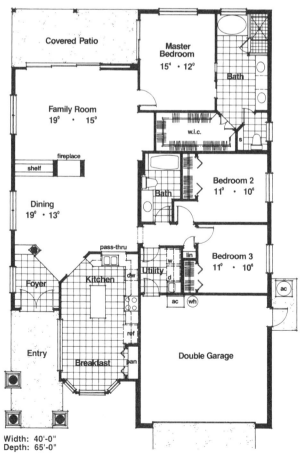

Covered Patio

Master Bedroom
15⁴ · 12⁰

Bath

Family Room
19⁰ · 15⁰

w.i.c.

fireplace

shelf

Bath

Bedroom 2
11⁰ · 10⁶

Dining
19⁰ · 13⁰

pass-thru

Utility

Bedroom 3
11⁰ · 10⁶

Foyer

Kitchen

dw

w

lin

d

ac

Entry

ac

wh

ref

Breakfast

pan

Double Garage

Width: 40'-0"
Depth: 65'-0"

PLAN DATA
Total Living Area: 1,787
Bedrooms: 3
Baths: 2
Garage: 2-car
Foundation Type:
  Slab

PLAN DATA

Total Living Area: 1,969
Bedrooms: 3
Baths: 2
Garage: 2-car
Foundation Types:
Crawl space standard
Slab

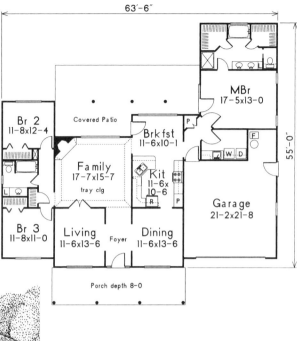

63'-6"

55'-0"

Br 2
11-8x12-4

Covered Patio

Brk fst
11-6x10-1

MBr
17-5x13-0

Family
17-7x15-7
tray clg

Kit
11-6x
10-6

Garage
21-2x21-8

Br 3
11-8x11-0

Living
11-6x13-6

Foyer

Dining
11-6x13-6

Porch depth 8-0

PLAN #563-RJ-A1485

Price Code A

PLAN DATA

Total Living Area: 1,436
Bedrooms: 3
Baths: 2
Garage: 2-car
Foundation Type:
Slab

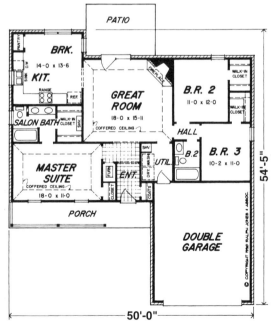

PATIO

BRK.
14-0 x 13-6

KIT.
SINK DW
RANGE
REF.

GREAT
ROOM
18-0 x 15-11
COFFERED CEILING

B.R. 2
11-0 x 12-0

WALK-IN
CLOSET

WALK-IN
CLOSET

SALON BATH
WALK-IN
CLOSET

HALL

MASTER
SUITE
COFFERED CEILING
18-0 x 11-0

B.2

ENT.

UTIL.

B.R. 3
10-2 x 11-0

PORCH

DOUBLE
GARAGE

54'-5"

50'-0"

First Floor
1,157 sq. ft.

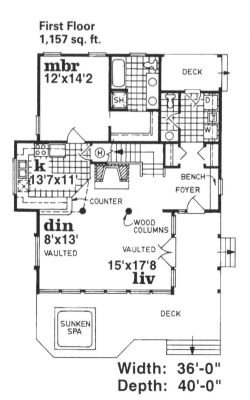

mbr
12'x14'2

DECK

SH.

D
W

k
13'7x11'

H

BENCH
FOYER

COUNTER

WOOD
COLUMNS

din
8'x13'
VAULTED

VAULTED
15'x17'8
liv

SUNKEN
SPA

DECK

Width: 36'-0"
Depth: 40'-0"

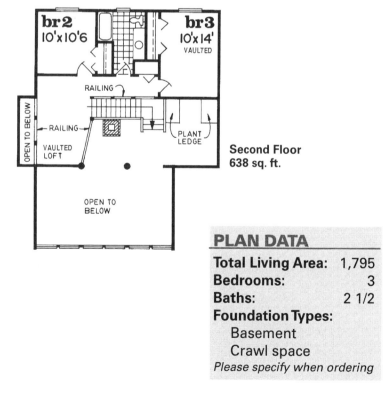

br2
10'x10'6

br3
10'x14'
VAULTED

RAILING

OPEN TO BELOW

RAILING

PLANT
LEDGE

VAULTED
LOFT

Second Floor
638 sq. ft.

OPEN TO
BELOW

PLAN DATA

Total Living Area:	1,795
Bedrooms:	3
Baths:	2 1/2
Foundation Types:	
Basement	
Crawl space	

Please specify when ordering

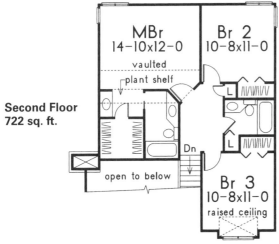

Second Floor
722 sq. ft.

MBr
14-10x12-0
vaulted

plant shelf

Br 2
10-8x11-0

L

Dn

open to below

Br 3
10-8x11-0
raised ceiling

PLAN DATA

Total Living Area:	1,556
Bedrooms:	3
Baths:	2 1/2
Garage:	2-car
Foundation Type:	
Basement	

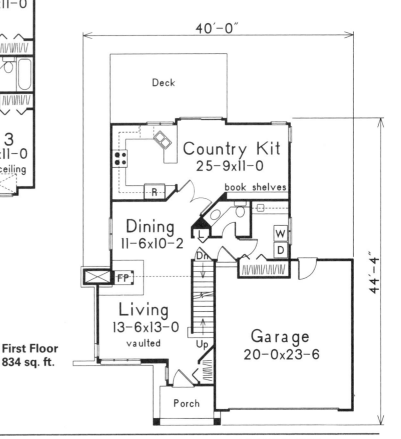

40'-0"

Deck

Country Kit
25-9x11-0

book shelves

R

L

W
D

Dining
11-6x10-2

Dn

44'-4"

FP

Living
13-6x13-0
vaulted

Up

Garage
20-0x23-6

First Floor
834 sq. ft.

Porch

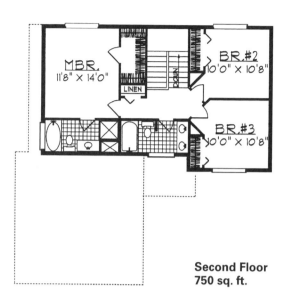

First Floor
786 sq. ft.

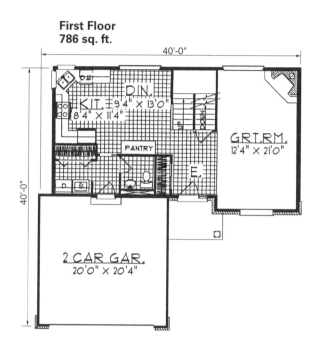

40'-0"

40'-0"

KIT. 8'4" × 11'4"

DIN. 9'4" × 13'0"

PANTRY

GRT. RM. 12'4" × 21'0"

2 CAR GAR. 20'0" × 20'4"

MBR. 11'8" × 14'0"

LINEN

BR. #2 10'0" × 10'8"

BR. #3 10'0" × 10'8"

Second Floor
750 sq. ft.

PLAN DATA

Total Living Area: 1,536
Bedrooms: 3
Baths: 2 1/2
Garage: 2-car
Foundation Type:
   Basement
Features:
   9' ceilings throughout

FREILING

26'-0"

30'-0"

R

Kit/
Dining
8-1x
16-6

D W W

Br 1
9-2x
12-9

L

Up

Living
25-5x12-11

Deck

First Floor
780 sq. ft.

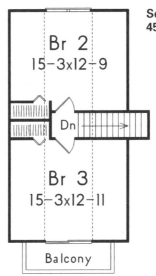

Second Floor
450 sq. ft.

Br 2
15-3x12-9

Dn

Br 3
15-3x12-11

Balcony

PLAN DATA
Total Living Area: 1,230
Bedrooms: 3
Baths: 1
Foundation Types:
  Crawl space standard
  Slab

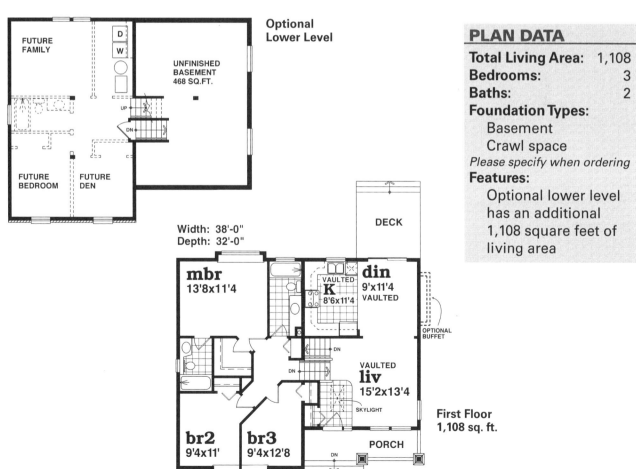

Optional Lower Level

FUTURE FAMILY

D
W

UNFINISHED BASEMENT 468 SQ. FT.

UP

DN

FUTURE BEDROOM   FUTURE DEN

PLAN DATA

Total Living Area: 1,108
Bedrooms: 3
Baths: 2
Foundation Types:
 Basement
 Crawl space
Please specify when ordering
Features:
 Optional lower level
 has an additional
 1,108 square feet of
 living area

Width: 38'-0"
Depth: 32'-0"

DECK

mbr
13'8x11'4

VAULTED
K
8'6x11'4

din
9'x11'4
VAULTED

OPTIONAL BUFFET

DN

VAULTED
liv
15'2x13'4

SKYLIGHT

First Floor
1,108 sq. ft.

br2
9'4x11'

br3
9'4x12'8

DN

PORCH

DN

Second Floor
1,080 sq. ft.

Br 3
10-0x
10-0

Bonus Rm
20-0x12-0

Dn

Dn

L

Br 2
14-0x11-0

MBr
13-8x15-0

52'-8"

Deck

Kit
12-10x10-0

Brk
10-10x
10-4

Garage
20-0x20-4

R

Dn

W D P

Dining
14-0x11-0

Family
13-8x16-8

Up

31'-4"

First Floor
878 sq. ft.

Porch depth 4-0

PLAN DATA

Total Living Area: 1,958
Bedrooms: 3
Baths: 2 1/2
Garage: 2-car
Foundation Types:
 Basement standard
 Crawl space
 Slab

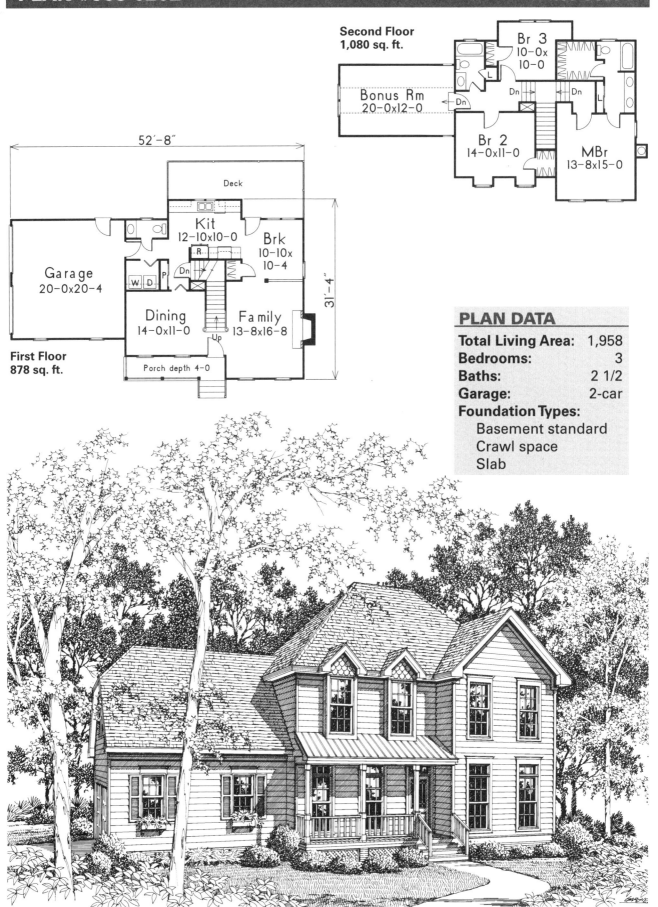

PLAN DATA

Total Living Area: 1,605
Bedrooms: 3
Baths: 2
Garage: 2-car
Foundation Types:
  Basement standard
  Crawl space
  Slab

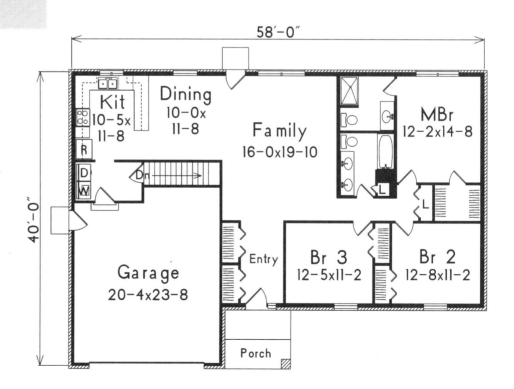

58'-0"

40'-0"

Kit
10-5x
11-8

Dining
10-0x
11-8

Family
16-0x19-10

MBr
12-2x14-8

R

D
W

Dn

L

L

Garage
20-4x23-8

Entry

Br 3
12-5x11-2

Br 2
12-8x11-2

Porch

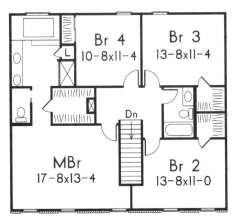

Second Floor
1,140 sq. ft.

Br 4
10-8x11-4

Br 3
13-8x11-4

Dn

MBr
17-8x13-4

Br 2
13-8x11-0

PLAN DATA

Total Living Area: 2,358
Bedrooms: 4
Baths: 2 1/2
Garage: 2-car
Foundation Types:
  Basement standard
  Crawl space
  Slab

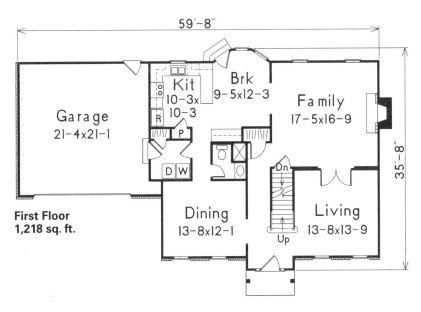

59'-8"

35'-8"

Garage
21-4x21-1

Kit
10-3x
10-3

Brk
9-5x12-3

Family
17-5x16-9

R

P

DW

Dn

Dining
13-8x12-1

Living
13-8x13-9

Up

First Floor
1,218 sq. ft.

PLAN #563-0485

Price Code AA

PLAN DATA

Total Living Area:	1,195
Bedrooms:	3
Baths:	2
Garage:	2-car
Foundation Type:	
Basement	

PLAN #563-0241

Price Code AAA

PLAN DATA

Total Living Area:	829
Bedrooms:	1
Baths:	1
Foundation Type:	
Slab	

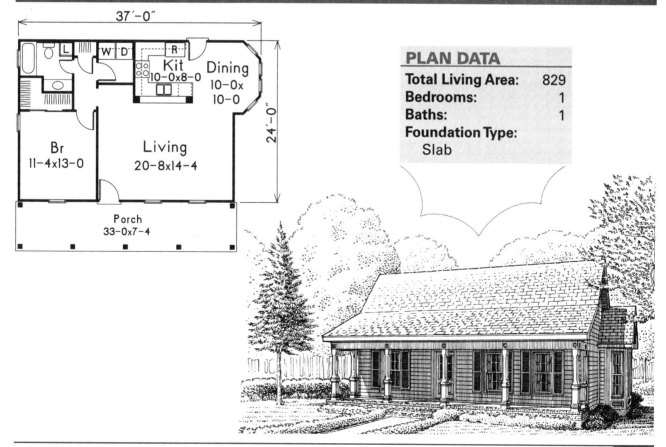

PLAN #563-RJ-A1369A

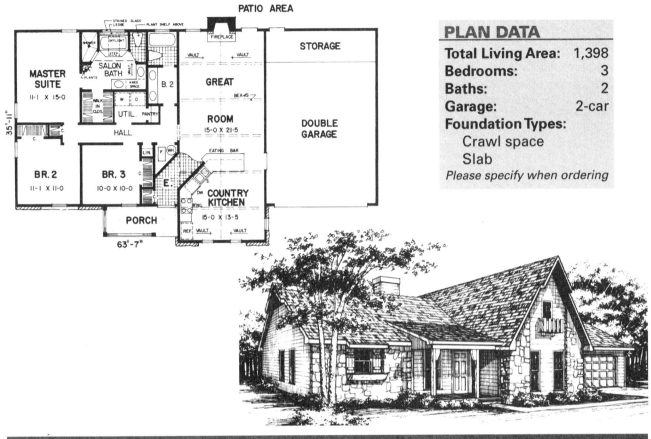

PLAN DATA
Total Living Area: 1,398
Bedrooms: 3
Baths: 2
Garage: 2-car
Foundation Types:
  Crawl space
  Slab
Please specify when ordering

PLAN #563-0176

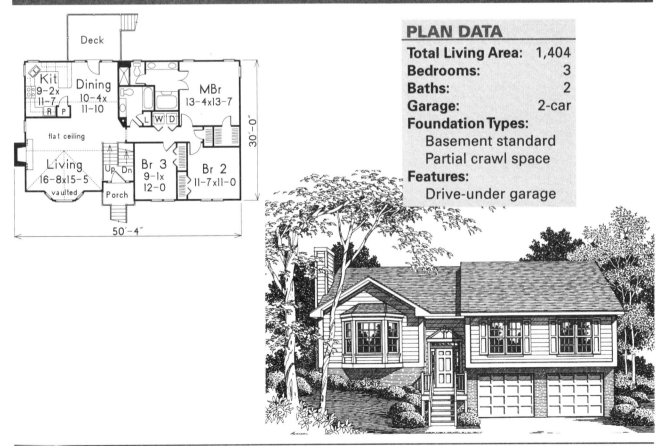

PLAN DATA
Total Living Area: 1,404
Bedrooms: 3
Baths: 2
Garage: 2-car
Foundation Types:
  Basement standard
  Partial crawl space
Features:
  Drive-under garage

PLAN DATA

Total Living Area: 1,824
Bedrooms: 3
Baths: 2
Garage: detached 2-car
Foundation Type:
  Slab
Features:
  10' ceiling in living
  room

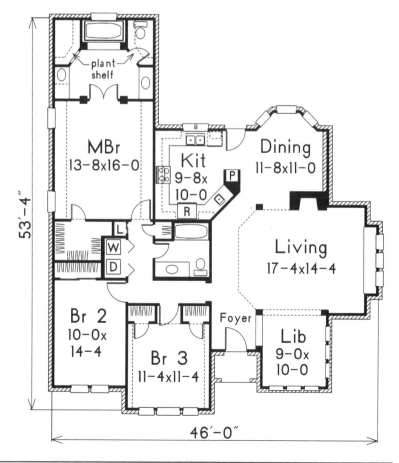

plant shelf

MBr
13-8x16-0

Kit
9-8x
10-0

Dining
11-8x11-0

Living
17-4x14-4

Br 2
10-0x
14-4

Br 3
11-4x11-4

Foyer

Lib
9-0x
10-0

53'-4"

46'-0"

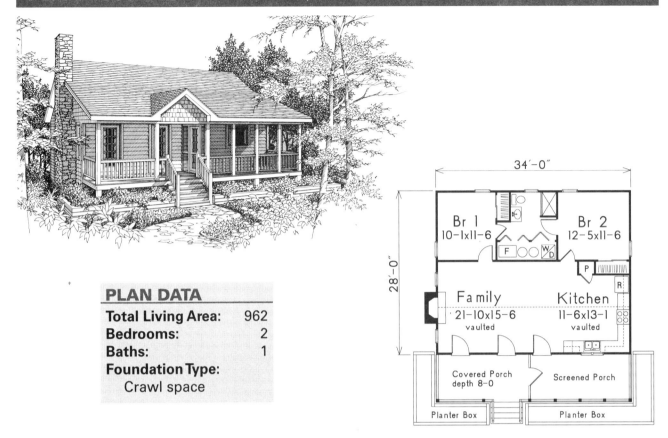

34´-0˝

28´-0˝

Br 1
10-1x11-6

Br 2
12-5x11-6

F

W
D

P

R

Family
21-10x15-6
vaulted

Kitchen
11-6x13-1
vaulted

Covered Porch
depth 8-0

Screened Porch

Planter Box

Planter Box

PLAN DATA

Total Living Area:	962
Bedrooms:	2
Baths:	1
Foundation Type:	
Crawl space	

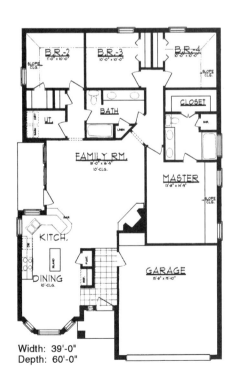

B.R.-2

B.R.-3

B.R.-4

SLOPE
CLG.

SLOPE
CLG.

UT.

BATH

CLOSET

LINEN

FAMILY RM.
10'-CLG.

MASTER
13'-8" x 14'-9"

SLOPE
CLG.

KITCH.

ISLAND

DINING
10'-CLG.

GARAGE
19'-8" x 19'-0"

Width: 39'-0"
Depth: 60'-0"

PLAN DATA

Total Living Area:	1,710
Bedrooms:	4
Baths:	2
Garage:	2-car
Foundation Type:	
Slab	

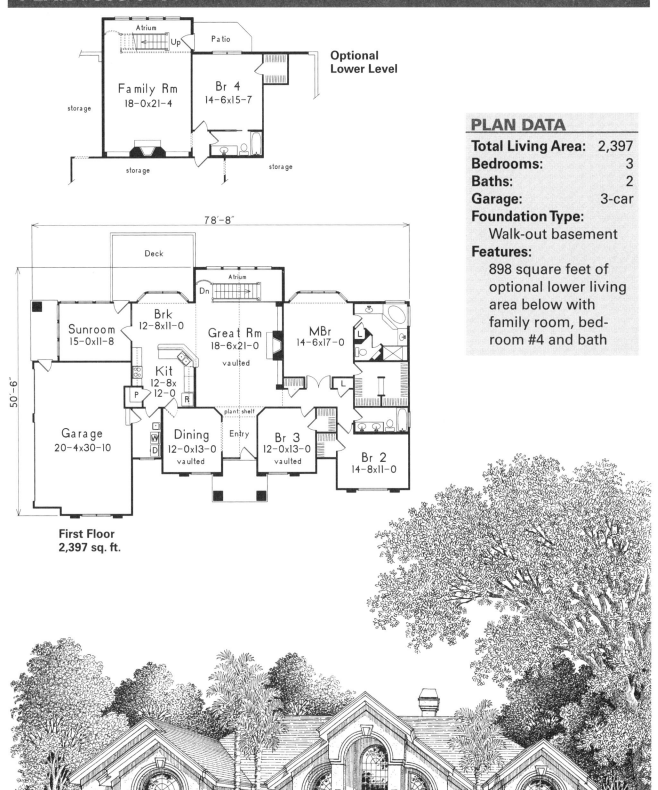

Optional Lower Level

Atrium
Up
Patio

Family Rm
18-0x21-4

Br 4
14-6x15-7

storage

storage

storage

PLAN DATA
Total Living Area: 2,397
Bedrooms: 3
Baths: 2
Garage: 3-car
Foundation Type:
  Walk-out basement
Features:
  898 square feet of
  optional lower living
  area below with
  family room, bed-
  room #4 and bath

78'-8"

Deck

Atrium
Dn

Brk
12-8x11-0

Great Rm
18-6x21-0
vaulted

MBr
14-6x17-0

L

Sunroom
15-0x11-8

Kit
12-8x
12-0

P

R

50'-6"

plant shelf

Dining
12-0x13-0
vaulted

Entry

Br 3
12-0x13-0
vaulted

L

Garage
20-4x30-10

W

D

Br 2
14-8x11-0

**First Floor
2,397 sq. ft.**

Second Floor
604 sq. ft.

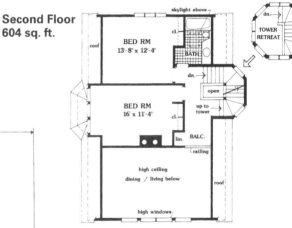

skylight above

dn.

TOWER
RETREAT

roof

BED RM
13'-8" x 12'-4"

cl.

BATH

dn.

open

BED RM
16' x 11'-4"

cl.

up to
tower

BALC.

lin.

railing

high ceiling
dining / living below

roof

high windows

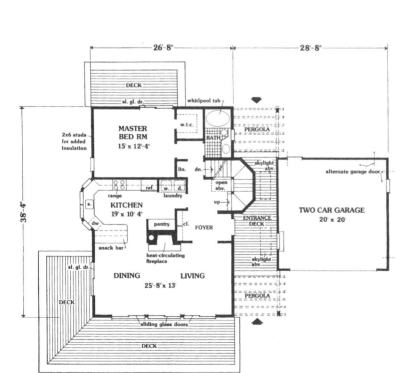

26'-8"   28'-8"

DECK

sl. gl. dr.

whirlpool tub

PERGOLA

w.i.c.

MASTER
BED RM
15' x 12'-4"

BATH

2x6 studs
for added
insulation

lin.

dn.

skylight
abv.

open
abv.

alternate garage door

ref.

w.   d.

up

range   laundry

KITCHEN
19' x 10' 4"

s.

ENTRANCE
DECK

TWO CAR GARAGE
20' x 20'

dw

pantry

cl.

FOYER

snack bar

heat-circulating
fireplace

38'-4"

sl. gl. dr.

skylight
abv.

DINING   LIVING
25'-8" x 13'

DECK

PERGOLA

sliding glass doors

DECK

First Floor
1,073 sq. ft.

PLAN DATA

Total Living Area: 1,677
Bedrooms: 3
Baths: 2
Garage: 2-car
Foundation Types:
  Basement
  Crawl space
  Slab
Please specify when ordering
Features:
  2" x 6" exterior walls

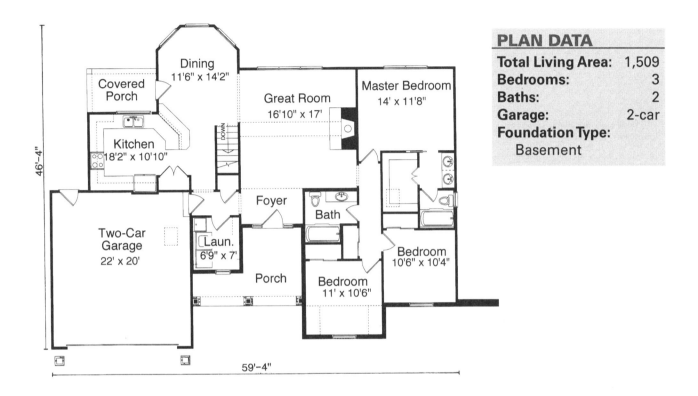

PLAN DATA

Total Living Area:	1,509
Bedrooms:	3
Baths:	2
Garage:	2-car
Foundation Type:	
Basement	

Dining
11'6" x 14'2"

Covered
Porch

Great Room
16'10" x 17'

Master Bedroom
14' x 11'8"

Kitchen
18'2" x 10'10"

Foyer

Bath

Bedroom
10'6" x 10'4"

Two-Car
Garage
22' x 20'

Laun.
6'9" x 7'

Porch

Bedroom
11' x 10'6"

46'-4"

59'-4"

PLAN #563-0274

PLAN DATA

Total Living Area: 1,020
Bedrooms: 2
Baths: 1
Garage: 2-car
Foundation Type:
  Basement

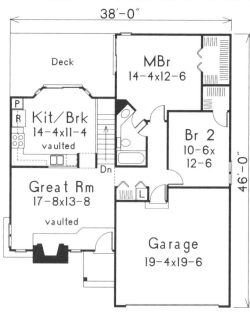

38'-0"

Deck

MBr
14-4x12-6

P
R

Kit/Brk
14-4x11-4
vaulted

Dn

Br 2
10-6x
12-6

Great Rm
17-8x13-8
vaulted

L

Garage
19-4x19-6

46'-0"

PLAN #563-0110

Price Code B

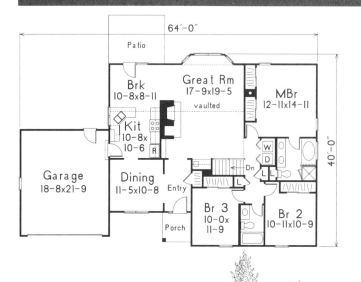

64'-0"

Patio

Brk
10-8x8-11

Great Rm
17-9x19-5
vaulted

MBr
12-11x14-11

Kit
10-8x
10-6
R

W
D
L

Garage
18-8x21-9

Dining
11-5x10-8

Entry

Dn

L

Br 3
10-0x
11-9

Br 2
10-11x10-9

Porch

40'-0"

PLAN DATA

Total Living Area: 1,605
Bedrooms: 3
Baths: 2
Garage: 2-car
Foundation Types:
  Basement standard
  Crawl space
  Slab

PLAN DATA

Total Living Area: 1,268

Bedrooms: 3

Baths: 2

Garage: 2-car

Foundation Type:

Basement

Features:

- Drive-under garage
- 10' ceilings through-
  out living/dining
  area

Sundeck
16-0 x 12-0

12-0

Bdrm. 3
11-2 x 10-0

Dining
9-8 x 10-0
(10'-0" Ceiling)

Ref.
Kitchen
10-0 x 10-0

M.Bath

Dw.

Pantry

Bath 2

Sloped
Floor

Master
Bdrm.
11-6 x 14-6

33-0

Bdrm. 2
11-2 x 10-0

Living Area
14-2 x 17-4
(10'-0" Ceiling)

Entry

Down

Sh

©1998, Jannis Vann & Associates, Inc.

46-0

PLAN DATA

Total Living Area: 1,281

Bedrooms: 3

Baths: 2

Garage: 2-car

Foundation Types:

Crawl space

Slab

Walk-out basement

Please specify when ordering

Features:

Drive-under garage

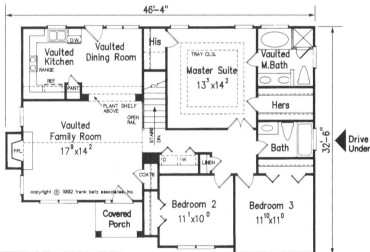

46'-4"

D.W.

Vaulted
Kitchen

RANGE

Vaulted
Dining Room

His

TRAY CLG.

Master Suite
13³x14²

Vaulted
M.Bath

REF

PANT

Hers

PLANT SHELF
ABOVE

OPEN
RAIL

Vaulted
Family Room
17⁹x14²

STAIRS
DN.

Bath

FPL

D W

LINEN

32'-6"

Drive
Under

COATS

copyright © 1992 frank betz associates, inc.

Covered
Porch

Bedroom 2
11¹x10⁰

Bedroom 3
11¹⁰x11⁰

PLAN DATA

Total Living Area: 1,340
Bedrooms: 3
Baths: 2
Garage: 2-car
Foundation Types:
  Slab standard
  Crawl space

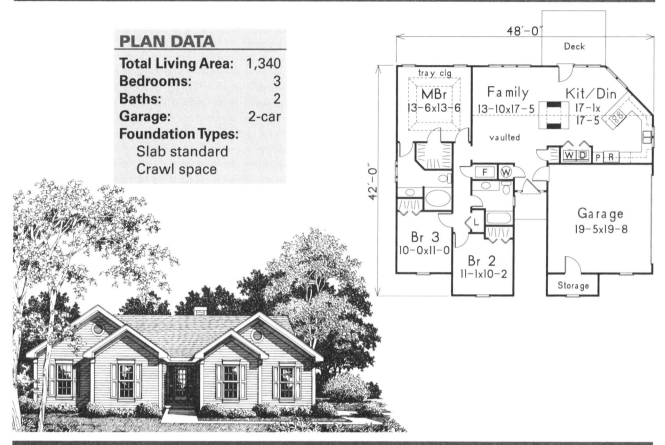

PLAN DATA

Total Living Area: 1,540
Bedrooms: 3
Baths: 2
Garage: 2-car
Foundation Types:
  Basement standard
  Crawl space
  Slab

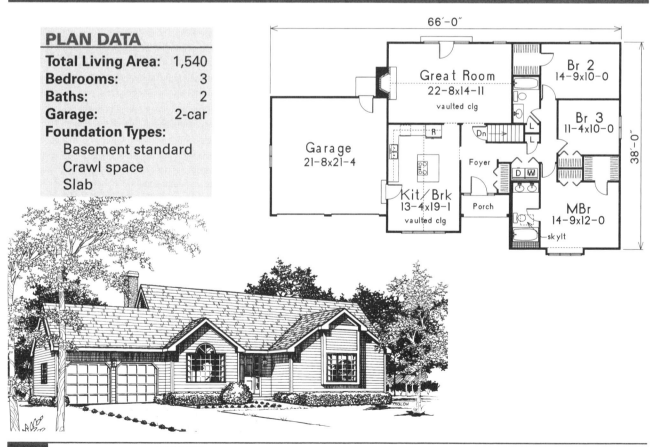

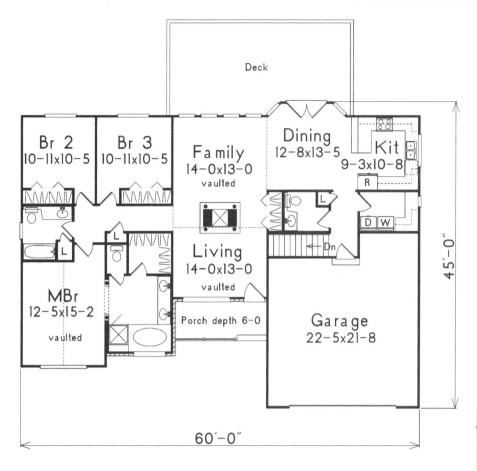

Deck

Br 2
10-11x10-5

Br 3
10-11x10-5

Family
14-0x13-0
vaulted

Dining
12-8x13-5

Kit
9-3x10-8

R

L

D W

MBr
12-5x15-2
vaulted

Living
14-0x13-0
vaulted

← Dn

Porch depth 6-0

Garage
22-5x21-8

45'-0"

60'-0"

PLAN DATA

Total Living Area:	1,684
Bedrooms:	3
Baths:	2 1/2
Garage:	2-car
Foundation Type:	
Basement	

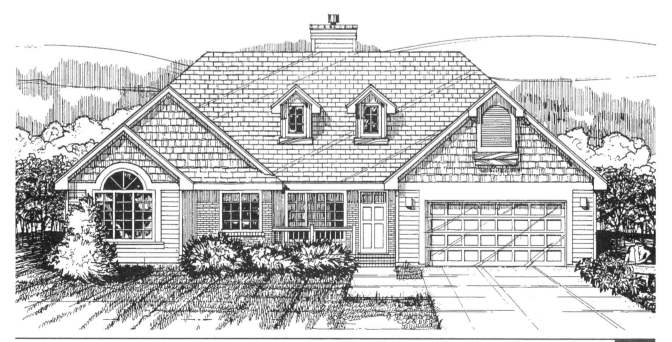

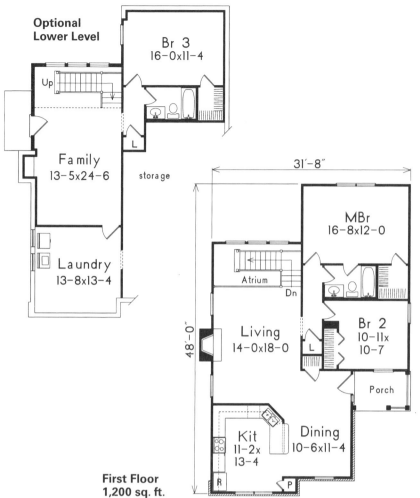

Optional Lower Level

Br 3
16-0x11-4

Up

L

Family
13-5x24-6

storage

Laundry
13-8x13-4

31'-8"

48'-0"

MBr
16-8x12-0

Atrium

Dn

Living
14-0x18-0

Br 2
10-11x 10-7

L

Porch

Kit
11-2x 13-4

Dining
10-6x11-4

R

P

First Floor
1,200 sq. ft.

PLAN DATA

Total Living Area: 1,200
Bedrooms: 2
Baths: 1
Foundation Type:
Walk-out basement
Features:
697 square feet of optional living area on the lower level

PLAN #563-0814

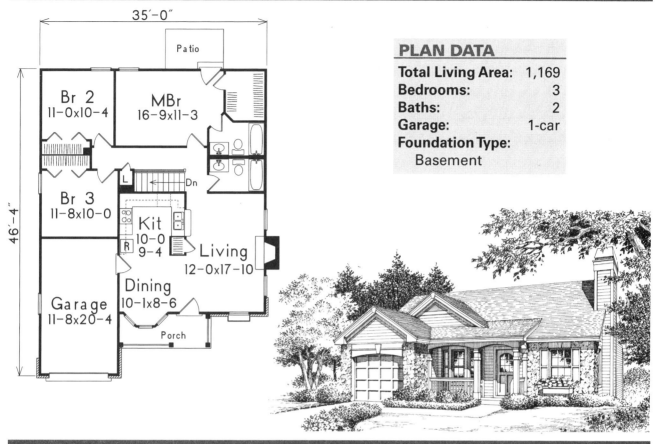

35'-0"

Patio

Br 2
11-0x10-4

MBr
16-9x11-3

46'-4"

Dn

Br 3
11-8x10-0

L

Kit
10-0
9-4

R

Living
12-0x17-10

Garage
11-8x20-4

Dining
10-1x8-6

Porch

PLAN DATA

Total Living Area:	1,169
Bedrooms:	3
Baths:	2
Garage:	1-car
Foundation Type:	
Basement	

PLAN #563-0808

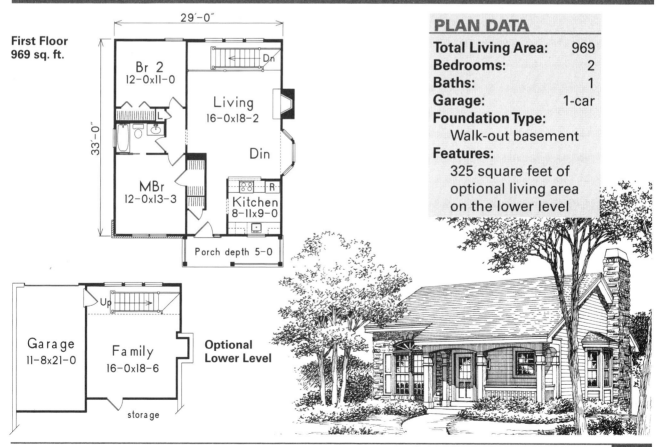

**First Floor
969 sq. ft.**

29'-0"

Br 2
12-0x11-0

Dn

33'-0"

L

Living
16-0x18-2

Din

MBr
12-0x13-3

R

Kitchen
8-11x9-0

Porch depth 5-0

Up

Garage
11-8x21-0

Family
16-0x18-6

**Optional
Lower Level**

storage

PLAN DATA

Total Living Area:	969
Bedrooms:	2
Baths:	1
Garage:	1-car
Foundation Type:	
Walk-out basement	
Features:	
325 square feet of optional living area on the lower level	

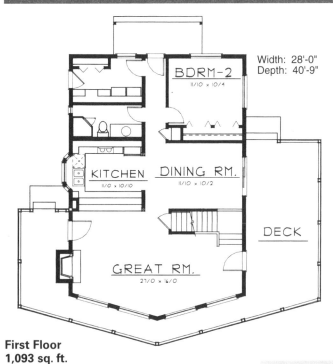

Width: 28'-0"
Depth: 40'-9"

First Floor
1,093 sq. ft.

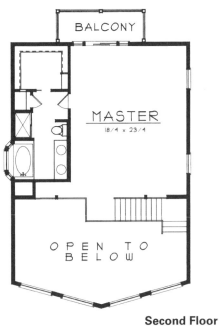

Second Floor
677 sq. ft.

PLAN DATA

Total Living Area: 1,770
Bedrooms: 2
Baths: 2
Foundation Types:
  Basement
  Walk-out basement
Please specify when ordering

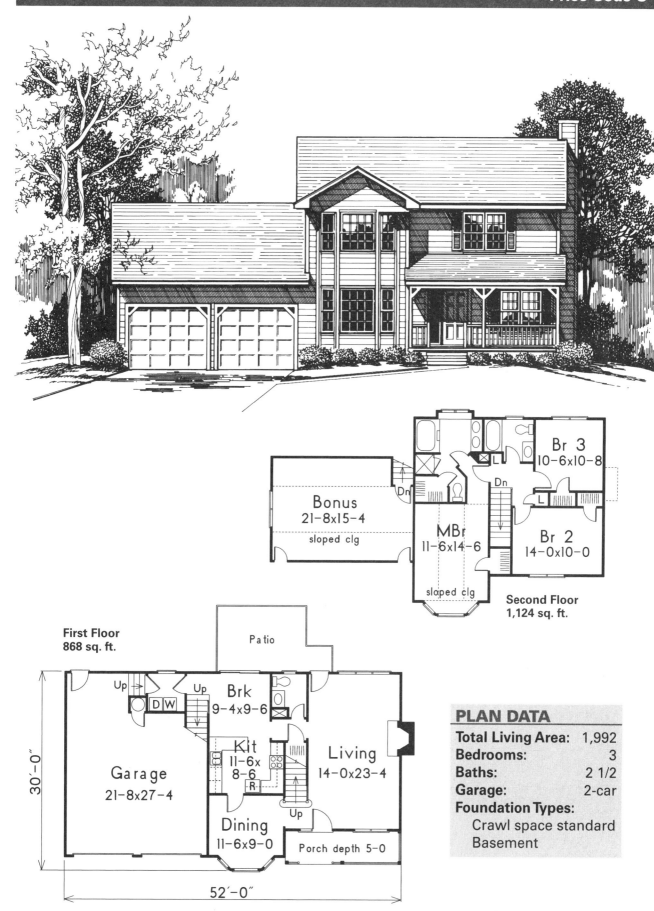

Bonus
21-8x15-4
sloped clg

Br 3
10-6x10-8

Dn

Dn

L

L

MBr
11-6x14-6
sloped clg

Br 2
14-0x10-0

Second Floor
1,124 sq. ft.

First Floor
868 sq. ft.

Patio

Up

Up

D W

Brk
9-4x9-6

Kit
11-6x
8-6

R

Living
14-0x23-4

Garage
21-8x27-4

Up

Dining
11-6x9-0

Porch depth 5-0

30'-0"

52'-0"

PLAN DATA

Total Living Area:	1,992
Bedrooms:	3
Baths:	2 1/2
Garage:	2-car
Foundation Types:	
Crawl space standard	
Basement	

**First Floor
982 sq. ft.**

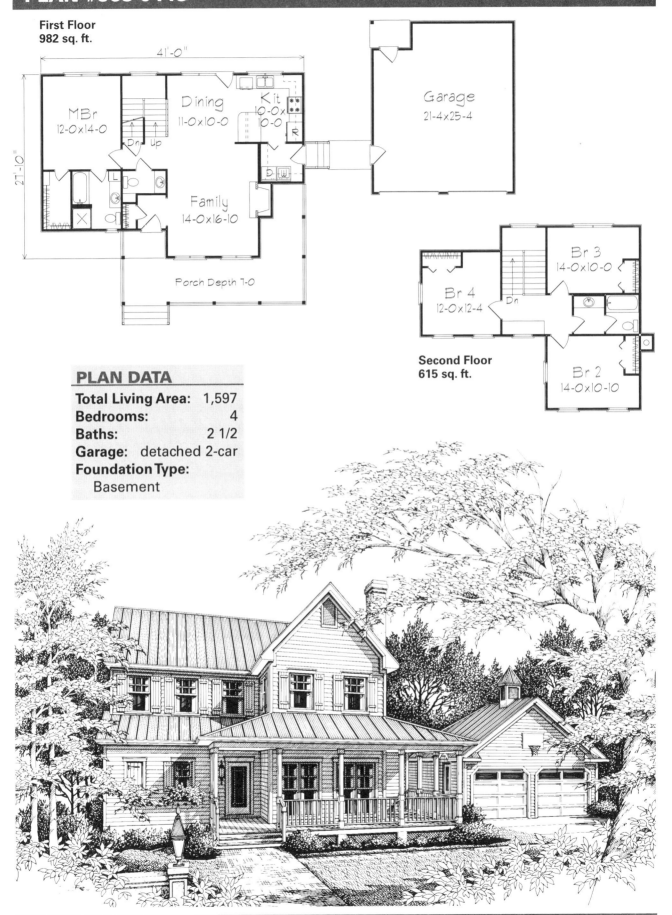

41'-0"

MBr
12-0x14-0

Dn Up

Dining
11-0x10-0

Kit
10-0x
10-0

Family
14-0x16-10

21'-10"

Porch Depth 7-0

Garage
21-4x25-4

**Second Floor
615 sq. ft.**

Br 4
12-0x12-4

Dn

Br 3
14-0x10-0

Br 2
14-0x10-10

PLAN DATA

Total Living Area: 1,597
Bedrooms: 4
Baths: 2 1/2
Garage: detached 2-car
Foundation Type:
  Basement

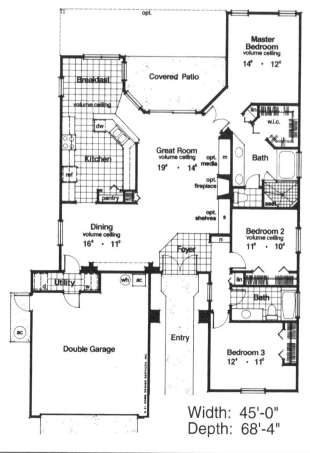

PLAN DATA

Total Living Area: 1,703
Bedrooms: 3
Baths: 2
Garage: 2-car
Foundation Type:
  Slab

Width: 45'-0"
Depth: 68'-4"

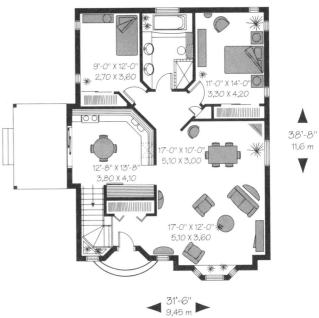

9'-0" X 12'-0"
2,70 X 3,60

11'-0" X 14'-0"
3,30 X 4,20

17'-0" X 10'-0"
5,10 X 3,00

12'-8" X 13'-8"
3,80 X 4,10

17'-0" X 12'-0"
5,10 X 3,60

38'-8"
11,6 m

31'-6"
9,45 m

PLAN DATA

Total Living Area:	1,199
Bedrooms:	2
Baths:	1
Foundation Type:	
Basement	

PLAN DATA

Total Living Area:	1,466
Bedrooms:	3
Baths:	2
Garage:	2-car
Foundation Types:	
Basement standard	
Slab	
Features:	
2" x 6" exterior walls	

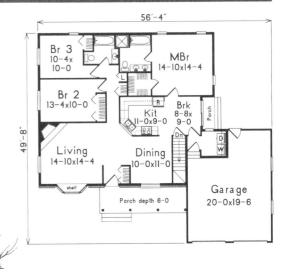

56'-4"

49'-8"

Br 3
10-4x
10-0

MBr
14-10x14-4

Br 2
13-4x10-0

Kit
11-0x9-0

Brk
8-8x
9-0

Porch

Living
14-10x14-4

Dining
10-0x11-0

Dn

D
W

Garage
20-0x19-6

shelf

Porch depth 6-0

PLAN DATA

Total Living Area:	1,707
Bedrooms:	3
Baths:	2
Garage:	2-car
Foundation Type:	
Slab	

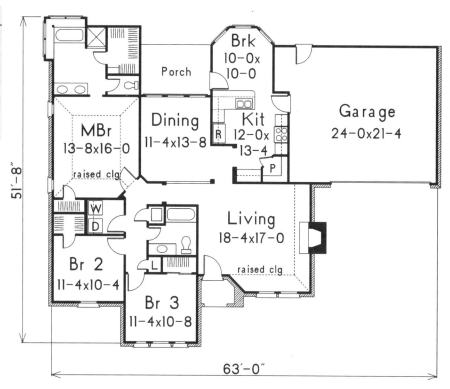

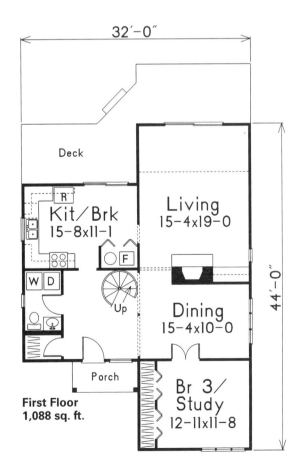

32'-0"

Deck

Kit/Brk
15-8x11-1

Living
15-4x19-0

R

F

W   D

Up

44'-0"

Dining
15-4x10-0

Porch

Br 3/
Study
12-11x11-8

First Floor
1,088 sq. ft.

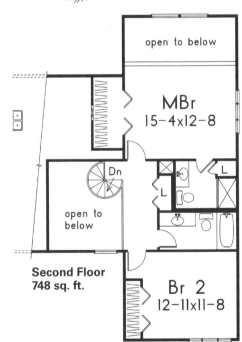

open to below

MBr
15-4x12-8

Dn

L

L

L

open to
below

Second Floor
748 sq. ft.

Br 2
12-11x11-8

PLAN DATA
Total Living Area: 1,836
Bedrooms: 3
Baths: 2 1/2
Foundation Types:
   Crawl space standard
   Slab

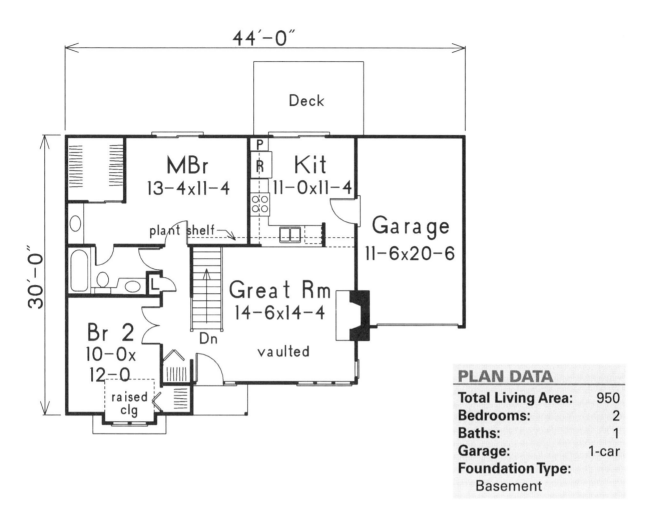

44'-0"

Deck

MBr
13-4x11-4

Kit
11-0x11-4

P
R

plant shelf

Garage
11-6x20-6

30'-0"

Great Rm
14-6x14-4

L

Dn

vaulted

Br 2
10-0x
12-0

raised
clg

PLAN DATA

Total Living Area:	950
Bedrooms:	2
Baths:	1
Garage:	1-car
Foundation Type:	
Basement	

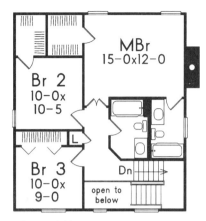

Second Floor
754 sq. ft.

MBr
15-0x12-0

Br 2
10-0x
10-5

Br 3
10-0x
9-0

Dn

open to
below

L

PLAN DATA

Total Living Area:	1,618
Bedrooms:	3
Baths:	2 1/2
Garage:	1-car
Foundation Type:	
Basement	

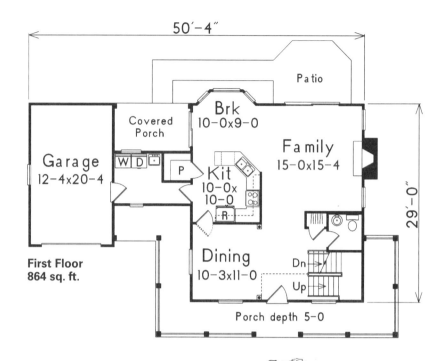

50'-4"

Patio

Covered
Porch

Brk
10-0x9-0

Family
15-0x15-4

Garage
12-4x20-4

W D

P

Kit
10-0x
10-0

R

First Floor
864 sq. ft.

Dining
10-3x11-0

Dn

Up

29'-0"

Porch depth 5-0

PLAN DATA
Total Living Area: 1,676
Bedrooms: 3
Baths: 2
Garage: 2-car
Foundation Types:
  Basement standard
  Crawl space
  Slab

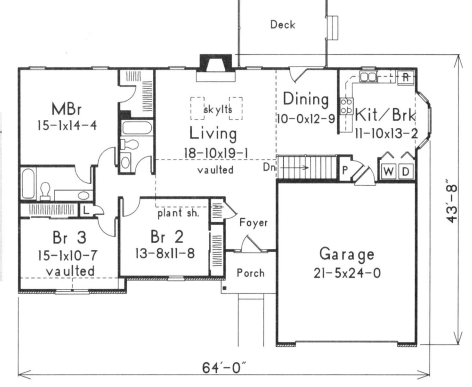

**Second Floor
504 sq. ft.**

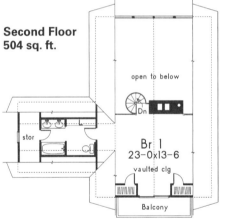

open to below

Dn

Br 1
23-0x13-6

vaulted clg

Balcony

stor

PLAN DATA

Total Living Area: 2,652
Bedrooms: 3
Baths: 2 1/2
Garage: 2-car
Foundation Type:
  Basement

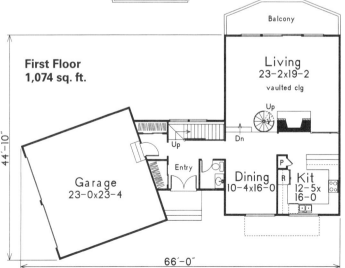

**First Floor
1,074 sq. ft.**

Balcony

Living
23-2x19-2
vaulted clg

Up

Dn

Up

Garage
23-0x23-4

Entry

Dining
10-4x16-0

P
R
Kit
12-5x
16-0

44'-10"

66'-0"

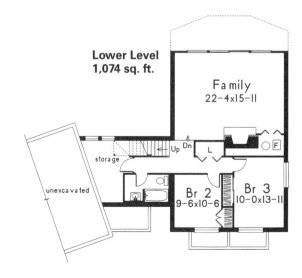

**Lower Level
1,074 sq. ft.**

Family
22-4x15-11

Up Dn
L
F

storage

unexcavated

Br 2
9-6x10-6

Br 3
10-0x13-11

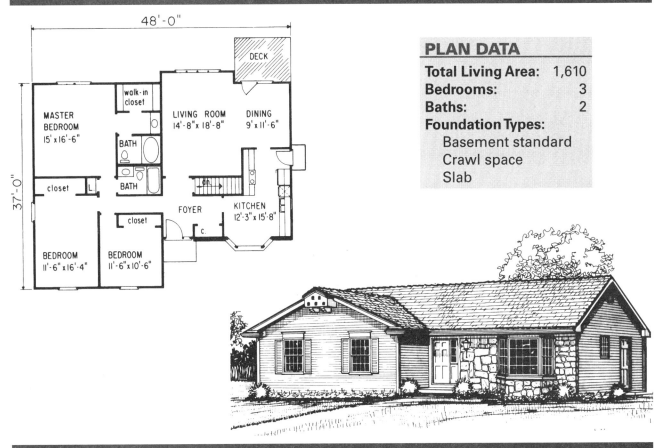

PLAN DATA

Total Living Area: 1,610
Bedrooms: 3
Baths: 2
Foundation Types:
   Basement standard
   Crawl space
   Slab

PLAN DATA

Total Living Area: 1,214
Bedrooms: 3
Baths: 2
Garage: optional 2-car
Foundation Types:
   Crawl space
   Slab
Please specify when ordering

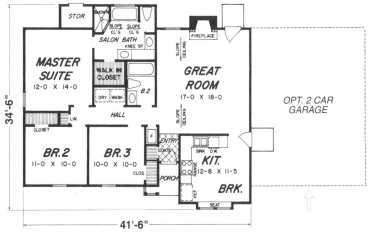

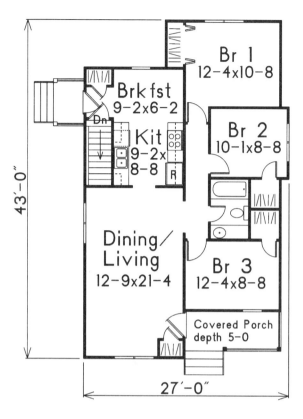

Br 1
12-4x10-8

Brkfst
9-2x6-2

Kit
9-2x8-8

Dn

Br 2
10-1x8-8

R

Dining/Living
12-9x21-4

Br 3
12-4x8-8

Covered Porch
depth 5-0

43'-0"

27'-0"

PLAN DATA

Total Living Area:	987
Bedrooms:	3
Baths:	1
Foundation Type:	
Basement	

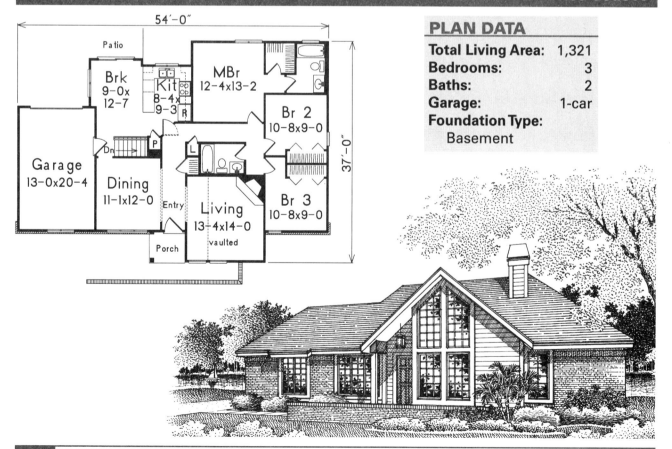

54'-0"

Patio

Brk
9-0x12-7

Kit
8-4x9-3

R

MBr
12-4x13-2

Br 2
10-8x9-0

Dn

P

L

Garage
13-0x20-4

Dining
11-1x12-0

Entry

Living
13-4x14-0
vaulted

Br 3
10-8x9-0

Porch

37'-0"

PLAN DATA

Total Living Area:	1,321
Bedrooms:	3
Baths:	2
Garage:	1-car
Foundation Type:	
Basement	

PLAN DATA

Total Living Area: 1,643
Bedrooms: 3
Baths: 2
Garage: 2-car
Foundation Types:
   Basement standard
   Crawl space
   Slab

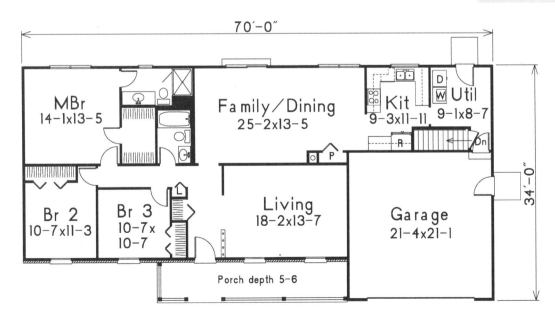

70'-0"

34'-0"

MBr
14-1x13-5

Family/Dining
25-2x13-5

Kit
9-3x11-11

Util
9-1x8-7

D
W

R

Dn

P

Br 2
10-7x11-3

Br 3
10-7x
10-7

Living
18-2x13-7

Garage
21-4x21-1

Porch depth 5-6

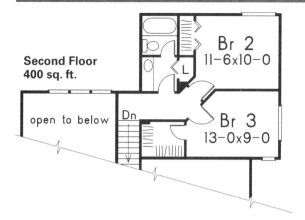

Second Floor
400 sq. ft.

open to below

Dn

Br 2
11-6x10-0

Br 3
13-0x9-0

L

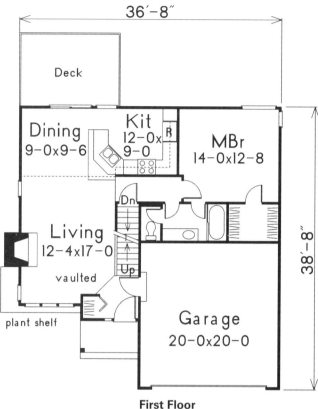

36'-8"

Deck

Dining
9-0x9-6

Kit
12-0x
9-0

R

MBr
14-0x12-8

Living
12-4x17-0

Dn

Up

vaulted

38'-8"

plant shelf

Garage
20-0x20-0

First Floor
846 sq. ft.

PLAN DATA

Total Living Area:	1,246
Bedrooms:	3
Baths:	2
Garage:	2-car
Foundation Type:	
Basement	

Second Floor
554 sq. ft.

Master Bedroom
vaulted ceiling
$20^2 \cdot 12^4$

shelf

Open To Living Room Below

dn

down

w.i.c.

w.i.c.

Bath
up

linen

shelf

shelf

PLAN DATA

Total Living Area: 1,679
Bedrooms: 3
Baths: 2
Garage: 3-car
Foundation Type:
  Pier
Features:
  Drive-under garage

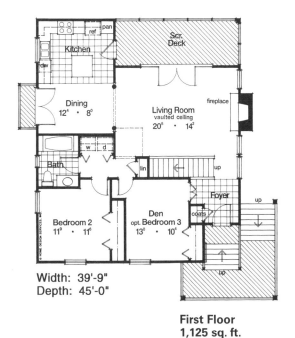

pan

ref

Scr. Deck

Kitchen

dw

Dining
$12^4 \cdot 8^0$

Living Room
vaulted ceiling
$20^5 \cdot 14^2$

fireplace

Bath

w   d

lin

up

Foyer

up

Bedroom 2
$11^9 \cdot 11^6$

Den
opt. Bedroom 3
$13^0 \cdot 10^4$

coats

up

Width: 39'-9"
Depth: 45'-0"

First Floor
1,125 sq. ft.

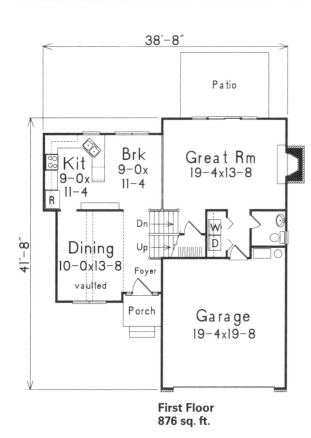

First Floor
876 sq. ft.

Second Floor
741 sq. ft.

PLAN DATA

Total Living Area:	1,617
Bedrooms:	3
Baths:	2 1/2
Garage:	2-car
Foundation Type:	Partial crawl space/ slab

PLAN DATA

Total Living Area:	960
Bedrooms:	3
Baths:	1
Garage:	2-car
Foundation Types:	

Basement standard
Crawl space
Slab

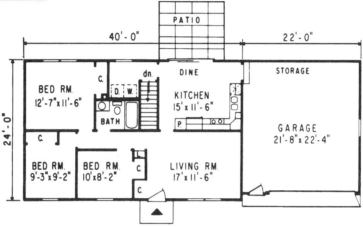

PLAN DATA

Total Living Area:	1,520
Bedrooms:	4
Baths:	2
Foundation Type:	

Pier

Features:
9' ceilings throughout

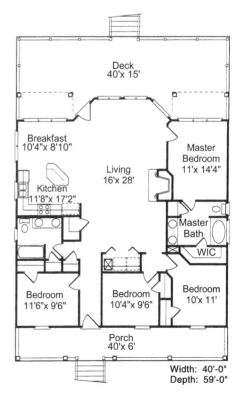

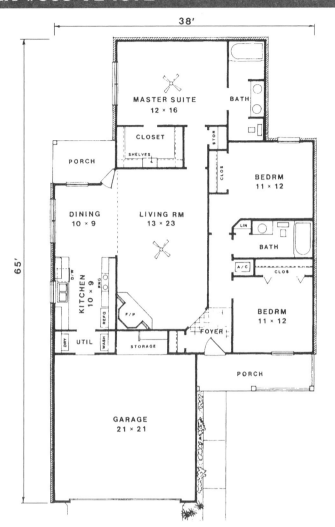

38'

65'

MASTER SUITE
12 × 16

BATH

CLOSET

SHELVES

STOR

CLOS

PORCH

BEDRM
11 × 12

DINING
10 × 9

LIVING RM
13 × 23

LIN

BATH

KITCHEN
10 × 9

D/W

RNG

REFG

F/P

A/C

CLOS

BEDRM
11 × 12

DRY

UTIL

WASH

STORAGE

FOYER

PORCH

GARAGE
21 × 21

PLAN DATA

Total Living Area: 1,372
Bedrooms: 3
Baths: 2
Garage: 2-car
Foundation Types:
  Crawl space
  Slab
Please specify when ordering

PLAN DATA

Total Living Area: 1,994
Bedrooms: 3
Baths: 2
Garage: 2-car
Foundation Type:
  Slab
Features:
  - 9' ceiling standard
  - 12' ceiling in
    bedroom #2
  - 10' ceiling in dining
    room

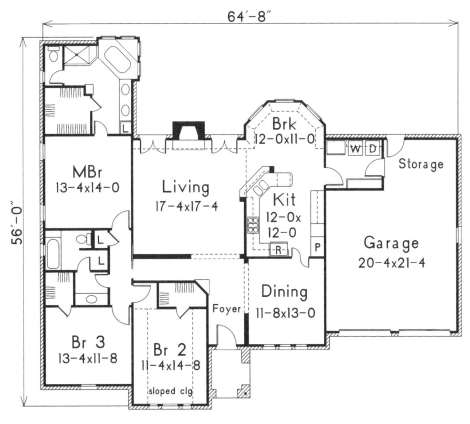

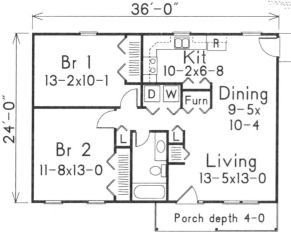

36'-0"

24'-0"

Br 1
13-2x10-1

Kit
10-2x6-8

R

D W Furn

Dining
9-5x
10-4

Br 2
11-8x13-0

Living
13-5x13-0

Porch depth 4-0

PLAN DATA
Total Living Area: 864
Bedrooms: 2
Baths: 1
Foundation Types:
  Crawl space standard
  Basement
  Slab

PLAN DATA
Total Living Area: 1,475
Bedrooms: 3
Baths: 2
Garage: optional 2-car
Foundation Types:
  Crawl space
  Slab
Please specify when ordering

PATIO

MASTER
SUITE
12-4 X 14-0

STOR.

BR. 2
11-0 X 11-0

OPTIONAL
DOUBLE
GARAGE
20-0 X 22-0

42'-8"

GREAT ROOM
15-0 X 19-0

WALK-IN
CLOSET

B.1

UTIL.

B.2

H.

BR. 3
10-0 X 11-0

© COPYRIGHT 1983 RALPH JONES & ASSOC.

BRK.
10-0 X 16-4

K.

DINING
10-0 X 11-0

ENT.

PORCH

45'-9"

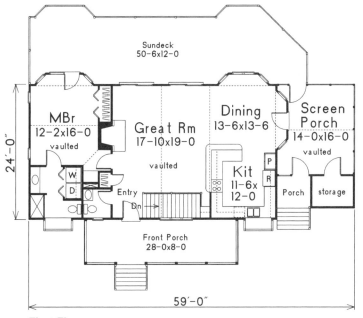

Sundeck
50-6x12-0

MBr
12-2x16-0
vaulted

Great Rm
17-10x19-0
vaulted

Dining
13-6x13-6

Screen Porch
14-0x16-0
vaulted

Kit
11-6x 12-0

W D

P R

Entry

Dn

Porch

storage

24'-0"

Front Porch
28-0x8-0

59'-0"

First Floor
1,158 sq. ft.

PLAN DATA

Total Living Area: 1,732
Bedrooms: 3
Baths: 2 1/2
Garage: 2-car
Foundation Type:
  Basement
Features:
  Drive-under garage

Garage
19-6x23-4

Br 2
11-8x11-6

Br 3
12-6x11-6

Up

Stor

L

Lower Level
574 sq. ft.

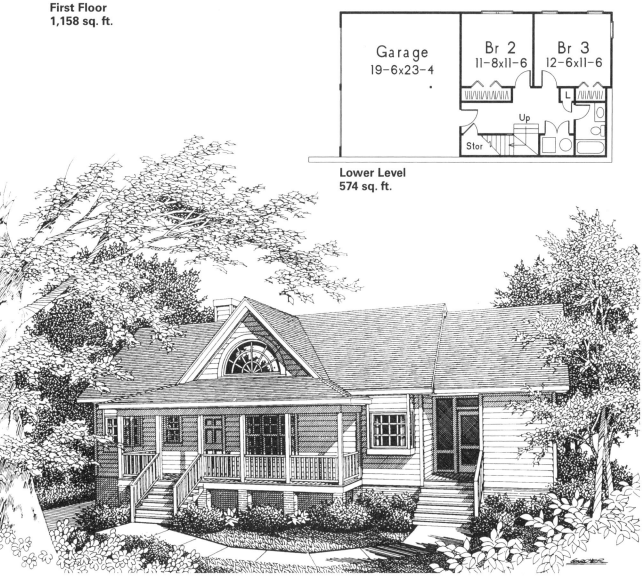

Second Floor
551 sq. ft.

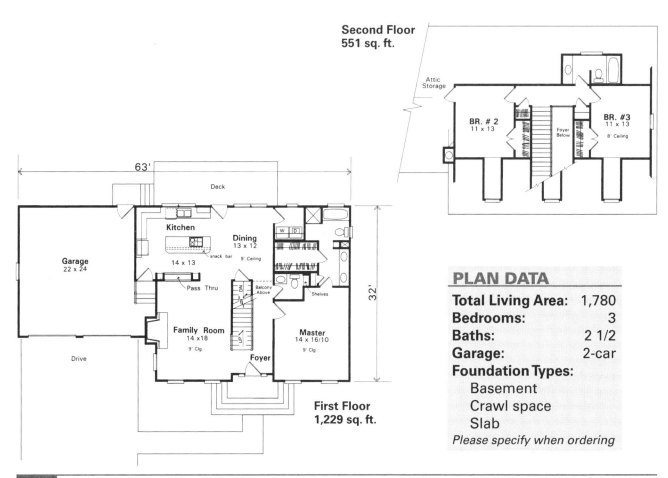

Attic
Storage

BR. # 2
11 x 13

Foyer
Below

BR. #3
11 x 13

8' Ceiling

63'

Deck

Kitchen

Dining
13 x 12

14 x 13

snack bar

9' Ceiling

W D

Garage
22 x 24

Pass Thru

Balcony
Above

Sheves

32'

Drive

Family Room
14 x18

9' Clg.

Master
14 x 16/10

9' Clg.

Foyer

First Floor
1,229 sq. ft.

PLAN DATA

Total Living Area: 1,780
Bedrooms: 3
Baths: 2 1/2
Garage: 2-car
Foundation Types:
  Basement
  Crawl space
  Slab
Please specify when ordering

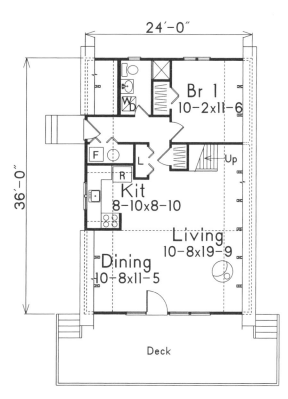

24'-0"

36'-0"

Br 1
10-2x11-6

Kit
8-10x8-10

Living
10-8x19-9

Dining
10-8x11-5

F

L

R

W/D

Up

Deck

First Floor
864 sq. ft.

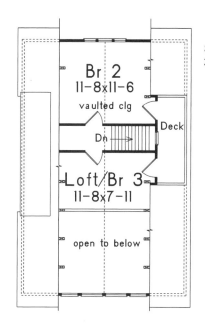

Second Floor
360 sq. ft.

Br 2
11-8x11-6
vaulted clg

Dn

Deck

Loft/Br 3
11-8x7-11

open to below

PLAN DATA

Total Living Area: 1,224
Bedrooms: 3
Baths: 1
Foundation Type:
Crawl space

PROJECT PLANS

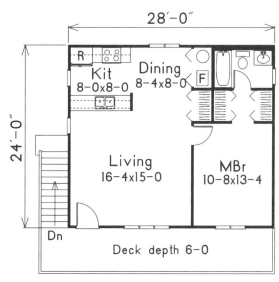

28'-0"

24'-0"

R

Kit
8-0x8-0

Dining
8-4x8-0

F

Living
16-4x15-0

MBr
10-8x13-4

Dn

Deck depth 6-0

PLAN DATA

Total Living Area: 672
Bedrooms: 1
Baths: 1
Garage: 3-car carport
Foundation Type:
 Pier
Features:
 - Building height - 22'-0"
 - Roof pitch - 4/12
 - Complete material list

PLAN DATA

Total Living Area: 576
Bedrooms: 1
Baths: 1
Foundation Type:
 Crawl space
Features:
 - Building height - 16'-0"
 - Roof pitch - 6/12
 - Complete material list

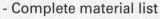

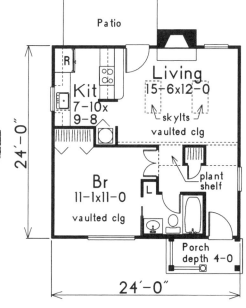

Patio

R

Kit
7-10x
9-8

Living
15-6x12-0
skylts
vaulted clg

24'-0"

Br
11-1x11-0
vaulted clg

L

plant
shelf

Porch
depth 4-0

24'-0"

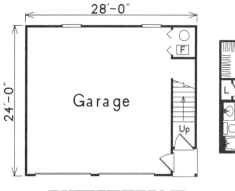

PLAN DATA

Total Living Area: 604
Bedrooms: 1
Baths: 1
Garage: 2-car
Foundation Type:
Slab
Features:
- Building height - 21'-4"
- Roof pitch - 4/12, 12/4.75
- Complete material list

PROJECT PLANS

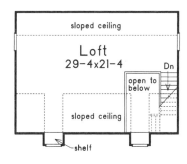

PLAN DATA

Size: 30' x 22'
Foundation Type:
Slab
Features:
- Building height - 20'-6"
- Roof pitch - 8/12, 6/12
- 8' x 7' overhead door
- Complete material list

PROJECT PLANS

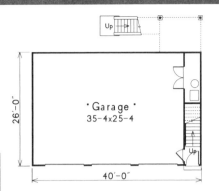

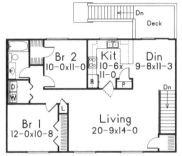

26'-0"

Garage
35-4x25-4

40'-0"

Br 2
10-0x11-0

Kit
10-6x
11-0

Din
9-8x11-3

Deck

Up

Dn

Br 1
12-0x10-8

Living
20-9x14-0

Dn

PLAN DATA

Total Living Area:	1,040
Bedrooms:	2
Baths:	1
Garage:	3-car

Foundation Type:
   Slab

Features:
   - Building height - 23'-0"
   - Roof pitch - 5/12
   - Complete material list

PLAN DATA

Total Living Area:	973
Bedrooms:	2
Baths:	1
Garage:	3-car

Foundation Type:
   Slab

Features:
   - Building height - 24'-8"
   - Roof pitch - 6/12
   - Complete material list

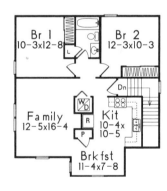

Br 1
10-3x12-8

Br 2
12-3x10-3

Dn

Family
12-5x16-4

Kit
10-4x
10-5

Brk fst
11-4x7-8

31'-4"

Storage
7-4x12-4

32'-0"

Garage
31-0x22-11

Up

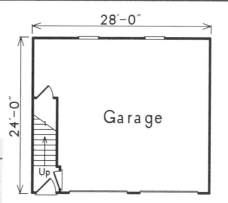

PLAN DATA

Total Living Area: 566
Bedroom/Studio: 1
Baths: 1
Garage: 2-car
Foundation Type:
  Slab
Features:
  - Building height - 22'-0"
  - Roof pitch - 12/12, 4.5/12
  - Complete material list

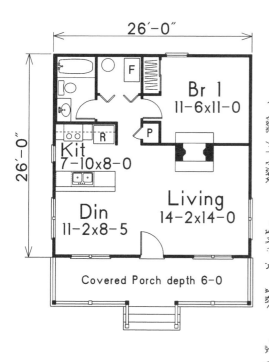

PLAN DATA

Total Living Area: 676
Bedrooms: 1
Baths: 1
Foundation Type:
  Crawl space
Features:
  - Building height - 17'-9"
  - Roof pitch - 6/12
  - Complete material list

PROJECT PLANS

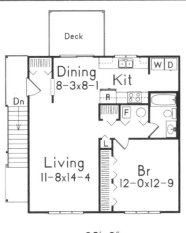

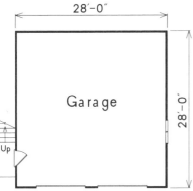

28'-0"

28'-0"

Garage

Up

PLAN DATA

Total Living Area:	784
Bedrooms:	1
Baths:	1
Garage:	2-car
Foundation Type:	
Slab	

Features:
- Building height - 24'-6"
- Roof pitch - 6/12
- Complete material list

PROJECT PLANS

PLAN DATA

Total Living Area:	416
Bedrooms:	1
Baths:	1
Foundation Type:	
Slab	

Features:
- Building height - 14'-0"
- Roof pitch - 6/12
- Complete material list

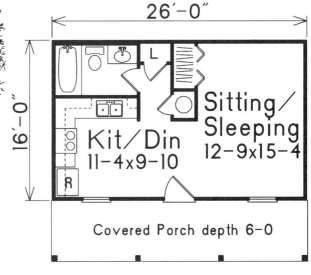

26'-0"

16'-0"

Kit/Din
11-4x9-10

Sitting/
Sleeping
12-9x15-4

Covered Porch depth 6-0

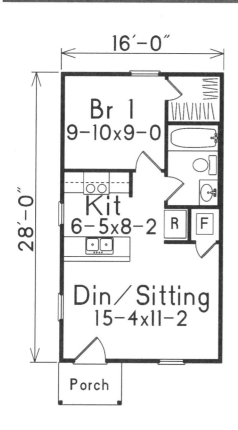

16'-0"

28'-0"

Br 1
9-10x9-0

Kit
6-5x8-2

R   F

Din/Sitting
15-4x11-2

Porch

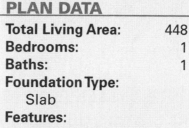

PLAN DATA

Total Living Area:	448
Bedrooms:	1
Baths:	1
Foundation Type:	
Slab	

Features:
- Building height - 14'-0"
- Roof pitch - 8/12
- Complete material list

PROJECT PLANS

Dn

R

Studio
14-11x22-3

PLAN DATA

Total Living Area:	438
Bedrooms/Studio:	1
Baths:	1
Garage:	2-car
Foundation Type:	
Slab	

Features:
- Building height - 21'-3"
- Roof pitch - 6/12, 12/6
- Complete material list

24'-0"

Up

26'-0"

Garage

PROJECT PLANS

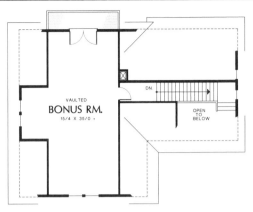

◄ 48' ►

36'

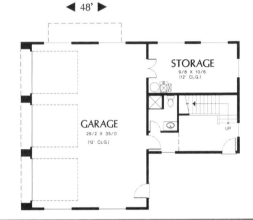

PLAN DATA

Total Living Area:	686
Baths:	1
Garage:	3-car
Foundation Type:	
Slab	

Features:
- Building height - 25'-6"
- Roof pitch - 10/12
- Complete material list

PLAN DATA

Total Living Area:	632
Bedrooms:	1
Baths:	1
Garage:	2-car
Foundation Type:	
Slab	

Features:
- Building height - 26'-6"
- Roof pitch - 8/12, 9/12
- Complete material list

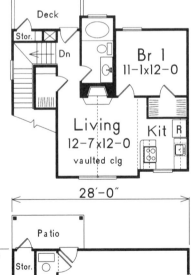

28'-0"

26'-0"

PLAN DATA

Total Living Area:	576
Bedroom/Studio:	1
Baths:	1
Garage:	2-car
Foundation Type:	
Slab	

Features:
- Building height - 21'-6"
- Roof pitch - 4/12
- Complete material list

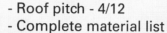

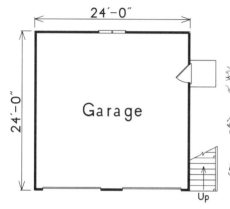

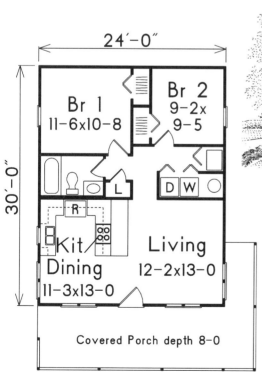

PLAN DATA

Total Living Area:	720
Bedrooms:	2
Baths:	1
Foundation Types:	
Crawl space standard	
Slab	

Features:
- Building height - 14'-0"
- Roof pitch - 4/12
- Complete material list

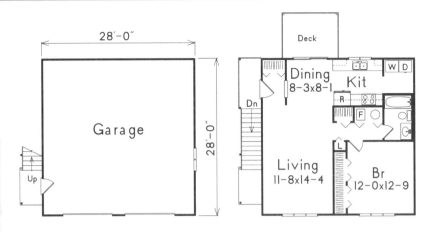

PLAN DATA

Total Living Area:	784
Bedrooms:	1
Baths:	1
Garage:	2-car
Foundation Type:	
Slab	
Features:	

- Building height - 24'-6"
- Roof pitch - 6/12
- Complete material list

PROJECT PLANS

PLAN DATA

Total Living Area:	633
Bedrooms:	1
Baths:	1
Garage:	2-car
Foundation Type:	
Slab	
Features:	

- Building height - 24'-0"
- Roof pitch - 9/12
- Complete material list

PLAN DATA

Total Living Area:	654
Bedrooms:	1
Baths:	1
Garage:	2-car
Foundation Type:	
Slab	
Features:	

- Building height - 24'-0"
- Roof pitch - 7/12
- Complete material list

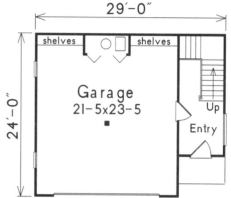

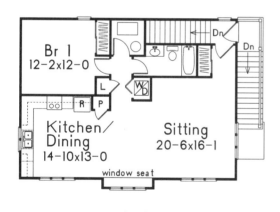

PLAN DATA

Total Living Area:	949
Bedrooms:	1
Baths:	1
Garage:	3-car
Foundation Type:	
Slab	
Features:	

- Building height - 24'-10"
- Roof pitch - 6/12
- Complete material list

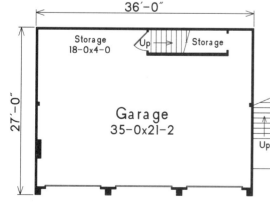

PROJECT PLANS

PLAN #563-15021

PLAN DATA

Size: 24' x 20'

Foundation Type:
Slab

Features:
- Building height - 13'-6"
- Roof pitch - 6/12
- Complete material list

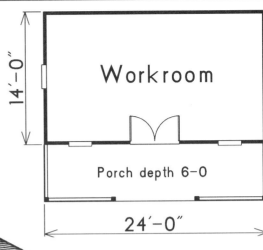

Workroom

14'-0"

Porch depth 6-0

24'-0"

PROJECT PLANS

PLAN #563-15507

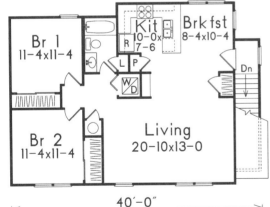

Br 1
11-4x11-4

Kit
10-0x
7-6

Brkfst
8-4x10-4

L P
R
W D

Dn

Br 2
11-4x11-4

Living
20-10x13-0

PLAN DATA

Total Living Area:	974
Bedrooms:	2
Baths:	1
Garage:	3-car

Foundation Type:
Slab

Features:
- Building height - 23'-2"
- Roof pitch - 5/12
- Complete material list

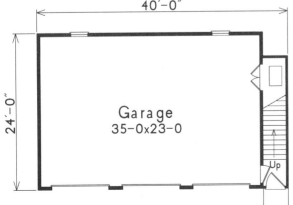

40'-0"

24'-0"

Garage
35-0x23-0

Up

PLAN #563-15504

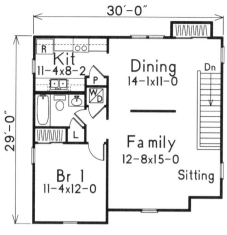

30'-0"

Kit
11-4x8-2

R

Dining
14-1x11-0

Dn

P

W/D

L

Family
12-8x15-0

Sitting

Br 1
11-4x12-0

29'-0"

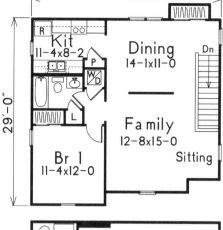

Stor

Garage
25-8x24-4

Up

PLAN DATA

Total Living Area:	840
Bedrooms:	1
Baths:	1
Garage:	2-car
Foundation Type:	
Slab	

Features:
- Building height - 25'-8"
- Roof pitch - 7/12
- Complete material list

PROJECT PLANS

PLAN #563-15032

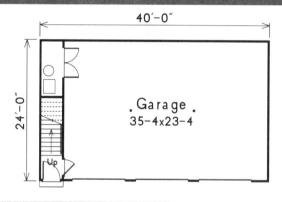

40'-0"

Garage
35-4x23-4

24'-0"

Up

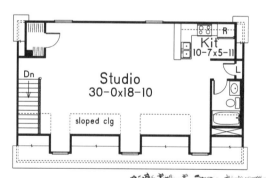

Dn

Kit
10-7x5-11

R

L

Studio
30-0x18-10

sloped clg

PLAN DATA

Total Living Area:	813
Bedroom/Studio:	1
Baths:	1
Garage:	3-car
Foundation Type:	
Slab	

Features:
- Building height - 22'-0"
- Roof pitch - 12/12, 4.25/12
- Complete material list

PLAN DATA

Total Living Area:	960
Bedrooms:	1
Baths:	1

Foundation Type:
- Pier

Features:
- Building height - 22'-0"
- Roof pitch -24/12
- Complete material list

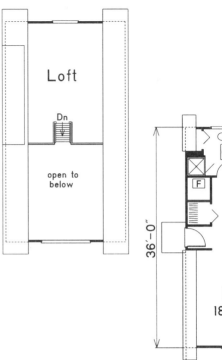

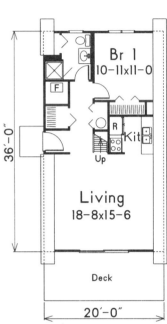

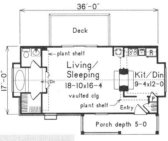

PLAN DATA

Total Living Area:	647

Features:
- 1 bedroom, 1 bath
- Crawl space foundation
- Building height - 17'-0"
- Roof pitch - 10/12
- Complete material list

PLAN DATA

Total Living Area:	480

Features:
- 1 bedroom, 1 bath
- Slab foundation
- Building height - 14'-2"
- Roof pitch - 6/12
- Complete material list

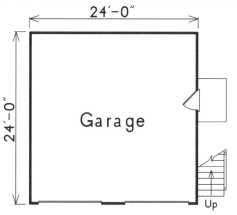

24'-0"

24'-0"

Garage

Up

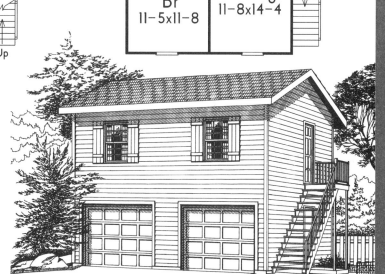

Kit/Dining
17-11x9-1

R

Br
11-5x11-8

Living
11-8x14-4

Dn

PLAN DATA

Total Living Area:	576
Bedrooms:	1
Baths:	1
Garage:	2-car
Foundation Type:	
Slab	

Features:
- Building height - 21'-5"
- Roof pitch - 4/12
- Complete material list

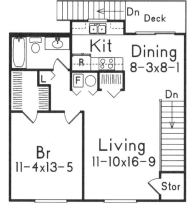

Dn Deck

Kit

Dining
8-3x8-1

R

F

L

Dn

Br
11-4x13-5

Living
11-10x16-9

Stor

PLAN DATA

Total Living Area:	746
Bedrooms:	1
Baths:	1
Garage:	2-car
Foundation Type:	
Slab	

Features:
- Building height - 22'-0"
- Roof pitch - 4/12
- Complete material list

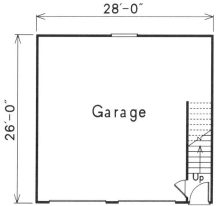

28'-0"

26'-0"

Garage

Up

PROJECT PLAN ORDER FORM

How To Order

For fastest service, Call Toll-Free 1-800-373-2646 day or night

Three Easy Ways To Order

1. CALL toll free 1-800-373-2646 for credit card orders. MasterCard, Visa, Discover and American Express are accepted.

2. FAX your order to 1-314-770-2226.

3. MAIL the Order Form to:

   HDA, Inc.
   4390 Green Ash Drive
   St. Louis, MO 63045

QUESTIONS?
Call Our Customer Service Number
314-770-2228

ORDER FORM

Please send me -

    PLAN NUMBER 563- _____

      PRICE CODE _____ (see Plan Page)
      (for plans on pgs. 340-353)

Reproducible Masters (see chart at right) $ _____
Initial Set of Plans $ _____
Additional Plan Sets (see chart at right)
   _____ (Qty) at $ _____ each $ _____

              SUBTOTAL $ _____
SALES TAX (MO residents add 6%) $ _____
☐ Shipping / Handling (see chart at right) $ _____
   (each additional set add $2.00 to shipping charges)

   TOTAL ENCLOSED (US funds only) $ _____

☐ Enclosed is my check or money order payable to HDA, Inc. (Sorry, no COD's)

I hereby authorize HDA, Inc. to charge this purchase to my credit card account (check one):

☐ MasterCard   ☐ VISA   ☐ DISCOVER NOVUS   ☐ AMERICAN EXPRESS Cards

Credit Card number _____

Expiration date _____

Signature _____

Name _____
        (Please print or type)
Street Address _____
        (Please **do not** use PO Box)
City _____

State _____ Zip _____

Daytime phone number (____) - _____

   Thank you for your order!

IMPORTANT INFORMATION TO KNOW BEFORE YOU ORDER

◆ **Exchange Policies -** Since blueprints are printed in response to your order, we cannot honor requests for refunds. However, if for some reason you find that the plan you have purchased does not meet your requirements, you may exchange that plan for another plan in our collection. At the time of the exchange, you will be charged a processing fee of 25% of your original plan package price, plus the difference in price between the plan packages (if applicable) and the cost to ship the new plans to you.

Please note: Reproducible drawings can only be exchanged if the package is unopened, and exchanges are allowed only within 90 days of purchase.

◆ **Building Codes & Requirements -** At the time the construction drawings were prepared, every effort was made to ensure that these plans and specifications meet nationally recognized codes. Our plans conform to most national building codes. Because building codes vary from area to area, some drawing modifications and/or the assistance of a professional designer or architect may be necessary to comply with your local codes or to accommodate specific building site conditions. We advise you to consult with your local building official for information regarding codes governing your area.

BLUEPRINT PRICE SCHEDULE

Price Code	1-Set	Additional Sets	Reproducible Masters
P3	$15.00	$10.00	$65.00
P4	$20.00	$10.00	$70.00
P5	$25.00	$10.00	$75.00
P6	$30.00	$10.00	$80.00
P7	$50.00	$10.00	$100.00
P8	$75.00	$10.00	$125.00
P9	$125.00	$20.00	$200.00
P10	$150.00	$20.00	$225.00
P11	$175.00	$20.00	$250.00
P12	$200.00	$20.00	$275.00
P13	$225.00	$45.00	$440.00

Plan prices guaranteed through December 31, 2004.
Please note that plans are not refundable.

SHIPPING & HANDLING CHARGES
EACH ADDITIONAL SET ADD $2.00 TO SHIPPING CHARGES

<u>U.S. SHIPPING</u>

Regular *(allow 7-10 business days)* $5.95
Priority *(allow 3-5 business days)* $15.00
Express* *(allow 1-2 business days)* $25.00

<u>CANADA SHIPPING</u>

Standard *(allow 8-12 business days)* $15.00
Express* *(allow 3-5 business days)* $40.00

<u>OVERSEAS SHIPPING/INTERNATIONAL</u>
Call, fax, or e-mail (plans@hdainc.com) for shipping costs.
* For express delivery please call us by 11:00 a.m. CST